ADVANCED TEXTS IN ECONOMETRICS

General Editors
C.W.J. Granger   G.E. Mizon

Other Advanced Texts in Econometrics

ARCH: Selected Readings
Edited by Robert F. Engle

Asymptotic Theory for Integrated Processes
By H. Peter Boswijk

Bayesian Inference in Dynamic Econometric Models
By Luc Bauwens, Michel Lubrano, and Jean-François Richard

Co-integration, Error Correction, and the Econometric Analysis of Non-Stationary Data
By Anindya Banerjee, Juan J. Dolado, John W. Galbraith, and David Hendry

Dynamic Econometrics
By David F. Hendry

Likelihood-Based Inference in Cointegrated Vector Autoregressive Models
By Søren Johansen

Long-Run Economic Relationships: Readings in Cointegration
Edited by R. F. Engle and C. W. J. Granger

Modelling Economic Series: Readings in Econometric Methodology
Edited by C. W. J. Granger

Modelling Non-Linear Economic Relationships
By Clive W. J. Granger and Timo Teräsvirta

Modelling Seasonality
Edited by S. Hylleberg

Non-Stationary Time Series Analysis and Cointegration
Edited by Colin P. Hargreaves

Outlier Robust Analysis of Economic Time Series
By André Lucas, Philip Hans Franses, and Dick van Dijk

Panel Data Econometrics
By Manuel Arellano

Periodicity and Stochastic Trends in Economic Time Series
By Philip Hans Franses

Progressive Modelling: Non-nested Testing and Encompassing
Edited by Massimiliano Marcellino and Grayham E. Mizon

Stochastic Limit Theory: An Introduction for Econometricians
By James Davidson

Stochastic Volatility
Edited by Neil Shephard

Testing Exogeneity
Edited by Neil R. Ericsson and John S. Irons

Time Series with Long Memory
Edited by Peter M. Robinson

Time-Series-Based Econometrics: Unit Roots and Co-integrations
By Michio Hatanaka

Workbook on Cointegration
By Peter Reinhard Hansen and Søren Johansen

Periodic Time Series Models

PHILIP HANS FRANSES
AND
RICHARD PAAP

OXFORD
UNIVERSITY PRESS

*This book has been printed digitally and produced in a standard specification
in order to ensure its continuing availability*

OXFORD
UNIVERSITY PRESS

Great Clarendon Street, Oxford OX2 6DP

Oxford University Press is a department of the University of Oxford.
It furthers the University's objective of excellence in research, scholarship,
and education by publishing worldwide in

Oxford New York

Auckland Cape Town Dar es Salaam Hong Kong Karachi
Kuala Lumpur Madrid Melbourne Mexico City Nairobi
New Delhi Shanghai Taipei Toronto
With offices in
Argentina Austria Brazil Chile Czech Republic France Greece
Guatemala Hungary Italy Japan South Korea Poland Portugal
Singapore Switzerland Thailand Turkey Ukraine Vietnam

Oxford is a registered trade mark of Oxford University Press
in the UK and in certain other countries

Published in the United States
by Oxford University Press Inc., New York

© Philip Hans Franses and Richard Paap 2004

The moral rights of the author have been asserted

Database right Oxford University Press (maker)

Reprinted 2006

ISBN 0-19-924203-8

Preface

This book deals with the analysis of economic time series with seasonality. There are many ways to model such series, where typically these models are to be used for out-of-sample forecasting. One class of models for seasonal series is the periodic time series model, and this class is the focus of the present book.

In a sense, our book can be seen as a second edition, or better, an updated edition, of *Periodicity and Stochastic Trends in Economic Time Series*, which was written by the first author and which was published in 1996, also by Oxford University Press. At that time, there were not many academics and practitioners who considered periodic models for their seasonal time series. Hence, the 1996 book aimed to provide arguments as to why periodic models could be useful. The first few chapters considered (seasonal) time series in general, and Chapter 6 in that book was meant to argue that perhaps it would be better to use periodic models, instead of the, at the time, popular models.

We believe that the current book no longer needs all these chapters. A casual look at the relevant literature suggests that periodic models are now accepted as a useful tool, although perhaps not implemented by many. Indeed, a recent more theoretical book on seasonality, *The Econometric Analysis of Seasonal Time Series* by Eric Ghysels and Denise Osborn (Cambridge University Press, 2001), dedicates an entire chapter to periodic models. As the authors state, that chapter discusses part of the theory, and therefore we will aim to give a more complete account, as well as to give ample empirical illustrations. Hence, one might view our book as a cookbook, which guides the reader towards the eventual empirical use of a periodic time series model.

Our book gives a review of everything we now know about periodic time series models. It summarizes a decade of research, and we currently believe that everything that is needed to be understood is now understood, although there are a few avenues for further research. In part, we ourselves contributed to the literature on periodic models, where we sometimes had the help of our co-authors Peter Boswijk, Jörg Breitung, Niels Haldrup, Frank Kleibergen, Gary Koop, and Marius Ooms. We are extremely grateful for their input.

This book will be most useful for readers who are interested in obtaining a comprehensive picture of periodic time series modeling. The list of references is up to date. The book can also be useful for readers who want to apply the models to their own time series, and who want to get an overview of which steps should be taken in practice. Indeed, we provide the relevant EViews 4.1 code, at least when tractable, and more extensive code can be obtained via our web sites.

Finally, we thank Andrew Schuller, Clive Granger, and Graham Mizon for their encouragement and for their willingness to incorporate this book in their prestigious series. We are also grateful to Eric Ghysels, Svend Hylleberg, and Denise Osborn for inspiration.

Rotterdam   Philip Hans Franses
August 2003   Richard Paap

Contents

List of Figures

List of Tables

Notation and abbreviations

Time series

$D_{s,t}$ Seasonal dummy variable, which takes the value 1 if t corresponds to the sth season and 0 otherwise for $t = 1, \ldots, n = SN$ and $s = 1, \ldots, S$.

T_t Linear deterministic trend defined by $T_t = [(t-1)/S] + 1$, where $[\cdot]$ is the integer function.

y_t (Seasonally-observed) time series for $t = 1, \ldots, n = SN$.

$Y_{s,T}$ Observation on variable y_t in season s of year T for $s = 1, \ldots, S$ and $T = 1, \ldots, N$.

Y_T S-dimensional vector $(Y'_{1,T}, Y'_{2,T}, \ldots, Y'_{S,T})'$ for $T = 1, \ldots, N$.

$\bar{y}_t$ m-dimensional vector of time series $(y_{1,t}, \ldots, y_{m,t})'$, for $t = 1, \ldots, n = SN$.

$y_{i,t}$ ith time series in $\bar{y}_t$ for $t = 1, \ldots, n = SN$ and $i = 1, \ldots, m$.

$\bar{Y}_{s,T}$ Observation on variable $\bar{y}_t$ in season s of year T for $s = 1, \ldots, S$ and $T = 1, \ldots, N$.

$\bar{Y}_T$ mS-dimensional vector $(\bar{Y}'_{1,T}, \ldots, \bar{Y}'_{S,T})'$.

$\Delta_k y_t$ kth difference of the time series y_t defined by $y_t - y_{t-k}$ for $k = 1, 2, 3, \ldots$ and $t = k+1, \ldots, n$.

$\Delta_k Y_T$ kth difference of the time series Y_T defined by $Y_T - Y_{T-k}$ for $k = 1, 2, 3, \ldots$ and $T = k+1, \ldots, N$.

Parameters

α_s, ϕ_s periodic autoregressive parameter in a PAR(1) model for $s = 1, \ldots, S$.

ϕ_{is} periodic autoregressive parameter for season s and lag i in a PAR(p) model, for $s = 1, \ldots, S$ and $i = 1, \ldots, p$.

Φ_i $S \times S$ matrix of autoregressive parameters of a PAR(p) model in VQ representation for $i = 1, \ldots, P$.

$\bar{\phi}_{is}$ $m \times m$ matrix of periodic autoregressive parameters for season s and lag i in an m-dimensional PVAR(p) model, for $s = 1, \ldots, S$ and $i = 1, \ldots, p$.

$\bar{\Phi}_i$ $Sm \times Sm$ matrix of periodic autoregressive parameters of a PVAR(p) model in VQ representation for $i = 1, \ldots, P$.

μ_s seasonal intercept parameters in a PAR model for $s = 1, \ldots, S$.

μ S-dimensional vector $(\mu_1, \ldots, \mu_S)'$.

$\bar{\mu}_s$ m-dimensional seasonal intercept parameter vector $(\mu_{1,s}, \ldots, \mu_{m,s})'$ in a PVAR model, where $\mu_{i,s}$ denotes the intercept of series i in season s, for $s = 1, \ldots, S$.

$\bar{\mu}$ Sm-dimensional vector $(\bar{\mu}_1', \ldots, \bar{\mu}_S')'$.

τ_s seasonal trend parameters in a PAR model for $s = 1, \ldots, S$.

τ S-dimensional vector $(\tau_1, \ldots, \tau_S)'$.

$\bar{\tau}_s$ m-dimensional seasonal trend parameter vector $(\tau_{1,s}, \ldots, \tau_{m,s})'$ in a PVAR model, where $\tau_{i,s}$ denotes the trend parameter of series i in season s, for $s = 1, \ldots, S$.

$\bar{\tau}$ Sm-dimensional vector $(\bar{\tau}_1', \ldots, \bar{\tau}_S')'$.

Abbreviations

ACF	autocorrelation function
AIC	Akaike information criterion
AR	autoregressive (or autoregression)
ARMA	autoregressive moving-average
CLT	common linear trends
CRDF	cointegration regression Dickey–Fuller
CRDW	cointegration regression Durbin–Watson
DF	Dickey–Fuller
DGP	data generating process
GARCH	generalized autoregressive conditional heteroskedasticity
GMM	generalized method of moments
HEGY	Hylleberg, Engle, Granger, and Yoo
I(k)	integrated of order k
IGARCH	integrated GARCH
LM	Lagrange multiplier
LR	likelihood ratio
MAPE	mean absolute percentage error
NLS	nonlinear least squares
NLT	no linear trends
NQT	no quadratic trends
OLS	ordinary least squares
PADF	periodic augmented Dickey–Fuller
PAR	periodic autoregressive (or autoregression)
PARMA	periodic autoregressive moving-average
PGARCH	periodic GARCH
PI	periodically integrated

PIAR	periodically-integrated autoregressive (or autoregression)
PIGARCH	periodically-integrated GARCH
PMA	periodic moving-average
PVAR	periodic vector autoregressive
RMSE	root mean squared error
RSS	residual sum of squares
SC	Schwarz criterion
VAR	vector autoregressive
VD	vector of days
VMA	vector moving-average
VQ	vector of quarters

1

Introduction

This book is concerned with modeling and forecasting seasonally-observed time series, predominantly in economics. Many macroeconomic time series display a trend and marked seasonal variation, while many variables in finance and marketing display seasonality but no trend. If there is a trend in the data, then often one is interested in examining the nature of this trend, as this can have implications for forecasting and for subsequent model building. Indeed, when the trend is found to be stochastic, one needs to resort to the so-called multivariate stochastic trend or cointegration models, whereas when the trend is found to be deterministic, one does not have to do so. Similar implications follow from the nature of seasonal variation. If seasonality is found to be stochastic, one tends to resort to models which include the relevant description in a subsequent multivariate model, whereas when it is deterministic, the subsequent models look different. Many time series also display features like aberrant observations, time-varying variance, and nonlinearity, see Franses (1998), but for the sake of brevity we confine ourselves to trend and seasonality. Indeed, this book is concerned with modeling and forecasting economic time series with seasonal variation and a trend, both of an a priori unknown type. It is the task of the practitioner to make a choice between the various models and to use the model for the relevant purpose.

1.1 Preliminaries

In recent years there has been an enormous interest in forecasting and modeling seasonal time series. This interest is reflected by the fact that many new models have been proposed (or introduced into economics) and many empirical studies have been carried out. The main reason for this is that it is now well understood that the inclusion of explicit descriptions of a trend and of seasonality in an econometric time series model is sensible from a modeling and forecasting point of view. Indeed, not including such a description would lead to nonsensical out-of-sample forecasts, which can easily be visualized. Additionally, there can be an interest in common patterns across economic variables, including common trends and common seasonality. Hence, it is worthwhile putting effort into eliciting the key features of economics time series data, and to incorporate these in models for description and for forecasting.

With the renewed interest in modeling seasonality, data providers also became aware of the relevance of making available the original data. For many people outside of macroeconomics, this may seem like an oddity, but indeed, until quite recently it was common practice to provide only so-called seasonally-adjusted data. Such data amount to somehow filtered original data. It was even common practice to replace the original data by these mechanically filtered data. Why did and do people seasonally adjust macroeconomic data? Well, it was (and still is) widely believed that policymakers (would) have trouble disentangling important data patterns like a trend and a business cycle in the presence of seasonality, and hence would be better off analyzing adjusted data. The most common approach, originating from the US Census Bureau, applies a series of data transformations, resulting in an estimated seasonality-free time series.

It is by now well documented that this approach is rather harmful, at least if one intends to use the estimated adjusted data for subsequent modeling. This holds in particular for cases in which one is interested in (i) examining the trend and the business cycle, (ii) when one wants to see how innovations get propagated through the model, and (iii) when one wants to forecast time series. There are many studies in the literature which substantiate these statements using simulated and real-life data. Hence, the very goal of seasonal adjustment seems cumbersome to achieve, and by now it seems to be held as common knowledge that there is perhaps simply no need to analyze such filtered data. If, in any case, one still is interested in separating seasonality from the time series, one seems better off using the so-called model-based methods, instead of the mechanical filtering methods of the Census Bureau. These methods also allow one to provide confidence bounds around the seasonally-adjusted data, thereby making it explicit that such data are estimates and should not be confused with the original data, see Koopman and Franses (2002) and the references cited therein. At present (that is, August 2003), we are witnessing a tendency of the US Census Bureau to gradually adopt ideas from the model-based methods, and hence perhaps in a few years from now the above remarks will no longer hold.

There are various approaches to the modeling and forecasting of trends in time series with seasonality, and, interestingly, there seems to be no consensus as to which of these approaches is best. It turns out that one approach is better for some data, while another approach works best for other data. There is also no consensus as to which approach is simpler or more meaningful, and hence it is all a matter of taste as to which method one prefers. One dominant approach is the method that builds on the notion of so-called seasonal stochastic trends, see, for example, Ghysels and Osborn (2001:ch.3) and the many references cited therein. Another approach allows for time-varying parameters. The nature of such time variations may range from a stochastic-trend-like variation to a more restrictive version in which the parameters vary across the seasons. This latter class of models is usually coined 'periodic models', and it is this class which is the key topic of this book. Note that the notion of periodicity does not entail things like nonlinear attractors, nor does it deal with spectral representations of time series data. When we use the phrase 'periodic' in this book, we basically mean time series data which seem to have different time series properties across different seasons. These properties concern the autocorrelations and the variances, as well as the links between two or more time series in a regression context. For example, we consider data for which it might hold that the correlation between March and February data is, say, 0.8, while it is -0.4 between April and March.

In Section 1.3 we discuss in more detail why periodic models can be relevant for empirical analysis. This relevance builds on practical findings and on considerations from economic theory. Next, we provide an outline of this book, by discussing the contents of the subsequent chapters. First, however, we now say something about how this book can best be read and appreciated.

1.2   Readership

Before we start off, it seems wise to provide the reader with some information on how to use this book. We assume that the reader has some basic knowledge of modeling economic time series data. This means that we assume familiarity with concepts such as a white noise series, the (partial) autocorrelation function, identification, parameter estimation, constructing forecasts and forecast intervals, and diagnostic checking. Almost all textbooks on time series analysis contain details of these topics, and it would be most helpful for the reader to use this book after consultation with one of these textbooks. We would recommend considering Fuller (1976) and Hamilton (1994) for advanced texts, or Mills (1991), Harvey (1993), and Franses (1998) for more introductory texts. Along the way we will deal with several of the above concepts, and, when we need them, we will provide formal definitions. However, to get the most out of this book, again it is helpful to have some prior knowledge about time series analysis. In the predecessor of this book, that is, Franses (1996*b*), there was a chapter on various concepts in time series, but this chapter has now been omitted.

The scope of this book is based on our belief that periodic models can be useful in practice. Also, we are strongly convinced that it is worthwhile paying attention to describing trends and seasonality in economic data. Periodic models, of course, amount to just one possible way to take account of seasonality and trends. Indeed, the recent survey book of Ghysels and Osborn (2001) contains several chapters on various approaches, of which periodic models is just one of these. Note, however, that we thus do not believe that periodic models are the only way to go, and hence they are not always to be preferred. In contrast, we believe that it is wise to include a wide range of possible models for practical problems, and then let the data help you to make a choice between them. In some cases, periodic models are more useful, and in other cases different models are preferable. The main reason for writing this book is that we believe that the most important developments for these models have now been made and published. Hence, it seems like the proper moment to put this knowledge together, and to summarize what has been achieved so far.

We adopt the viewpoint of someone who is interested in practical modeling and forecasting. As such, we exclude detailed discussions of technical matters, in particular asymptotic theory concerning the properties of estimators and tests. When needed, we refer to the relevant articles or books, but we may sometimes present a few results when they are required for further understanding. We merely focus on the empirical analysis of periodic time series models, and address issues such as specification, estimation, diagnostics, and implementation of these models in substantial detail. In a sense, one can view this book as a cookbook, which enables one to generate one's own forecasts or to construct a useful model linking two or more economic time series. When relevant, we also elaborate on matters such as which statistical package to use. In fact, we give some examples of EViews 4.1 programs and provide Gauss and EViews code on our web sites.

In accordance with our emphasis on empirical work, we do not discuss matters at their most general level, which usually involves messy notation and hard-to-understand expressions. Instead, we choose to consider the typical case of a quarterly time series variable with observations spanning three to four decades. Sometimes we discuss other frequencies, like daily data or monthly data, but the main focus is on four seasons. In principle, everything we say for quarterly data can be extended to data measured at other frequencies, although we must warn the reader that they will find the practical application of periodic models to even monthly data already not straightforward due to the potentially large amount of parameters. Having said this, we will continue to focus on quarterly data, since many published applications of periodic models also concern such data. We will illustrate all theoretical material using fourteen US production time series, including total manufacturing but also less aggregated series such as the production of paper products.

Our intention is to give an up-to-date survey of what has happened in the last ten to fifteen years in the area of periodic models for economic time series data. The book of Franses (1996b), which also dealt with periodic models, and on which we build in several chapters, was written while many new developments were happening. At present, we believe that we can look back at more than a decade of research, and it seems that we can summarize the available knowledge. This does not mean that all has been said and done, although we think that the major steps have been made. Of course, there is always a need for further developments, and this is indicated at times in the various chapters.

The analysis of seasonal time series using periodic models is a rather specific area within econometric time series modeling. Indeed, it covers only two of the five salient features of economic time series data, albeit that these features dominate within-sample fluctuations and out-of-sample forecasts. On the other hand, forecasts of quarterly data will have to be made in the future too, and hence any possible model class which can lead to accurate forecasts deserves attention. As stressed before, we aim to convey to the reader that periodic models can be plausible from an economic perspective, that they are easy to analyze, and that they can lead to accurate forecasts. Indeed, they are easy to analyze, as most steps in the analysis concern only standard regression techniques. Admittedly, the asymptotic theory can be a little more complicated than for other models, but in practice the use of periodic models is not difficult, at least not for quarterly data.

1.3 Why periodic models?

To be able to provide some motivation for our choice of discussing periodic models, we need to establish some notation. Consider a time series variable y_t, which has been observed for $t = 1, 2, \ldots, n$. Usually, at least in economics, y_t is a natural logarithmic transformation of a variable, say, x_t. This is done as various economic series tend to grow exponentially, and taking natural logs dampens this trend and facilitates econometric analysis. Of course, in other applications one may want to consider the original series.

A typical seasonal series in macroeconomics, which is used for out-of-sample forecasting and econometric modeling, is observed monthly or quarterly, covering data from, say, the late 1940s onwards. At present, this would amount to n being equal to 240 data points in the case of quarterly data. This number is around the maximum number that one can obtain, and sample sizes of 100 or 120 are more common. This is important to bear in mind, as we will look at models that treat the seasonal data differently, and for 100 quarterly data points there are only 25 that concern each season. Hence, we have to deal with reasonably small samples.

To further set notation, consider the variable $Y_{s,T}$, which denotes the observation on variable y_t in season s and in year T. Obviously, s runs from 1 to S, where for quarterly data S equals 4. To standardize notation we let T run from 1 to N. Hence, if one would have N years of quarterly data, then n equals $4N$. One may now want to write y_t as y_{ST+s}, but this is not necessary and can even become confusing in cases for which one does not want to consider periodic models. In essence, a periodic time series model permits a different model for $Y_{s,T}$ for each season s, where we mean that, depending on the season, one would make use of a different forecasting model. Of course, these models do not have to be different across all seasons. It can also happen that there is, say, a model for the first quarter, while there is another model for the second, third, and fourth quarters. We will indicate that easy-to-use diagnostic tests can be used to suggest the most adequate type of model.

A simple, but rather useful, illustrative model is a so-called first-order periodic autoregression, abbreviated as PAR(1), that is,

$$y_{s,T} = \phi_s y_{s-1,T} + \varepsilon_{s,T}, \tag{1.1}$$

for s is either 2, 3, or 4, and

$$y_{1,T} = \phi_1 y_{4,T-1} + \varepsilon_{1,T}, \tag{1.2}$$

for the first-quarter observations, where the $\varepsilon_{s,T}$ amount to standard white noise time series. Now we know how periodic models can look, it is quite common to proceed with the short-hand notation

$$y_t = \phi_s y_{t-1} + \varepsilon_t, \tag{1.3}$$

where ε_t again denotes a standard white noise series, which means that it has mean zero, a fixed variance, and it is linearly unpredictable. Clearly, a periodic model effectively encapsulates S models, which are all potentially different. Again, it may be that just a single model differs from the other $S - 1$ models.

Periodic models seem to have been in use in the environmental, water resources, and meteorological disciplines for a long time, see Jones and Brelsford (1967), Pagano (1978), Troutman (1979), Tiao and Grupe (1980), Salas *et al.* (1982), Vecchia *et al.* (1983), and Vecchia (1985). In the case of water resources, it seems reasonable to believe that water supply differs with the seasonal rainfall. As another example, one may expect the effect of carbon dioxide emissions to differ across the seasons. These early references are mainly concerned with estimating model parameters and applications to non-trending data. In fact, for non-trending data, the statistical theory was already well developed quite some time ago. The main reason why economists became interested in periodic models is that (macro-)economic data typically display trends, and that these trends seem to be best characterized as stochastic trends. Naturally, the choice of the trend representation is of tantamount importance for out-of-sample forecasting. The interplay between periodic models and stochastic trends is not that straightforward, and it is in this area in particular where one could see most developments during the 1990s.

The introduction of periodic models into economics dates back to the late 1980s, see Osborn (1988), Birchenhall *et al.* (1989), and Osborn and Smith (1989). By then, the focus was on describing trending consumption and income data, and the use of periodic models for out-of-sample forecasting. These studies did not include a formal analysis of the type of trends, simply as the relevant tools were only developed in the mid 1990s, see Boswijk and Franses (1996) and Boswijk *et al.* (1997). Other new developments were extensions to multivariate periodic models for trending data and formal model selection strategies. A detailed account of all this material will be given in this book.

The PAR(1) model above is a special case of

$$y_t = \phi_t y_{t-1} + \varepsilon_t, \tag{1.4}$$

which is usually called a random-coefficient autoregression of order 1. As such, this model cannot be used for practical purposes as it needs further assumptions on the parameters ϕ_t. One such assumption amounts to restricting them to be equal to ϕ_s when $t = ST + s$, which brings us back to the PAR(1) model in (1.3).

The PAR(1) model itself encompasses the non-periodic AR(1) model, that is,

$$y_t = \phi y_{t-1} + \varepsilon_t, \tag{1.5}$$

by assuming that ϕ_s equals ϕ for all s. From a general-to-specific modeling perspective, this suggests that it makes sense to first examine whether a periodic model fits the data and next to see if it can be reduced to a non-periodic model, instead of the other way around. Indeed, we will demonstrate in Chapter 4 that the analysis of stochastic trends runs better from periodic models to non-periodic models than the other way around, see also Boswijk *et al.* (1997). For example, in Chapter 3 we will also demonstrate that the reduction from a periodic model to a non-periodic one can be simply achieved using an *F*-test with a standard distribution, no matter what the trend looks like.

Hence, a first motivation for using a periodic model is that it allows for more flexibility to describe economic data, although not too much, and that it nests other potentially relevant models. This is particularly relevant in practice as this means that periodic models can generate data that look like data generated by non-periodic models, but that this does not hold true the other way around. In fact, if we were to analyze PAR(1) data using a non-periodic model, we could derive how this model would look. For example, if a PAR(1) model generates the data, then a non-periodic model for these data would most likely have the form

$$y_t = \alpha y_{t-4} + \varepsilon_t + \theta_1 \varepsilon_{t-1} + \theta_2 \varepsilon_{t-2} + \theta_3 \varepsilon_{t-3}, \tag{1.6}$$

see Osborn (1991) and Section 3.5. In contrast, however, if one generated data from this non-periodic autoregressive moving-average model of order (4,3) [ARMA(4,3)], a PAR(1) model would not fit at all, as would be indicated by proper diagnostic tests. In other words, it makes sense to start with models with periodic parameters and to see if there really is such a periodic variation.

A second motivation for the use of periodic models is that there are a few economic theories, with the appropriate modifications to incorporate seasonality, which predict that certain macroeconomic data should show periodic behavior that can be picked up by PAR-type models. Examples of these theories are Gersovitz and MacKinnon (1978), Osborn (1988), Todd (1990), and Hansen and Sargent (1993). These theories incorporate the fact that consumers may have different loss (or utility) functions throughout the year, that agents can adapt disequilibrium errors differently throughout the year, or that technology shocks show seasonality. In those cases, one can derive that variables like consumption and production show seasonality of the periodic type.

A third motivation for periodic models has to do with seasonal adjustment. It can happen that somehow seasonally-adjusted data still display seasonality. One possible cause may be that the data show periodic properties, and if so, then seasonal adjustment does not make much sense. Periodic data cannot be seasonally adjusted, and the supposedly adjusted series will continue to show signs of seasonality. This holds both in theory and in practice, albeit that it is not always immediately obvious and is not easy to detect in real-life data. The implication is that seasonal adjustment, by definition, assumes that a time series y_t can be split up into two independent components, a seasonal and a non-seasonal component. It is easy to understand that this is impossible, for example, for the PAR(1) model. Hence, a periodic model allows the trend and the seasonal fluctuations to be related.

Finally, sometimes the periodic model is easier to extend. For example, multivariate periodic models are not difficult to analyze, and, more importantly, they also have interpretable parameters. Certain other models for more than two trending time series concern model representations for which the parameters are difficult to interpret. See Osborn (1993) for a discussion of the interpretation of the so-called seasonal cointegration model. Of course, one can still use these models for out-of-sample forecasting purposes, but if one aims to provide an economically meaningful description of a multivariate process then periodic models sometimes make more sense. Also, extending periodic models to include descriptions of nonlinearity is easily achieved, see, for example, Franses and van Dijk (2000), whereas this does not hold for various other models for seasonal time series.

In conclusion, we believe that periodic time series models are useful models for various reasons, and therefore we summarize the current state of the art in this book.

1.4   Outline of this book

This book contains four further chapters. Chapter 2 aims to convince the reader that economic time series show marked seasonality and an obvious trend, and, foremost, that the patterns of these trends and seasonal fluctuations do not seem to be very stable over time, nor do they seem to be similar across time series. We illustrate this for a range of quarterly US industrial production series, but other quarterly series from other countries would have yielded the same qualitative conclusion, as a glance at the relevant literature will indicate. We use graphical techniques and recently developed tests for unit roots. When economic data show evidence of unit roots, then one can conclude that the trend or the seasonal patterns are of a stochastic nature. This observation provides motivation for considering periodic models for economic data with a stochastic trend, as we will do in Chapter 4.

In Chapter 3 we outline the basics of periodic models for univariate time series data. In that chapter we abstain from a discussion of trending data, and assume there are no stochastic trends. This will be relaxed in Chapter 4. An important feature of time series models is that the model implies properties of the data that it aims to describe, see Franses (1998), among others. This is an extremely powerful result, as it implies that one can consider features of the observed data and let these indicate which time series model might be a good first guess model. For example, the first-order (non-periodic) autoregressive model implies that the data have an autocorrelation function which dies out geometrically. If one has such data, then one might start fitting such a first-order model. In other words, it is important to study the properties of time series models in order to know (or have an idea) when they can be useful in practice. This is what we shall do in Chapter 3, where we discuss two types of representation of periodic models. We discuss how parameters can be estimated, how the lag structures can be determined, and we give diagnostic measures to examine if the models are properly specified. Next, we show how one can generate forecasts from periodic models. As it is of interest to see what happens when one neglects periodicity, we also dedicate a section to this topic. Finally, we discuss periodic models for the conditional second moment, that is, models for volatility. Mention is made of periodic models for nonlinear data as well.

In Chapter 4 we address the issue of how to incorporate descriptions of trends in periodic models. It is well known that the trend in many economic time series may be characterized by a so-called unit root in the autoregressive part of the model, together with a nonzero intercept, although several variables allow for a purely deterministic trend. For periodic models, the notions of unit roots and deterministic trends become a little more complicated as there might be different trends across the seasons, thereby, for example, allowing for increasing or decreasing seasonal variation. If a periodic autoregression has a single unit root, this will appear as a function of all parameters in the model. If this restriction does not coincide with the well-known $(1, -1)$ filter, that is, the first-differencing filter, then the data are periodically integrated. As periodic integration nests non-periodic integration, we will argue that a sensible test strategy in practice begins with testing for periodic integration and then continues with examining non-periodic integration. This is sensible for various reasons, one of these being that no new asymptotic theory is needed. We derive the relevant parameter restrictions for periodic integration, and put forward statistics to test for unit roots. We need to be careful about how we handle deterministics in periodic models when we perform these tests, and therefore we dedicate an entire section to this issue. In the same chapter, we also show how one can forecast from periodic models with unit roots, and we say something about the consequences of neglecting periodicity. All material is again illustrated using the US production series.

In Chapter 5 we aim to extend all material in Chapter 4 to the case of more than a single time series. It turns out that in principle it is easy to extend univariate periodic models, by simply adding a subscript s, but that subsequent models can be cumbersome, if not impossible, to analyze for unit roots. Hence, we first outline various representations and discuss which ones are more useful than others in different situations. We devote two sections to the topic of testing for cointegration in periodic models, and indicate how one can best proceed in practice.

2

Properties of seasonal
time series

In this chapter we review typical properties of quarterly seasonal time series in economics. These properties are that there is substantial seasonality, next to a dominant trend. This seasonality sometimes seems to change over time. Trends in seasonal variation are rare in macroeconomics, but can be found in tourism and marketing, while they can also be found for data which have not been transformed using the logarithmic transformation.

As mentioned earlier, this book intends to suggest that periodic models can be useful, but other models can be useful too. We aim to outline how one can specify periodic models in practice, given that one has an interest in doing so. These models can be evaluated against other models in descriptive and forecasting exercises. Some of these alternative models are based on the results of seasonal unit tests discussed in this chapter, and hence a few remarks on these models need to be made. This chapter will not be very extensive as an excellent survey recently appeared in Ghysels and Osborn (2001:ch.3).

2.1   Graphs and basic regressions

This section contains a summary of the data used in this book, in terms of graphs and simple regression models. The next section will rely on more elaborate methods, but here we stick to simple tools.

For illustrative purposes, we use a set of fourteen US industrial production series. The data are available at the monthly level and can be downloaded from www.economagic.com. We consider both the unadjusted, that is, the original data and the seasonally-adjusted data. The latter data series have been adjusted using the Census X-12 method (or, perhaps the X-11 version, but this we do not know), and we will consider these when evaluating the

11

consequences of seasonal adjustment for potentially periodic data in forth-coming chapters. We aggregated the data to quarterly data by taking simple averages. Perhaps this is a redundant statement, but we take as the first quarter the months January to March, and so on. The quarterly data used in this book can be downloaded from `www.few.eur.nl/few/people/franses` or `www.few.eur.nl/few/people/paap`.

The fourteen series concern the total index (1919.1–2000.4), total products, final products, and consumer goods (all three observed for 1939.1–2000.4), durable consumer goods, automotive products, auto parts and allied goods, other durable goods, foods and tobacco, and clothing (all six observed for 1947.1–2000.4), and, finally, chemical products, paper products, energy products, and fuels (these last four series are observed for 1954.1–2000.4). These series concern a wide array of products. Also, it is our experience that the time series properties of the series amount to a rather representative sample of possible properties across quarterly observed macroeconomic time series. Hence, series based on consumption, income, imports, and exports, and also for other industrialized countries, display similar kinds of features as those considered in this book.

In Fig. 2.1 we present the graph of the total index, which concerns the longest sample. This graph conveys two important features of typical macroeconomic data, that is, the data have an upward trend and it seems that this trend is not linear but something close to exponential. This last observation usually leads to the application of the natural logarithmic transformation. There are various studies that question the automatic use of this transformation, but we take this issue to be outside the scope of this book. Hence, when we discuss models for the fourteen variables below, and when we write y_t, then we mean

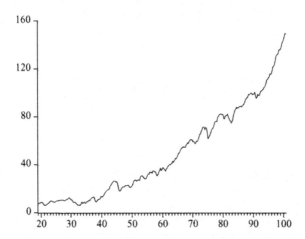

Figure 2.1: Index of total industrial production, 1919.1–2000.4

the natural logarithm of the original series. Another feature of the total industrial production index in Fig. 2.1 is that the upward trend in the data seems disrupted once in a while by short periods of downturn. Although perhaps not easy to see at first sight, there are many studies that suggest that such data are best described by nonlinear time series models, thereby allowing for different dynamic properties of the data across different regimes, which here might be associated with expansions and recessions. Most of the material in this book, however, assumes that the model is linear. But, at the end of Chapter 3, we discuss how such models can be modified to allow for nonlinear features, even though we do not provide explicit estimation results.

Any seasonal variation is not very obvious from Fig. 2.1, but it is clearer from Fig. 2.2, which concerns the index for foods and tobacco. Again, an upward trend can be discerned, but what is most obvious is the marked seasonal pattern, to be recognized by the sawtooth-like pattern. Comparing the graph with the numbers on the vertical axis, one can already get an impression that seasonal variation can be pretty large.

Although graphs like Fig. 2.2 do indicate that there is a trend and seasonal variation, they are not very informative as to how substantial this seasonal variation is, nor whether seasonal variation is constant over time. Indeed, it is difficult to infer from Fig. 2.2 whether the sawtooth pattern at the end of the sample is the same as the one in the beginning. For that purpose, it is perhaps better to look at the graphs as depicted in, for example, Fig. 2.3. This graph contains four lines, each of which is associated with one of the four quarters, and which concern detrended data. One way to detrend the data is by taking first differences of natural logarithmic transformed data, as this comes close to quarterly growth rates. In Chapter 4 we will see that other detrending methods can be applied to periodic time series data, but for the moment the

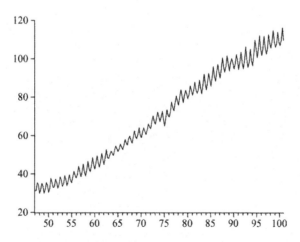

Figure 2.2: Index of production of foods and tobacco, 1947.1–2000.4

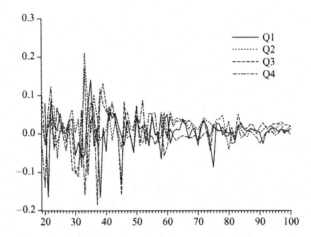

Figure 2.3: Quarterly growth rate of total industrial production, 1919–2000

detrending method taken here suffices. Figure 2.3 gives the quarterly growth
rates for total industrial production in each of the quarters from the year 1919
onwards. Graphs like this were apparently first advocated in Franses (1991),
which eventually got published in revised form as Franses (1994), see also Engle
et al. (1993: p. 280). These graphs have recently been included in EViews 4.1,
where they are labeled as 'seasonal split line'. These four graphs can provide
a first impression as to whether seasonal variation is large, as in that case the
four lines are rather distinct and their separation is relatively large, and as to
whether seasonality changes over time, which would appear as lines crossing
each other (and suggesting notions like 'summer becomes winter').

Indeed, the graphs in Fig. 2.3 suggest that there is not much seasonal variation in total industrial production, which is most likely due to the high level of
aggregation. In cases when there are seasonal fluctuations which are common
across disaggregated series, one might expect that cross-sectional aggregation
removes seasonality to some degree. In contrast, the graphs in Fig. 2.4 show
substantial seasonality (average growth varying from about 5 per cent in the
second quarter to about minus 5 per cent in the fourth quarter) for food and
tobacco production. Finally, the graphs in Fig. 2.5 provide an example of data
where seasonal fluctuations display a rather erratic behavior, where there are
many intersections across the four lines.

To provide some further insights into the size of seasonal variation, we
consider a very simple exercise, that is, we regress the quarterly growth rates,
which are thus $y_t - y_{t-1}$, on four seasonal dummies. Seasonal dummies $D_{s,t}$ are
equal to 1 if t corresponds to the sth season and 0 otherwise, for $s = 1, 2, 3, 4$. It
is well known that it can be hazardous to interpret this regression as a measure
of the size and type of deterministic seasonality, see Franses *et al.* (1995), but

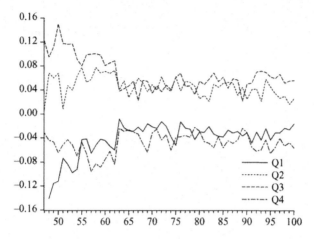

Figure 2.4: Quarterly growth rate of food and tobacco production, 1947–2000

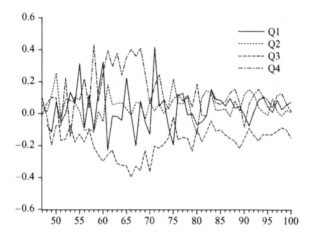

Figure 2.5: Quarterly growth rate of automotive products, 1947–2000

it can give a first and useful impression. The most relevant results appear in Table 2.1.

The parameter estimates concern the four seasonal dummy variables, and hence one can interpret δ_s as the average value of growth in quarter s, with $s = 1, 2, 3, 4$, assuming this to be the proper model. For some series it is clear that the growth values differ substantially across quarters, see, for example, automotive products, food and tobacco, and energy products, while for other series the differences are much smaller, see, for example, total production and clothing. The final column of Table 2.1 gives the R^2 of the regression. Obviously, when there is not much variation across estimates of δ_s, this R^2 is

Table 2.1

Regressing quarterly growth rates on four seasonal dummy variables:
parameter estimates

Production series	Sample	Parameter estimates				R^2
		δ_1	δ_2	δ_3	δ_4	
Total	327	0.453	1.748	0.735	0.755	0.011
Products	247	−0.032	1.673	1.905	0.502	0.076
Final products	247	0.598	0.899	1.744	0.892	0.021
Consumer goods	247	0.300	0.394	2.746	0.075	0.137
Durable consumer goods	215	−0.136	2.297	−6.513	8.251	0.458
Automotive products	215	3.069	4.379	−16.386	12.550	0.471
Auto parts	215	−0.192	2.346	1.903	−0.545	0.071
Other durable goods	215	−2.202	1.049	−0.380	5.604	0.267
Food and tobacco	215	−4.166	4.596	6.704	−4.875	0.837
Clothing	215	2.549	0.053	0.687	−2.636	0.158
Chemical products	187	−2.653	5.278	7.334	−4.757	0.593
Paper products	187	−1.019	1.715	4.985	−3.056	0.464
Energy products	187	13.420	−18.668	7.138	1.667	0.723
Fuels	187	−2.740	0.921	3.156	0.521	0.278

The parameter estimates are the growth rates (in percentages) for each quarter. The residuals of the auxiliary regression are unlikely to be white noise, and perhaps not even stationary, and hence no estimated standard errors are reported. The sample size concerns the effective sample size and R^2 denotes the coefficient of determination.

likely to be small too, although one should of course take account of the total variation in a time series. For series like food and tobacco (see also Fig. 2.4), chemical products, and energy products, the R^2 value is rather high. This can be interpreted to mean that, for these series in particular, it may matter later on which model one takes for modeling and forecasting. In contrast, for the series with very low R^2 values, one may expect that various models do not yield very different conclusions on forecasts. Additionally, if seasonality is strong, one wants to make the best decision in terms of selecting a model.

Finally, Table 2.2 concerns the possibility that there is not only seasonality in the mean but also in the variance, see also Jaditz (2000). This will become more important in Chapter 3, as periodic models often imply seasonality in variance, and a first impression might be useful. This table reports on a test of common variance of the estimated residuals from an autoregression for the growth

Table 2.2
Regressing quarterly growth rates on four seasonal dummy variables:
evidence of seasonal heteroskedasticity

Variable	Lags	Sample	Test statistic
Total	8	319	1.229
Products	7	240	0.599
Final products	7	240	0.896
Consumer goods	8	239	0.893
Durable consumer goods	8	207	2.902**
Automotive products	8	207	5.440***
Auto parts	5	210	1.495
Other durable goods	6	209	0.663
Food and tobacco	7	208	0.204
Clothing	16	199	0.274
Chemical products	8	179	0.134
Paper products	5	182	0.831
Energy products	10	177	0.997
Fuels	4	187	5.886***

***Significant at the 0.01 level, **at the 0.05 level, *at the 0.10 level.
The test statistic is based on an auxiliary regression in which the squares of
the estimated residuals from an autoregression of lag order k are regressed on
an intercept and three seasonal dummy variables. The statistic itself is the
F-test for the joint significance of the three dummy variables. The lag order
k is determined by the familiar Lagrange Multiplier (LM)-test for first-to-
fourth-order residual autocorrelation. The order is set to be the smallest
order for which this LM-test does not reject the null hypothesis. The sample
size concerns the effective sample size.

rates against the alternative that there is deterministic seasonal variation in
this variance. The last column of Table 2.2 suggests that there is evidence of
such seasonal variation in only three of the fourteen cases. Note, however, that
the number of lags for most variables, in order for the estimated residuals to
behave a bit like a white-noise-type error process, is quite large. As will become
clear in Chapter 3, this might also be a sign of the usefulness of periodic models,
as neglecting periodicity leads to many lags in non-periodic models.

2.2   Typical features of seasonal time series

The graphical and basic regression results in the previous section indicated that
the data have a trend, and that many of the fourteen series show substantial

seasonal variation, while only a few show seasonal heteroskedasticity. In this section we elaborate a bit more on the idea that seasonal variation might not be constant over time. For this purpose, we use tests for so-called seasonal unit roots, see Ghysels and Osborn (2001:ch.3) for a survey.

A time series variable is said to have a unit root if the autoregressive polynomial, of the autoregressive model that best describes this variable, contains the component $1 - L$, and the moving-average part does not, where L denotes the familiar lag operator defined by $L^k y_t = y_{t-k}$, for $k = \ldots, -2, -1, 0, 1, 2, \ldots$. For example, the model $y_t = y_{t-1} + \varepsilon_t$ has a first-order autoregressive polynomial $1 - L$, as it can be written as $(1 - L)y_t = \varepsilon_t$, and hence data that can be described by this model, which is the so-called random walk model, are said to have a unit root. The same holds of course for the model $y_t = \mu + y_{t-1} + \varepsilon_t$, which is called a random walk with drift. Solving this last model to the first observation, that is, $y_t = y_0 + \mu t + \varepsilon_t + \varepsilon_{t-1} + \cdots + \varepsilon_1$, shows that such data display a trend. Due to the summation of the error terms, it is possible that data diverge from the overall trend μt for a long time, and hence at first sight one would conclude from a graph that there are all kinds of temporary trends. Therefore, such data are sometimes said to have a stochastic trend.

The unit roots in seasonal data, which can be associated with changing seasonality, are the so-called seasonal unit roots, see Hylleberg *et al.* (1990). For quarterly data, these roots are -1, i, and $-$i. For example, data generated from the model $y_t = -y_{t-1} + \varepsilon_t$ would display seasonality, but if one were to make graphs with the seasonals split then one could observe that the quarterly data within a year shift places quite frequently. Similar observations hold for the model $y_t = -y_{t-2} + \varepsilon_t$, which can be written as $(1 + L^2)y_t = \varepsilon_t$, where the autoregressive polynomial $1 + L^2$ corresponds to the seasonal unit roots i and $-$i, as these two values solve the equation $1 + z^2 = 0$. Hence, when a model for y_t contains an autoregressive polynomial with roots -1 and/or i, $-$i, the data are said to have seasonal unit roots.

Autocorrelations

If a time series has all four unit roots, that is, 1, -1, i, and $-$i, the autoregressive polynomial contains the component $(1 - L)(1 + L)(1 + L^2)$, which equals $1 - L^4$. This so-called differencing filter is the annual filter, and the resulting data are approximately the annual growth rates, which are usually denoted as $\Delta_4 y_t = y_t - y_{t-4}$. Note that this again assumes that the data are analyzed after the natural logarithmic transformation has been applied, which is quite common for macroeconomic data.

There seems to be a consensus amongst applied econometricians that the above four unit roots are the only ones of interest. That is, many economic series (at least after natural logarithmic transformation) do not have two sets of unit roots of either type. This seems to be confirmed by the application of

Table 2.3

An informal check for the maximum number of possible unit roots by considering the estimated values of the first five autocorrelations of the $\Delta_4 y_t$ time series

Variable	$\hat{\rho}_1$	$\hat{\rho}_2$	$\hat{\rho}_3$	$\hat{\rho}_4$	$\hat{\rho}_5$
Total	0.827	0.540	0.242	−0.059	−0.181
Products	0.878	0.626	0.345	0.099	−0.049
Final products	0.884	0.648	0.382	0.146	0.002
Consumer goods	0.784	0.440	0.088	−0.237	−0.346
Durable consumer goods	0.771	0.405	0.027	−0.308	−0.422
Automotive products	0.646	0.325	0.035	−0.273	−0.235
Auto parts	0.785	0.494	0.178	−0.109	−0.188
Other durable goods	0.802	0.404	−0.032	−0.397	−0.538
Food and tobacco	0.600	0.429	0.285	−0.001	−0.002
Clothing	0.771	0.375	−0.009	−0.281	−0.288
Chemical products	0.735	0.536	0.402	0.237	0.299
Paper products	0.777	0.498	0.251	0.031	−0.027
Energy products	0.493	0.316	0.233	0.115	0.244
Fuels	0.612	0.477	0.306	0.097	0.157

formal methods like those developed in Franses and Koehler (1998) and Franses and Taylor (2000). A more informal check is also possible by considering the estimated autocorrelation function of $\Delta_4 y_t$, and investigating if it rapidly dies out. Indeed, the unit root 1 typically generates an autocorrelation function which takes high values even at longer lags, while seasonal unit roots would establish a similar phenomenon at lags which are multiples of two.

Table 2.3 displays the first five autocorrelations, which we denote by ρ_1 to ρ_5, for the annual growth rates of the fourteen series under scrutiny. It is evident that the values of the estimated autocorrelations die out rather quickly. Hence, it seems that we can safely assume that the Δ_4 filter is associated with the maximum number of unit roots. A word of caution is relevant here, though. Models of the form $\Delta_4 \Delta_1 y_t = (1 - \theta L)\varepsilon_t$, with θ very close to unity, also generate autocorrelations like those in Table 2.3. Now, the debate is of course what 'very close' means, and if the value of θ can be somehow useful for forecasting. In the literature there are two trains of thought. The first does not mind considering filters like $\Delta_4 \Delta_1$, which assume five(!) unit roots, while allowing for MA parameters close to the unit circle. The other view is that it may be odd for economic time series to be driven by so much random-walk-like uncertainty. In this book we adopt a middle view by taking the Δ_4 filter as the maximum. In Section 4.5, we will demonstrate that a misinterpretation of

periodic data with a single(!) unit root makes one think that the $\Delta_4\Delta_1$ filter
is needed, but we save this illustration for later on.

Seasonal unit roots

In order to examine if a time series has seasonal unit roots, one can nowadays
choose from a wide range of methods. Some methods take the presence of the
unit roots as the null hypothesis, like Hylleberg *et al.* (1990), Kunst (1997), and
Breitung and Franses (1998), while others take stable seasonality as the null
hypothesis, see Canova and Hansen (1995). While most methods follow classical inference techniques, there are also Bayesian methods, see Franses *et al.*
(1997). There are methods that can handle structural breaks in deterministic seasonality, while testing for seasonal unit roots, see Franses *et al.* (1997),
Franses and Vogelsang (1998), and Balcombe (1999). There are methods that
make use of recursive and rolling samples, see Smith and Taylor (2001), methods that can handle seasonal heteroskedasticity of the type discussed in the
previous section, see Burridge and Taylor (2001), and methods that take other
alternatives, for example, Taylor and Smith (2001).

   Although there are many methods, it seems that the most basic one, that
is the one developed in Hylleberg *et al.* (1990), the so-called HEGY method, is
still the most popular. We do not intend to discuss the various methods, and
we are aware of the possibility that different methods might lead to different
conclusions. Hence, here we simply take this basic method. So, it is possible
that alternative methods, such as allowing for breaks or for periodic variances,
would have resulted in other conclusions for some series, but now we are only
interested in a quick-and-ready overall picture.

   The HEGY method amounts to a regression of $\Delta_4 y_t$ on deterministic terms
like seasonal dummies, and a trend on $(1 + L + L^2 + L^3)y_{t-1}$, $(-1 + L - L^2 + L^3)y_{t-1}$, $-(1 + L^2)y_{t-1}$, $-(1 + L^2)y_{t-2}$, and on lags of $\Delta_4 y_t$. The t-test for
the significance of the parameter for $(1 + L + L^2 + L^3)y_{t-1}$ is denoted by t_1,
the t-test for $(-1 + L - L^2 + L^3)y_{t-1}$ by t_2, and the joint significance test
for $-(1 + L^2)y_{t-1}$ and $-(1 + L^2)y_{t-2}$ is denoted by F_{34}. An insignificant test
value indicates the presence of the associated root(s), which are 1, -1, and the
pair i, $-$i, respectively. Asymptotic theory for the tests is developed in various
studies, see Ghysels and Osborn (2001) and Osborn and Rodrigues (2002) for
reviews.

   We summarize the most relevant critical values for most economic data
in Table 2.4. The last panel contains the critical values in the case where
one restricts the seasonal intercepts when they correspond with a certain unit
root, see Smith and Taylor (1999). The first panel assumes that the regression
contains the seasonal dummies $D_{s,t}$, with $s = 1, 2, 3, 4$ and the trend t, while the
second panel assumes that the model contains the same four seasonal dummies
but also seasonal trends, given by $D_{s,t}t$. The third panel does not include the

Table 2.4
Critical values for test statistics for non-seasonal and seasonal unit roots in
quarterly time series

The regression model includes	Test	0.90	0.95	0.99
Seasonal dummies and trend	t_1	−3.10	−3.39	−3.96
	t_2	−2.53	−2.82	−3.41
	F_{34}	5.48	6.55	8.79
Seasonal dummies and seasonal trends	t_1	−3.11	−3.41	−3.97
	t_2	−3.11	−3.41	−3.97
	F_{34}	8.51	9.72	12.32
Alternating dummies and trend	Φ_1	5.34	6.25	8.27
	Φ_2	3.76	4.62	6.41
	Φ_{34}	3.25	3.77	5.01

The critical values for the case of seasonal dummies and trend can be found in
Hylleberg *et al.* (1990). Those for the case of seasonal dummies and seasonal
trends are from Smith and Taylor (1998*a*). The critical values in the last
panel are based on Smith and Taylor (1999), and the unpublished working
paper Smith and Taylor (1998*b*) cited therein, except for those for Φ_1 which
can be found in Dickey and Fuller (1981). The tests in the panel also assume
that the relevant parameters for alternating dummy variables are zero under
the null hypothesis of corresponding seasonal unit roots.

dummy variables $D_{s,t}$, but includes the alternating dummy variables $D_{1,t} -$
$D_{2,t} + D_{3,t} - D_{4,t}$, $D_{1,t} - D_{3,t}$, and $D_{2,t} - D_{4,t}$. Under the null hypothesis
that there is a unit root -1, the parameter for the first of these alternating
dummies should also be zero. The test statistic for this joint hypothesis is
denoted by Φ_2. The null hypothesis of roots i and $-i$ corresponds to zero
values of the parameters for the last two alternating dummies, and the test
statistic for this joint hypothesis is denoted by Φ_{34}. The Φ_1 statistic is the
familiar Dickey and Fuller (1981) test.

The application of the three test strategies yields the outcomes reported
in Tables 2.5–2.7. Interestingly, whichever method one takes, the qualitative
conclusion across the three tables appears to be the same. About half the series
does not have seasonal unit roots, while the other half does. It also seems that
the more disaggregated the data are, the more seasonal unit roots one tends
to find. Note again that for some series one needs a large number of lagged
annual growth rates, in order to obtain an approximately white noise error
series.

Table 2.5

Testing for unit roots in quarterly data using the method of Hylleberg et al. (1990)

Variable	Lags	Sample	Test statistics			Roots
			t_1	t_2	F_{34}	
Total	5	319	-2.736	-5.960***	36.805***	1
Products	3	241	-4.322***	-3.934***	33.662***	–
Final products	3	241	-4.675***	-4.166***	36.677***	–
Consumer goods	5	239	-1.005	-3.092**	17.532***	1
Durable consumer goods	2	210	-2.955	-3.861***	30.627***	1
Automotive products	5	207	-3.668**	-2.647*	12.470***	-1
Auto parts	5	207	-1.899	-4.719***	19.057***	1
Other durable goods	2	210	-2.340	-5.773***	19.842***	1
Food and tobacco	6	206	0.376	-4.306***	5.929*	1, i, -i
Clothing	13	199	0.742	-3.030**	3.335	1, i, -i
Chemical products	5	179	-2.598	-1.964	5.847*	1, -1, i, -i
Paper products	2	182	-2.050	-1.983	5.608*	1, -1, i, -i
Energy products	1	183	-2.583	-2.904**	2.726	1, i, -i
Fuels	1	183	-1.636	-2.744*	20.267***	1, -1

***Significant at the 0.01 level, **at the 0.05 level, *at the 0.10 level.

The number of lags of $\Delta_4 y_t$ in the auxiliary test regression is selected using an LM-test for first-to-fourth-order residual autocorrelation. The order is set at the value for which this LM-test statistic is not significant. The maximum lag length is set at 8. When the test is insignificant at the 0.05 level, the lag length gets reduced to 7, and so on. The number of lags is fixed at k, when the test rejects the null hypothesis for lag $k-1$ and not for k. For the clothing data, we need to expand the model as the test indicates misspecification for lags below 8. The sample size concerns the effective sample size. The decision on the number and type of unit roots is based on a 0.05 significance level.

Table 2.6

Testing for unit roots in quarterly data using the method of Smith and Taylor (1998a)

Variable	Lags	Sample	Test statistics			Roots
			t_1	t_2	F_{34}	
Total	5	319	−2.758	−5.705***	36.827***	1
Products	3	241	−4.249***	−4.054***	41.434***	–
Final products	3	241	−4.620***	−4.190***	40.008***	–
Consumer goods	5	239	−1.013	−3.257*	20.142***	1, −1
Durable consumer goods	2	210	−2.846	−3.928**	35.188***	1
Automotive products	5	207	−3.655**	−2.704	12.645***	−1
Auto parts	5	207	−1.856	−4.692***	19.774***	1
Other durable goods	2	210	−2.277	−6.179***	25.920***	1
Food and tobacco	6	206	0.378	−4.251***	5.882	1, i, −i
Clothing	13	199	0.724	−3.353*	6.567	1, −1, i, −i
Chemical products	5	179	−2.583	−1.915	2.174	1, −1, i, −i
Paper products	2	182	−2.028	−1.907	5.731	1, −1, i, −i
Energy products	1	183	−2.500	−4.344***	9.371*	1, i, −i
Fuels	1	183	−1.656	−5.111***	35.698***	1

***Significant at the 0.01 level, **at the 0.05 level, *at the 0.10 level.
See note of Table 2.5.

Table 2.7
Testing for unit roots in quarterly data using the method of Smith and Taylor (1999)

Variable	Lags	Sample	Test statistics			Roots
			Φ_1	Φ_2	Φ_{34}	
Total	5	319	4.009	16.289***	18.432***	1
Products	3	241	10.053***	7.802***	16.856***	–
Final products	3	241	11.452***	8.705***	18.353***	–
Consumer goods	5	239	2.823	4.817**	8.786***	1
Durable consumer goods	2	210	4.394	7.459***	15.336***	1
Automotive products	5	207	6.768**	3.504	6.281***	–1
Auto parts	5	207	2.158	11.207***	9.697***	1
Other durable goods	2	210	2.738	16.679***	9.948***	1
Food and tobacco	6	206	4.470	9.431***	3.376*	1, i, –i
Clothing	13	199	4.671	7.863***	2.558	1, i, –i
Chemical products	5	179	6.135*	1.987	3.016	1, –1, i, –i
Paper products	2	182	3.580	1.965	2.804	1, –1, i, –i
Energy products	1	183	12.221***	4.274*	1.462	i, –i
Fuels	1	183	2.574	3.809*	10.218***	1, –1

***Significant at the 0.01 level, **at the 0.05 level, *at the 0.10 level.
See note of Table 2.5.

2.3   Summary and outlook

This chapter has documented, for the fourteen sample series at hand, that typical macroeconomic data can display trends, that these trends tend to look like stochastic trends as the unit root 1 is often found, that there is substantial seasonal variation and that this variation can sometimes be described by seasonal unit root models, and that sometimes it seems close to deterministic.

One possible strategy would now be to take the outcomes of seasonal unit root tests seriously and build univariate or multivariate models with such unit roots. Applications of this strategy are given in Lee (1992), Engle *et al.* (1993), Kunst (1993), Franses and Kunst (1999), and Johansen and Shaumburg (1999). However, in the present book, we only use these tests to suggest that economic data have certain properties. At a later stage, and if needed, when we have postulated periodic models for the fourteen series at hand, we will return to seasonal unit root models as they provide a sensible benchmark for evaluating out-of-sample forecasting of periodic models.

In the next chapter we will present the details of linear time series models for periodic data. We did not explicitly test for periodicity in the present chapter to justify our focus on periodic models, but the reader has to trust us that later on we will see that for several of the fourteen series at hand we can fit such periodic models. At this stage, we have not said much about their representation and properties, and therefore we have not said much about tests to diagnose periodicity.

3

Univariate periodic time series models

In this chapter we focus on periodic autoregressive models for univariate economic time series, as these models might be able to capture the features of seasonal time series, discussed in the previous chapter. A periodic autoregression (PAR) extends a non-periodic AR model by allowing the autoregressive parameters to vary with the seasons. This allowance can concern all parameters, but it can also be confined to just a few. A PAR model assumes that the observations in each of the seasons might be described by a different model. Such a property may be useful to describe certain economic time series data, as one sometimes may expect that economic agents behave differently in different seasons. If so, then the memory structure, which in turn gets reflected by the autoregressive components, can vary with the season. For example, technological advances through the years have now made it possible to buy certain vegetables in almost all seasons, while these products were available in, say, only the summer season several years ago. Hence, one may observe an increasing trend in the consumption of these vegetables in one or more seasons but see no trend in the summer season. Another example is that tax measures can become effective in, say, the first part of the year, and this may lead to seasonal variation in inflation. In turn, this may lead to economic agents increasingly anticipating this inflation peak. Yet another example is that, due to increasing personal disposable income and increasing leisure time in developed countries, consumer spending on holidays has changed over the years. Hence, there seem to be theoretical motivations for the possible usefulness of PAR models, in addition to the empirical evidence on the data features which also suggests their potential.

In this chapter we examine the econometric properties of PAR models. As mentioned before, it is important to do this, as knowledge of these properties

makes one able to recognize the potential usefulness of PAR models when analyzing actual data. In Section 3.1 we discuss notation and representation issues
for PAR models for univariate quarterly time series. In this chapter we do not
consider trending periodic data, as the analysis of such data actually requires
a separate chapter, see Chapter 4.

A PAR model can be represented in at least two ways. We will see that
a multivariate representation appears to be most useful for analyzing the stationarity properties of the model, see Section 3.2, which is quite important
when it comes to analyzing unit roots. We only consider quarterly time series,
although all material naturally extends to, for example, monthly time series.
We must stress though that these extensions are straightforward in theory, but
in practice they might not be. Indeed, periodic models for monthly data can
involve a huge number of parameters.

In the present chapter, we abstain from a detailed analysis of periodic
MA models (PMA) or periodic ARMA models (PARMA). This is due to our
personal experience of working with periodic data. Often it turns out that low-
order PAR models are sufficiently adequate to describe periodic time series, see
also McLeod (1994), for example.

Next, in Section 3.3, we discuss model selection and estimation in PAR
models. It appears that standard model selection techniques can readily be
applied. We also discuss simple methods to select between periodic and non-
periodic AR models. We illustrate these tools for the fourteen US production
series under scrutiny. Upon application of the various tests, we find much
evidence of periodic patterns in the time series properties. Section 3.4 deals with
forecasting from stationary PAR models. In Section 3.5 we study the impact of
neglecting periodicity, that is, the effects of considering non-periodic models for
periodic time series, and we illustrate the consequences for the autocorrelation
functions. We also examine what happens when one applies linear seasonal
adjustment filters to otherwise periodic data. This is also illustrated by the
fact that several of our seasonally-adjusted production series still display strong
signs of periodic patterns. Finally, in Section 3.6, we briefly discuss periodic
models for modeling the conditional variances of time series, which we illustrate
for S&P 500 returns. Most sections, however, contain empirical investigations
using the example series which were also analyzed in the previous chapter. It
should again be mentioned that the explicit analysis of stochastic trends (unit
roots) in PAR models is postponed until Chapter 4. The last section of this
chapter discusses some further topics, such as nonlinear periodic models and
structural breaks.

3.1   Representation

In this section we consider notation and representation issues. The notation
used is a simplified form of that used in, for example, Vecchia (1985), and hence

in order to avoid confusion we put some effort into giving notational details. Early references to PAR models are Gladyshev (1961), Jones and Brelsford (1967), Pagano (1978), Cleveland and Tiao (1979), Parzen and Pagano (1979), Troutman (1979), and Andel (1983), where these models were used to analyze water resources and environmental data.

Univariate representation

Consider a univariate time series y_t, which is observed quarterly for N years, that is, $t = 1, 2, \ldots, n$. Without loss of generality, it is assumed that $n = 4N$. A periodic autoregressive model of order p [PAR(p)] can be written as

$$y_t = \mu_s + \phi_{1s} y_{t-1} + \cdots + \phi_{ps} y_{t-p} + \varepsilon_t, \tag{3.1}$$

or

$$\phi_{p,s}(L) y_t = \mu_s + \varepsilon_t \tag{3.2}$$

with

$$\phi_{p,s}(L) = 1 - \phi_{1s} L - \cdots - \phi_{ps} L^p, \tag{3.3}$$

where μ_s is a seasonally-varying intercept term. The $\phi_{1s}, \ldots, \phi_{ps}$ are auto-regressive parameters up to order p_s which may vary with the season s, where $s = 1, 2, 3, 4$. We choose to use the notation ϕ_{1s}, and not $\phi_{1,s}$, for parameters, while we will use $y_{s,t}$ for variables. The ε_t is assumed to be a standard white noise process with constant variance σ^2. This assumption may be relaxed by allowing ε_t to have seasonal variance σ_s^2. Below, we will consider a simple test statistic for such seasonal heteroskedasticity, which is effectively the same as the one used in Table 2.2. For the moment, however, we abstain from seasonal variation in σ^2 and focus on (3.1). As some ϕ_{is}, $i = 1, 2, \ldots, p$, can take zero values, the order p in (3.1) is the maximum of all p_s, where p_s denotes the AR order per season s. Hence, one may also wish to consider so-called subset periodic autoregressions, which are investigated in Franses (1993). It must be mentioned though that, for the analysis of unit roots in periodic models, it is better to first examine their presence, and perhaps later on to reduce the model to a subset model.

A periodic moving average model of order q [PMA(q)] for y_t can be written as

$$y_t = \mu_s + \theta_{q,s}(L) \varepsilon_t, \tag{3.4}$$

with

$$\theta_{q,s}(L) = 1 + \theta_{1s} L + \cdots + \theta_{qs} L^q. \tag{3.5}$$

See Cipra (1985) for a theoretical analysis of a PMA(q) model. Naturally, one can combine (3.1) and (3.4) into a PARMA(p, q) model, see Vecchia (1985) for an analysis of a PARMA model. Although PMA and PARMA models may be useful for describing some time series, in this book we limit the discussion to PAR models as, firstly, these can be usefully analyzed for stochastic trends, and, secondly, empirical experience with economic time series shows that low-order PAR models often fit periodic time series data rather well—see the empirical results below, where p is often found to be smaller than six for the running example of industrial production series. Hence, the gain from using MA structures to deal with lengthy AR structures is perhaps not very large.

The μ_s parameters in (3.1) do not necessarily imply that the mean of y_t is also seasonally varying. This can be observed from rewriting a PAR process for y_t with a constant mean μ, that is,

$$\phi_{p,s}(L)(y_t - \mu) = \varepsilon_t, \tag{3.6}$$

as (3.1). It is then clear that $\mu_s = \phi_{p,s}(1)\mu$, and hence that μ_s is seasonally varying because the autoregressive parameters are varying. Similar results apply when a linear deterministic trend component $\tau_s T_t$ is added to (3.1) in a linear way, where τ_s are seasonally-varying parameters. We define the linear deterministic trend as $T_t = [(t-1)/4] + 1$, where $[\cdot]$ is the integer function such that the value of the trend is constant across the year. Note that this means that for quarterly data T_t equals $1, 1, 1, 1, 2, 2, 2, 2, \ldots$. This notation will turn out to be convenient when testing for unit roots. In the next chapter we will elaborate more on the analysis of trends in periodic data.

Obviously, the number of autoregressive parameters in a PAR(p) model for a quarterly time series is four times as many as that in a non-periodic AR(p) model, at least for the same value of p. For example, when p equals 4 in (3.1), one needs to estimate $16 + 4 = 20$ parameters in the PAR model, where 4 parameters concern the intercepts. In practice, this may become too large a number of parameters, given the possibly limited number of observations. Therefore, Gersovitz and MacKinnon (1978) proposed the imposition of some smoothness restrictions on the autoregressive parameters, which can be useful when analyzing, for example, monthly data. On the other hand, recent empirical results on the application of PAR models to monthly time series, as in Noakes *et al.* (1985) and McLeod (1994), indicate that such restrictions may not be strictly necessary in order to obtain useful estimation results. We will also abstain from such restrictions in further analysis, although we aim to be careful in the practical application of PAR(p) models.

Finally, it should be mentioned that one can already observe from (3.1) that, for data generated from a PAR model, the time series cannot be decomposed into seasonal and non-seasonal components. In fact, as the autoregressive parameters show seasonal variation, and as these cannot be separated from the y_t series, it is obvious that linear seasonal adjustment filters would not yield a non-periodic time series. Indeed, linear seasonal adjustment methods treat the observations in all quarters in the same way. As a consequence, one might still find evidence of autoregressive periodicity in seasonally-adjusted data. In Section 3.5 we will analyze this implication in more detail.

Multivariate representation

Strictly speaking, the periodic time series model in (3.1) or (3.4) is a non-stationary model as the variance and autocovariances take different values in different seasons. Consider, for example, the PMA(1) model

$$y_t = \varepsilon_t + \theta_{1s}\varepsilon_t, \tag{3.7}$$

for which it is easily shown that the variance and first-order autocovariance in season s, to be denoted by γ_{0s} and γ_{1s}, respectively, are given by

$$\begin{aligned} \gamma_{0s} &= \sigma^2(1 + \theta_{1s}^2), \\ \gamma_{1s} &= \sigma^2\theta_{1s}, \end{aligned} \tag{3.8}$$

and hence that the first-order autocorrelation per season s, ρ_{1s}, equals

$$\rho_{1s} = \frac{\theta_{1s}}{1 + \theta_{1s}^2}. \tag{3.9}$$

Obviously, this result violates the assumption of time-invariant correlations, which is one of the assumptions for stationarity. This indicates that, in order to also facilitate the analysis of stationarity, a more convenient representation of a PAR(p) process is a time-invariant form. As the PAR(p) model considers different AR(p) models for different seasons, it seems natural to rewrite it as a model for annual observations, see also Gladyshev (1961), Tiao and Grupe (1980), Lütkepohl (1991), and Osborn (1991).

In general, the PAR(p) process in (3.1) can be rewritten as an AR(P) model for the 4×1 vector process $Y_T = (Y_{1,T}, Y_{2,T}, Y_{3,T}, Y_{4,T})'$, $T = 1, 2, \ldots, N$, where $Y_{s,T}$ is the observation of y_t in season s of year T, $s = 1, 2, 3, 4$. The model is then

$$\Phi_0 Y_T = \mu + \Phi_1 Y_{T-1} + \cdots + \Phi_P Y_{T-P} + \varepsilon_T, \tag{3.10}$$

or

$$\Phi(L)Y_T = \mu + \varepsilon_T \tag{3.11}$$

with

$$\Phi(L) = \Phi_0 - \Phi_1 L - \cdots - \Phi_P L^P, \tag{3.12}$$

where $\mu = (\mu_1, \mu_2, \mu_3, \mu_4)'$ and $\varepsilon_T = (\varepsilon_{1,T}, \varepsilon_{2,T}, \varepsilon_{3,T}, \varepsilon_{4,T})'$, and $\varepsilon_{s,T}$ is the observation on the error process ε_t in season s of year T. Note that the lag operator L applies to data at frequencies t and to T, that is, $Ly_t = y_{t-1}$ and

$LY_T = Y_{T-1}$. The $\Phi_0, \Phi_1, \ldots, \Phi_P$ are 4×4 parameter matrices with elements

$$\Phi_0[i,j] = \begin{cases} 1 & \text{if } i = j, \\ 0 & \text{if } j > i, \\ -\phi_{i-j,i} & \text{if } i < j, \end{cases} \tag{3.13}$$

$$\Phi_k[i,j] = \phi_{i+4k-j,i},$$

for $i = 1, 2, 3, 4$, $j = 1, 2, 3, 4$, and $k = 1, 2, \ldots, P$. For the model order P in (3.10) it holds that $P = 1 + [(p-1)/4]$, where $[\cdot]$ is again the integer function. Hence, when p is less than or equal to 4, the value of P is only 1. Note that the notation is slightly different from that in Lütkepohl (1991), where the convention is followed that the Y_T vector denotes the stacked $Y_{4,T}$ to $Y_{1,T}$ series.

As Φ_0 is a lower triangular matrix, model (3.10) is a recursive model. This means that the observations in the fourth quarter, that is, $Y_{4,T}$, depend on the preceding observations in the same year, that is $Y_{3,T}$, $Y_{2,T}$, and $Y_{1,T}$, and observations in past years. Similarly, $Y_{3,T}$ depends on $Y_{2,T}$ and $Y_{1,T}$, and $Y_{2,T}$ on $Y_{1,T}$ and observations in past years.

As an example of (3.10), consider the PAR(2) process

$$y_t = \phi_{1s}y_{t-1} + \phi_{2s}y_{t-2} + \varepsilon_t, \tag{3.14}$$

which can be written as

$$\Phi_0 Y_T = \Phi_1 Y_{T-1} + \varepsilon_T, \tag{3.15}$$

with

$$\Phi_0 = \begin{pmatrix} 1 & 0 & 0 & 0 \\ -\phi_{12} & 1 & 0 & 0 \\ -\phi_{23} & -\phi_{13} & 1 & 0 \\ 0 & -\phi_{24} & -\phi_{14} & 1 \end{pmatrix} \quad \text{and} \quad \Phi_1 = \begin{pmatrix} 0 & 0 & \phi_{21} & \phi_{11} \\ 0 & 0 & 0 & \phi_{22} \\ 0 & 0 & 0 & 0 \\ 0 & 0 & 0 & 0 \end{pmatrix}. \tag{3.16}$$

In order to avoid confusion with multivariate time series models, we refer to models like (3.10) as the vector of quarters (VQ) representation, as advocated in Franses (1991). Sometimes we will refer to a VQ of order P, which then corresponds to (3.10). Notice from (3.10) and (3.16) that one can always write a non-periodic AR model using a VQ representation, hence this notation is not introducing any new parameters or structures. Also, it suggests that one can first analyze the data in VQ format, and next, if there is reason to do so, write the model in univariate format. The example in (3.16) also indicates that a PAR(4) model can still be written in VQ(1) format, since then the first row of the Φ_1 matrix does not contain zeros. Furthermore, it can be seen that such a VQ format of order 1 is still useful when $p_s = s + 3$. For example, when the order of the AR polynomial in quarter four is 7, that in quarter three is 6, and so on, the Φ_1 matrix does not contain any zero-valued parameters, while Φ_2 only has zeros.

There are two versions of (3.10) that will sometimes be considered below, as these are useful for the analysis of unit roots (for which more details are included in the next chapter) and for forecasting. The first is given by simply pre-multiplying (3.10) with Φ_0^{-1}, that is,

$$Y_T = \Phi_0^{-1}\mu + \Phi_0^{-1}\Phi_1 Y_{T-1} + \cdots + \Phi_0^{-1}\Phi_P Y_{T-P} + \Phi_0^{-1}\varepsilon_T. \tag{3.17}$$

As Φ_0 for a PAR(P) series is a lower triangular matrix with no zeros on the diagonal, it is always invertible. The expression in (3.17) is a vector autoregressive (VAR) model of order P for the Y_T process. When $\varepsilon_T \sim \mathrm{N}(0, \sigma^2 I_4)$, it follows that

$$\Phi_0^{-1}\varepsilon_T \sim \mathrm{N}(0, \sigma^2 \Phi_0^{-1}(\Phi_0^{-1})'). \tag{3.18}$$

Note that Φ_0^{-1} for any PAR process is again a lower triangular matrix. For example, for the PAR(2) case in (3.15) it can be found that

$$\Phi_0^{-1} = \begin{pmatrix} 1 & 0 & 0 & 0 \\ \phi_{12} & 1 & 0 & 0 \\ \phi_{12}\phi_{13} + \phi_{23} & \phi_{13} & 1 & 0 \\ \phi_{12}\phi_{13}\phi_{14} + \phi_{12}\phi_{24} + \phi_{23}\phi_{14} & \phi_{13}\phi_{14} + \phi_{24} & \phi_{14} & 1 \end{pmatrix}. \tag{3.19}$$

This implies that the first two columns of $\Phi_0^{-1}\Phi_1$ contain only zeros, that is,

$\Phi_0^{-1}\Phi_1$

$$= \begin{pmatrix} 0 & 0 & \phi_{21} & \phi_{11} \\ 0 & 0 & \phi_{12}\phi_{21} & \phi_{12}\phi_{11} + \phi_{22} \\ 0 & 0 & (\phi_{12}\phi_{13} + \phi_{23})\phi_{21} & \phi_{11}\phi_{12}\phi_{13} + \phi_{11}\phi_{23} + \phi_{13}\phi_{22} \\ 0 & 0 & (\phi_{12}\phi_{13}\phi_{14} + \phi_{12}\phi_{24} + \phi_{23}\phi_{14})\phi_{21} & (\phi_{12}\phi_{13}\phi_{14} + \phi_{12}\phi_{24} + \phi_{23}\phi_{14})\phi_{11} \end{pmatrix}. \tag{3.20}$$

For a PAR(1) model, the first three columns of $\Phi_0^{-1}\Phi_1$ contain only zero-valued parameters. For a PAR(2) process this holds for the first two columns, see (3.20). For the PAR(p) process with $p \geq 4$ it holds that $\Phi_0^{-1}\Phi_1$ does not contain columns with only zeros. These expressions suggest that one can retrieve the parameters in, say, a PAR(2) model, by regressing $Y_{s,T}$ on $Y_{2,T-1}$ and $Y_{1,T-1}$, although this is of course not the easiest way as these nonlinear functions are not simple.

A second version of (3.10), which is sometimes useful, is based on the possibility of decomposing a non-periodic AR(p) polynomial as $(1 - \alpha_1 L)(1 - \alpha_2 L) \cdots (1 - \alpha_p L)$. Note that this can only be done when the solutions to the characteristic equation for this AR(p) polynomial are all real valued. Similar results hold for the multivariate representation of a PAR(p) process, and it can be useful to rewrite (3.10) as

$$\prod_{i=1}^{P} \Xi_i(L)Y_T = \mu + \varepsilon_T, \tag{3.21}$$

where the $\Xi_i(L)$ are 4×4 matrices with elements which are polynomials in L. A simple example is again the PAR(2) process in (3.14), which may be written as

$$\Xi_1(L)\Xi_2(L)Y_T = \varepsilon_T, \tag{3.22}$$

with

$$\Xi_1(L) = \begin{pmatrix} 1 & 0 & 0 & -\beta_1 L \\ -\beta_2 & 1 & 0 & 0 \\ 0 & -\beta_3 & 1 & 0 \\ 0 & 0 & -\beta_4 & 1 \end{pmatrix}, \quad \Xi_2(L) = \begin{pmatrix} 1 & 0 & 0 & -\alpha_1 L \\ -\alpha_2 & 1 & 0 & 0 \\ 0 & -\alpha_3 & 1 & 0 \\ 0 & 0 & -\alpha_4 & 1 \end{pmatrix}, \tag{3.23}$$

where we leave the derivation as an exercise to the reader. Now, (3.14) can be written as

$$(1 - \beta_s L)(1 - \alpha_s L)y_t = \mu_s + \varepsilon_t. \tag{3.24}$$

This expression equals

$$y_t - \alpha_s y_{t-1} = \mu_s + \beta_s(y_{t-1} - \alpha_{s-1}y_{t-2}) + \varepsilon_t, \tag{3.25}$$

as, and this is quite important, the lag operator L also operates on α_s, that is, $L\alpha_s = \alpha_{s-1}$ for all $s = 1, 2, 3, 4$ and with $\alpha_0 = \alpha_4$. This last representation will come in handy when analyzing multiple unit roots in periodic time series data, see Chapter 4.

The analogy of a univariate PAR process with a multivariate time series process can also be exploited to derive explicit formulae for one- and multi-step ahead forecasting, see Section 3.4. In that case it should be noted that the one-step ahead forecasts concern one-year ahead forecasts for all four $Y_{s,T}$ series. For example, for the model $Y_T = \Phi_0^{-1}\Phi_1 Y_{T-1} + \omega_T$, where $\omega_T = \Phi_0^{-1}\varepsilon_T$, the forecast for $N + 1$ is $Y_{N+1} = \Phi_0^{-1}\Phi_1 Y_N$. Of course, if one wants to forecast one-step ahead for any other season than the first quarter, one may want to use the univariate representation, see Section 3.4.

3.2   Stationarity in periodic autoregressions

There are two approaches to investigating the stationarity properties of a PAR process, that is, to investigate whether it contains unit roots. To know whether or not there are unit roots is important for subsequent statistical analysis of the model, and also for the width of the confidence bounds around forecasts.

The first approach is to rewrite the process (3.1) as an infinite moving average process, and to check for parameter restrictions which establish that the effects of previous shocks do not die out. For simple PMA or PAR processes this may be a useful method, see Cipra (1985) for an application to PMA processes. For PAR processes of higher order, this may however become analytically cumbersome. A second method, which utilizes the link between a PAR model and a multivariate VQ time series model as in (3.10), is then more convenient. This method is also used in Bentarzi and Hallin (1994) for the analysis of the invertibility of a PMA process.

For a PAR(p) process, an investigation of the presence of unit roots in y_t amounts to investigating the solutions of the characteristic equation of (3.10), that is, the solutions of

$$|\Phi_0 - \Phi_1 z - \cdots - \Phi_P z^P| = 0. \tag{3.26}$$

When k solutions of (3.26) are on the unit circle, the Y_T process, and also the y_t process, have k unit roots. Indeed, it is important to understand (in order to avoid serious misinterpretation) that the number of unit roots in y_t equals that in Y_T, and hence that no additional unit roots are introduced in the multivariate representation. Also, no unit root disappears during the process of writing a model in another representation. This is all due to the fact that the number of unit roots is determined by the number of lags in the AR model for y_t. We now illustrate this with several examples.

As a first example, consider the PAR(2) process in (3.14) for which the characteristic equation is

$$|\Phi_0 - \Phi_1 z| = \begin{vmatrix} 1 & 0 & -\phi_{21}z & -\phi_{11}z \\ -\phi_{12} & 1 & 0 & -\phi_{22}z \\ -\phi_{23} & -\phi_{13} & 1 & 0 \\ 0 & -\phi_{24} & -\phi_{41} & 1 \end{vmatrix} = 0, \tag{3.27}$$

which becomes

$$1 - (\phi_{22}\phi_{13}\phi_{14} + \phi_{22}\phi_{24} + \phi_{21}\phi_{12}\phi_{13} + \phi_{21}\phi_{23} + \phi_{11}\phi_{12}\phi_{13}\phi_{14}$$
$$+ \phi_{11}\phi_{12}\phi_{24} + \phi_{11}\phi_{14}\phi_{23})z + \phi_{21}\phi_{22}\phi_{23}\phi_{24}z^2 = 0. \tag{3.28}$$

Hence, when the nonlinear parameter restriction

$$\phi_{22}\phi_{13}\phi_{14} + \phi_{22}\phi_{24} + \phi_{21}\phi_{12}\phi_{13} + \phi_{21}\phi_{23} + \phi_{11}\phi_{12}\phi_{13}\phi_{14}$$
$$+ \phi_{11}\phi_{12}\phi_{24} + \phi_{11}\phi_{14}\phi_{23} - \phi_{21}\phi_{22}\phi_{23}\phi_{24} = 1 \tag{3.29}$$

is imposed on the parameters of the PAR(2) model in (3.14), the PAR(2) model contains a single unit root. In principle, one can impose this restriction on the parameters using EViews code, for example. However, it is easy to appreciate that such restrictions can become rather involved when analyzing higher-order models. Also, the restricted parameters in the periodic model become more difficult to interpret as these are highly nonlinear functions of the other parameters.

If the characteristic equation for a PAR(2) process, that is, (3.26), yields two real-valued solutions, one can also analyze the characteristic equation of (3.22), which is

$$|\Xi_1(z)\Xi_2(z)| = 0. \tag{3.30}$$

Given (3.23) it is easy to see that this equation is equivalent to

$$(1 - \beta_1\beta_2\beta_3\beta_4 z)(1 - \alpha_1\alpha_2\alpha_3\alpha_4 z) = 0, \tag{3.31}$$

and hence that the PAR(2) model in the format of (3.25) has one unit root when either $\beta_1\beta_2\beta_3\beta_4 = 1$ or $\alpha_1\alpha_2\alpha_3\alpha_4 = 1$, and has at most two unit roots when both products equal unity. Obviously, the maximum number of unity solutions to the characteristic equation of a PAR(p) process is equal to p, which is again rather crucial to bear in mind.

To continue with our discussion on unit roots and also on seasonal unit roots, and how they appear in the VQ representation, consider the simple PAR(1) model, that is,

$$y_t = \alpha_s y_{t-1} + \varepsilon_t. \tag{3.32}$$

Note that this notation corresponds to that in (3.25), when β_s is set equal to zero for all s, and that it does not correspond to (3.1) as we changed from ϕ parameters to α parameters. We choose to use (3.32) for notational convenience, and also as this notation will turn out to be useful in the next chapter, where the models written in the format of (3.25) will be considered.

The PAR(1) model can be written as

$$\Phi_0 Y_T = \Phi_1 Y_{T-1} + \varepsilon_T, \tag{3.33}$$

with

$$\Phi_0 = \begin{pmatrix} 1 & 0 & 0 & 0 \\ -\alpha_2 & 1 & 0 & 0 \\ 0 & -\alpha_3 & 1 & 0 \\ 0 & 0 & -\alpha_4 & 1 \end{pmatrix} \quad \text{and} \quad \Phi_1 = \begin{pmatrix} 0 & 0 & 0 & \alpha_1 \\ 0 & 0 & 0 & 0 \\ 0 & 0 & 0 & 0 \\ 0 & 0 & 0 & 0 \end{pmatrix}. \tag{3.34}$$

The characteristic equation is

$$|\Phi_0 - \Phi_1 z| = 1 - \alpha_1\alpha_2\alpha_3\alpha_4 z = 0, \tag{3.35}$$

and hence the PAR(1) process has a unit root when $\alpha_1\alpha_2\alpha_3\alpha_4 = 1$. Note that this means that some of the α parameters can be in excess of 1, while others are below 1. In the case where one or more α_s values are not equal to α, that is, when $\alpha_s \neq \alpha$ for some or all s, and $\alpha_1\alpha_2\alpha_3\alpha_4 = 1$, the y_t process in (3.32) is said to be periodically integrated of order 1 [PI(1)]. Periodic integration of order 2 can be similarly defined in terms of the α_s and β_s parameters in the PAR(2) process using (3.30). The concept of periodic integration was first defined in Osborn *et al.* (1988). In Chapter 4 we will discuss the concept of periodic integration in more detail, and give a slightly more precise definition than this one, as it will appear to be a useful concept in practice.

The PAR(1) process nests the non-periodic AR(1) model. When $\alpha_s = \alpha$ for all s, (3.32) becomes

$$y_t = \alpha y_{t-1} + \varepsilon_t. \tag{3.36}$$

It is obvious that a unit root in a PAR(1) process implies a unit root in the AR(1) process (3.36), that is, $\alpha^4 = 1$ implies that α is either 1 or -1. For (3.36), the characteristic equation (3.35) is $1 - \alpha^4 z = 0$. Hence, when $\alpha = 1$, the Y_T process has a single unit root. Also, when $\alpha = -1$, the process Y_T has a unit root. The first case corresponds to the simple random walk process, that is, the case where y_t has a non-seasonal unit root, while the second case corresponds to the case where y_t has a seasonal unit root -1. In other words, both the non-seasonal and the seasonal unit root processes are nested within the PAR(1) process. This suggests a natural and simple testing strategy. Firstly, one investigates the presence of a unit root by testing whether $\alpha_1 \alpha_2 \alpha_3 \alpha_4 = 1$. Secondly, one tests whether $\alpha_s = 1$ or $\alpha_s = -1$ for all s. In the next chapter we will consider the issue of testing for certain unit roots in more detail, where we also follow this strategy.

The main implication of this analysis of a PAR(1) process is that seasonal unit roots do not disappear when analyzing y_t in the VQ representation, but in fact they appear as regular unit roots for annual data. Indeed, this is to be expected as the VQ model concerns annual data and one would want to associate seasonal unit roots with non-seasonal data. This can also be made clear when considering the seasonally-integrated model, that is,

$$y_t = y_{t-4} + \varepsilon_t, \tag{3.37}$$

which can easily be written as a VQ(1) model, with characteristic equation

$$|\Phi_0 - \Phi_1 z| = (1 - z)^4 = 0. \tag{3.38}$$

Obviously, for the seasonally-integrated process, which has one non-seasonal unit root and three seasonal unit roots, as was discussed in Chapter 2, the corresponding Y_T process has four unit roots equal to 1. Hence, the seasonal unit roots -1 and $\pm i$ appear as unit roots of 1 when one analyzes the y_t variable in the Y_T format. Notice that the seasonally-integrated process assumes three more unit roots in the Y_T process than the periodically-integrated process does. There are similarities however between these two processes, and this will be discussed in Chapter 4.

Furthermore, when there are $4 - r$ unit roots in the Y_T process, there are r linear combinations of variables without such unit roots. Usually, this is referred to as there being r cointegration relations between the four elements of Y_T. This will also be exploited in a test procedure for unit roots in the next chapter. Finally, note that the seasonally-integrated process as above implies that each $Y_{s,T}$ series is a random walk. Such an assumption surely allows 'summer to become winter', as the seasonal data are allowed to fluctuate randomly, but perhaps this fits the data in Fig. 2.5.

A final example in this section concerns I(2)-type processes, where I(k) denotes that the process contains k unit roots at the zero frequency. We contrast these with seasonal unit root processes, which we discuss first, and look at how such processes are reflected by the number of unit roots in a VQ model for the Y_T process, even though we do not consider these processes in our empirical work. Consider first the simplest process with a non-seasonal and a seasonal unit root. As $1 - L^2$ is equal to $(1 - L)(1 + L)$, that is,

$$y_t = y_{t-2} + \varepsilon_t, \tag{3.39}$$

it can be written as a VQ(1) process with

$$\Phi_0 = \begin{pmatrix} 1 & 0 & 0 & 0 \\ 0 & 1 & 0 & 0 \\ -1 & 0 & 1 & 0 \\ 0 & -1 & 0 & 1 \end{pmatrix} \quad \text{and} \quad \Phi_1 = \begin{pmatrix} 0 & 0 & 1 & 0 \\ 0 & 0 & 0 & 1 \\ 0 & 0 & 0 & 0 \\ 0 & 0 & 0 & 0 \end{pmatrix} \tag{3.40}$$

such that

$$\Phi_0^{-1}\Phi_1 = \begin{pmatrix} 0 & 0 & 1 & 0 \\ 0 & 0 & 0 & 1 \\ 0 & 0 & 1 & 0 \\ 0 & 0 & 0 & 1 \end{pmatrix} \quad \text{and} \quad \Phi_0^{-1}\Phi_1 - I_4 = \begin{pmatrix} -1 & 0 & 1 & 0 \\ 0 & -1 & 0 & 1 \\ 0 & 0 & 0 & 0 \\ 0 & 0 & 0 & 0 \end{pmatrix}. \tag{3.41}$$

Clearly, the eigenvalues of $\Phi_0^{-1}\Phi_1$ are 0, 0, 1, and 1, and the rank of $\Phi_0^{-1}\Phi_1 - I_4$ is 2. Hence, there are two cointegrating relations between the Y_T variables and y_t has two unit roots. When, however, the time series is an I(2) process with two unit roots 1, that is, when

$$(1 - L)^2 y_t = \varepsilon_t \tag{3.42}$$

for example, is a useful model to describe y_t, the various parameter matrices in the VQ(1) model are

$$\Phi_0^{-1}\Phi_1 = \begin{pmatrix} 0 & 0 & -1 & 0 \\ 0 & 0 & -2 & 1 \\ 0 & 0 & -3 & 0 \\ 0 & 0 & -4 & 1 \end{pmatrix} \quad \text{and} \quad \Phi_0^{-1}\Phi_1 - I_4 = \begin{pmatrix} -1 & 0 & -1 & 0 \\ 0 & -1 & -2 & 1 \\ 0 & 0 & -4 & 0 \\ 0 & 0 & -4 & 0 \end{pmatrix}. \tag{3.43}$$

The eigenvalues of $\Phi_0^{-1}\Phi_1$ are 0, 0, 1, and 1, similar to the process in (3.39), but note that the rank of $\Phi_0^{-1}\Phi_1 - I_4$ now equals 3, see Johansen (1992a) for details of the representation of vector autoregressive models for I(2) processes. For practical purposes these examples suggest that it is useful to calculate the eigenvalues of $\Phi_0^{-1}\Phi_1$, since these may convey information on the maximum number of possible unit roots in y_t.

In this and the preceding section several notation and representation issues of PAR(p) models have been discussed. We believe that the multivariate VQ representation is most useful for analyzing the stationarity properties of the periodic models. Although some implications of unit roots in periodic time series models have been considered, a formal statistical analysis of such roots is postponed to Chapter 4. In this chapter we now proceed with the estimation of the parameters in a PAR(p) model and with model selection.

3.3 Model selection and parameter estimation

There are various ways to specify a periodic time series model in practice. A first approach is to decide on the order p of a PAR(p) process by using estimated so-called periodic autocorrelation and partial autocorrelation functions, as is standard in the Box and Jenkins (1970) type of approach. Definitions of these functions are given in McLeod (1993) and Sakai (1982), respectively. Vecchia and Ballerini (1991) derive the asymptotic distributions of the estimated periodic autocorrelation function, and use it as a method to identify a PARMA(1,1) model for a monthly river flow series. Note, however, that the identification of a periodic time series model is not as straightforward as it sometimes is for non-periodic time series models. One way to understand this is that periodic models can be seen to correspond to multivariate models, for which it is also sometimes found that the various autocorrelation functions may not be easy to use in practice.

Secondly, one can rely on the graphical approaches proposed in Hurd and Gerr (1991) and Bloomfield *et al.* (1994). Thirdly, one can use a method based on rank statistics, as proposed in Bentarzi and Hallin (1996).

In many practical situations, the above methods are perhaps unnecessarily cumbersome. We therefore advocate two alternative and somewhat simpler approaches to arrive at a practically useful PAR(p) model. The first is to investigate the potential usefulness of periodic time series models by checking the properties of estimated residuals from non-periodic models, which is in fact a simple-to-general strategy. The second, general-to-specific, approach amounts to estimating a PAR(p) model, where p is selected using conventional model selection criteria, and to test whether there is indeed periodic variation in the autoregressive parameters.

There are at least two ways to test for periodicity in the estimated residuals. One way is to investigate periodic correlation using a modified version of the Box–Pierce test. Another is to consider a variant of an LM-test statistic, see, for example, Franses (1993). This last approach amounts to first fitting a non-periodic AR(p) model to the time series x_t, where $x_t = \Delta_1 y_t$ with $\Delta_1 = 1 - L$ or an otherwise transformed series, depending on the outcome of tests for seasonal unit roots. This gives the estimated residuals $\hat{\nu}_t$. Next, one considers the auxiliary regression

$$\hat{\nu}_t = \sum_{s=1}^{4} \delta_s D_{s,t} + \sum_{i=1}^{p} \gamma_i x_{t-i} + \sum_{s=1}^{4} (\psi_{1s} D_{s,t} \hat{\nu}_{t-1} + \cdots + \psi_{ms} D_{s,t} \hat{\nu}_{t-m}) + u_t, \quad (3.44)$$

where $D_{s,t}$ are seasonal dummy variables, to investigate the presence of periodicity in the estimated residuals. The F-test for $\psi_{1s} = 0, \ldots, \psi_{ms} = 0$ can be used to test the null hypothesis of no periodic autocorrelation of order m. We denote this F-test as F_{pser}, where the subscript 'pser' reflects periodic serial correlation. Under the null hypothesis, this F-statistic is asymptotically F distributed with $(4m, n - p - 4m)$ degrees of freedom. Simulations in Franses and Paap (1994) support this distributional result.

To examine periodicity in the error variance, one can rely on the same approach as before and consider the auxiliary regression

$$\hat{\nu}_t^2 = \omega_0 + \omega_1 D_{1,t} + \omega_2 D_{2,t} + \omega_3 D_{3,t} + \lambda_t. \quad (3.45)$$

Note that, when periodic variation in the AR parameters is neglected, this variation may show up in the variance of the residual process. Under the null hypothesis of no seasonal heteroskedasticity, the F-test statistic for the significance of the ω_1, ω_2, and ω_3 parameters in (3.45), which is denoted as F_{sh}, is asymptotically F distributed with $(3, n - k)$ degrees of freedom. Of course, one may extend (3.45) to include periodic ARCH components in the case of, for example, financial time series where one may expect monthly or daily effects. The F_{sh}-test may also be useful in cases where one wants to consider non-periodic models with seasonal variances, as in, for example, Burridge and Wallis (1990). Finally, one can also apply a likelihood ratio (LR) test for equal variances across the seasons, corresponding to the null hypothesis

$$H_0: \sigma_s^2 = \sigma^2 \quad \text{for } s = 1, 2, 3, 4. \quad (3.46)$$

This LR-test denoted by LR_{sh} is asymptotically χ^2 distributed with 3 degrees of freedom. Below we will use these tests when analyzing the industrial production series under scrutiny.

To illustrate the above tests for various forms of periodicity, we consider again the fourteen industrial production series. The results are summarized in Table 3.1. In the second column we show the differencing filter as indicated by the HEGY results in Table 2.5. Furthermore, we display which deterministic terms are included in the models. The inclusion of these deterministics is guided by the applied filter.

Table 3.1

Testing for periodic patterns in the estimated residuals of non-periodic models (p values in parentheses)

Variable	Filter[1]	Order[2]	Test statistics[2]			
			$F_{ser}(1)$	$F_{ser}(4)$	$F_{pser}(1)$	F_{sh}^3
Total	$\Delta_1 y_t + SD$	8	1.039(0.309)	0.793(0.531)	2.503(0.042)	1.229(0.299)
Products	$y_t + SD + T$	7	1.869(0.173)	1.982(0.098)	2.587(0.038)	0.364(0.779)
	$y_t + SD + ST$	7	1.602(0.207)	1.168(0.326)	3.387(0.010)	0.375(0.771)
Final products	$y_t + SD + T$	7	0.652(0.420)	0.833(0.506)	1.702(0.150)	0.512(0.674)
	$y_t + SD + ST$	7	0.597(0.441)	0.638(0.425)	1.873(0.116)	0.515(0.672)
Consumer goods	$\Delta_1 y_t + SD$	8	2.733(0.099)	2.228(0.067)	2.658(0.034)	0.693(0.557)
Durable consumer goods	$\Delta_1 y_t + SD$	8	0.192(0.662)	1.132(0.343)	1.099(0.358)	2.902(0.036)
Automotive products	$(1+L)y_t + SD + T$	11	1.398(0.239)	1.876(0.117)	2.372(0.054)	4.764(0.003)
	$(1+L)y_t + SD + ST$	12	0.308(0.579)	2.211(0.070)	1.029(0.393)	5.287(0.002)
Auto parts	$\Delta_1 y_t + SD$	8	0.317(0.574)	0.891(0.470)	1.248(0.292)	2.411(0.068)
Other durable goods	$\Delta_1 y_t + SD$	6	1.574(0.211)	1.020(0.398)	3.655(0.007)	0.663(0.576)
Food and tobacco	$(1+L^2)\Delta_1 y_t + SD$	5	0.636(0.426)	2.253(0.065)	0.855(0.492)	0.288(0.834)
Clothing	$(1+L^2)\Delta_1 y_t + SD$	14	0.008(0.929)	0.851(0.495)	0.825(0.511)	0.172(0.915)
Chemical products	$\Delta_4 y_t + IC$	7	2.566(0.111)	2.037(0.916)	1.812(0.129)	0.106(0.957)
Paper products	$\Delta_4 y_t + IC$	5	0.987(0.322)	1.327(0.262)	2.469(0.047)	0.542(0.654)
Energy products	$(1+L^2)\Delta_1 y_t + SD$	8	0.001(0.973)	2.375(0.054)	6.464(0.000)	0.893(0.446)
Fuels	$(1+L)\Delta_1 y_t + SD$	3	0.041(0.840)	2.090(0.084)	2.308(0.060)	4.058(0.008)

[1]The variables have been transformed as indicated by the output of tests for seasonal unit roots, see Chapter 2. We give the filter and the deterministic terms (IC = intercept, SD = seasonal dummies, T = non-seasonal trend, ST = seasonal trends).

[2]The number of lags is based on F-type versions of LM-tests for first-order and first-to-fourth-order non-periodic residual correlation starting at lag length 8.

[3]F-test for the significance of the seasonal dummies in a regression of the squared residuals on an intercept and three seasonal dummies.

For each series, after any relevant transformation, we construct a non-periodic AR model. The order of this model is based on the standard LM-type diagnostics for first-order and first-to-fourth-order non-periodic serial correlation in the residuals at the 5 per cent level of significance. The appropriate lag order is shown in the third column of Table 3.1. The first model for which this test does not reject the null hypothesis is selected. The next four columns give these test statistics, as well as the associated p values.

The final four columns of Table 3.1 give the outcomes of two tests for periodicity in the residuals. We see that for seven out of the fourteen series we reject the absence of first-order periodic serial correlation in the residuals at the 5 per cent level of significance. Next, for three out of the fourteen series we reject homoskedasticity in favor of seasonal variance in the error term at the 5 per cent level of significance. These are the same series as those in Table 2.2 with seasonality in variance. Note that for none of the series can we reject both hypotheses. In summary, we find evidence of periodic patterns in nine of the fourteen series. Interestingly, the non-periodic tests do not find evidence of neglected seasonality, while the periodic tests do, which can be seen from comparing the p values for F_{pser} with those of F_{ser}.

Simulation results in Franses (1995b) imply that non-periodic tests have a low ability to indicate whether the series are perhaps better described by a periodic model. Therefore, in order to test for remaining or neglected seasonality, we recommend the use of a test based on a periodic model.

A second, but now general-to-specific, approach for investigating periodic variation in the autoregressive parameters is to estimate a PAR(p) model for y_t and to test if the null hypothesis of no periodic variation can be rejected. The parameters in a PAR(p) model can be estimated by considering the regression model

$$y_t = \sum_{s=1}^{4} \mu_s D_{s,t} + \sum_{s=1}^{4} \phi_{1s} D_{s,t} y_{t-1} + \cdots + \sum_{s=1}^{4} \phi_{ps} D_{s,t} y_{t-p} + \varepsilon_t. \qquad (3.47)$$

Under normality of the error process ε_t and with fixed starting values, the maximum likelihood estimators of the parameters ϕ_{is}, $i = 1, 2, \ldots, p$ and $s = 1, 2, 3, 4$, are obtained from ordinary least squares (OLS) estimation of (3.47). For alternative estimation methods and asymptotic results see Pagano (1978) and Troutman (1979). Other relevant references are Cipra (1985) for the estimation of PMA(q), Andel (1983) and Franses and Koop (1997) for a Bayesian analysis of PAR models, Vecchia (1985) and Anderson and Vecchia (1993) for maximum likelihood estimation of PARMA models, and Adams and Goodwin (1995) for yet another approach. It is important to be aware of the fact that the available sample for estimating each of the periodic parameters is $N = n/4$, that is, the number of observations can be small. This could also be understood from the link between periodic models and the VQ representation for annual data discussed earlier.

Once the parameters in a PAR(p) process have been estimated, a next step is to test for periodic variation in the autoregressive parameters. In Boswijk and Franses (1996) it is proved that the likelihood ratio test for the null hypothesis

$$H_0 \colon \phi_{is} = \phi_i \quad \text{for } s = 1, 2, 3, 4 \text{ and } i = 1, 2, \ldots, p \qquad (3.48)$$

has an asymptotic $\chi^2(3p)$ distribution, *irrespective* of whether the y_t series has non-seasonal or seasonal unit roots. The intuition behind this result is that these parameter restrictions do not in any way restrict the possible number of unit roots prior to examining periodicity. Hence, an F-test for this H_0, which is denoted by F_{per}, has asymptotically an $F(3p, n - (4 + 4p))$ distribution in the case of a PAR(p) process with four seasonal intercepts. Simulation evidence in Franses and Paap (1994) supports this theoretical result.

An important implication is that (3.47) can be estimated for the y_t series itself, that is, there is no need to a priori transform the y_t series to remove unit roots of whatever kind, when one wants to test for periodicity. Hence, there is no need to start with tests for unit roots. In turn, this suggests that, for practical purposes, it seems most convenient to start with estimating the model in (3.47) and testing the H_0 in (3.48). In a second step, one can test for unit roots. An additional advantage is that this sequence of steps allows the possibility of having a periodic differencing filter, which is useful in the case of periodic integration, as we will discuss extensively in Chapter 4. As a periodic differencing filter has to be estimated from the data, that is, the α_s in (3.32), it is therefore not sensible to start an analysis of periodic variation in a model for, for example, $\Delta_1 y_t$ or $\Delta_4 y_t$, see again the next chapter for more details.

Order selection in periodic autoregression

The order of a periodic autoregression for actual data is, of course, not known and it has to be estimated using the available data. Similar to non-periodic AR models, there are several criteria for model selection. One can use model selection criteria such as Akaike's (1969) information criterion (AIC),

$$\text{AIC}(p) = n \log \hat{\sigma}^2 + 8p, \qquad (3.49)$$

where $\hat{\sigma}^2$ is the residual sum of squares divided by the effective sample size n, or the Schwarz criterion (SC),

$$\text{SC}(p) = n \log \hat{\sigma}^2 + 4p \log n, \qquad (3.50)$$

see Schwarz (1978). Note that in (3.49) and (3.50) account has been taken of the fact that one estimates parameters for each of the four seasons. An alternative approach is given by using an F-test for the deletion of the parameters ϕ_{ls} for some value of l. The order of a PAR model can be set equal to p when some or all $\phi_{ps} \neq 0$, while the $\phi_{p+1,s} = 0$ for all s. This F-test would then be applied to PAR models with decreasing orders, where the initial order may be set at 4 or 8. Alternatively, one may estimate PAR models of order 8, 7, and so on, and test whether the residuals display periodic autocorrelation. The order p is chosen when the LM-test statistic calculated from the auxiliary regression (3.44) indicates that the hypothesis of no periodic autocorrelation cannot be rejected.

Franses and Paap (1994) perform an extensive Monte Carlo experiment to investigate the performance of lag order selection methods in periodic auto-regressions. The results of their study suggest that for practical purposes a convenient strategy is to use the Schwarz criterion to obtain a first indication of the lag order. Next, one uses diagnostic tests for neglected periodic and non-periodic serial correlation in the residuals, similar to (3.44), to investigate whether this lag length is appropriate. If this is not the case, one should extend the model with extra lags until the model passes these diagnostic tests. This strategy will also be followed here.

Illustration

To illustrate the selection of PAR models, we consider again the fourteen indus-trial production series. As the data display trends, and as we are yet uncertain as to what kind of trends these are, we include seasonal linear trends in the models, that is, we estimate the parameters of

$$y_t = \mu_s + \tau_s T_t + \phi_{1s} y_{t-1} + \cdots + \phi_{ps} y_{t-p} + \varepsilon_t. \qquad (3.51)$$

We summarize the results in Table 3.2. The second column shows the lag order selected by the Schwarz criterion, possibly increased by the number of lags as indicated by the outcomes of diagnostic tests. These are the F-type versions of LM-tests for first-order periodic serial correlation in the residuals denoted by $F_{\mathrm{pser}}(1)$, and first-order and first-to-fourth-order non-periodic serial correlation in the residuals denoted by $F_{\mathrm{ser}}(1)$ and $F_{\mathrm{ser}}(4)$, respectively. The relevant panel in this table indicates that the fourteen models all seem well specified.

If we look at the model orders, we see that the appropriate lag order is smaller than 5 for ten out of the fourteen series. For two series, that is, total index and chemical products, we need a periodic autoregression of order 6. It is important to see that all models pass the diagnostic tests for residual autocorrelation. Hence, the dynamics are reasonably short. This is in contrast to the findings in Chapter 2, where we sometimes needed many lags in non-periodic models to whiten the errors. This suggests that there is some kind of trade-off between the number of lags in non-periodic models and the intra-year parameter fluctuations in periodic models with shorter dynamics. We will return to this issue in Section 3.5.

It is a misconception to think that evidence of periodicity appears because one does not include enough lags. Of course, if one starts off with a very lengthy periodic autoregression, the power of tests becomes low. Therefore, we recom-mend first choosing the appropriate form of a PAR model and then working

Table 3.2

Lag order selection, diagnostics tests and tests for periodicity (p values in parentheses)

Variable	Order[1]	Serial correlation tests[2]			Periodicity tests[3]	
		$F_{ser}(1)$	$F_{ser}(4)$	$F_{pser}(1)$	F_{per}	LR_{sh}
Total	4+2	3.152(0.077)	1.587(0.178)	1.661(0.159)	3.274(0.000)	18.765(0.000)
Products	2+2	0.721(0.397)	1.955(0.102)	0.320(0.864)	3.139(0.000)	1.508(0.680)
Final products	2+2	0.521(0.417)	0.930(0.427)	0.773(0.544)	3.394(0.000)	5.310(0.150)
Consumer goods	1+1	0.054(0.817)	0.033(0.998)	0.161(0.958)	4.384(0.000)	18.569(0.000)
Durable consumer goods	1+1	0.101(0.751)	1.042(0.387)	0.655(0.624)	3.152(0.001)	9.641(0.021)
Automotive products	2	0.571(0.451)	1.878(0.116)	0.794(0.530)	6.954(0.000)	12.380(0.006)
Auto parts	1+1	1.244(0.266)	0.505(0.732)	0.601(0.662)	3.028(0.007)	8.072(0.045)
Other durable goods	2+1	3.057(0.082)	1.212(0.307)	1.111(0.352)	3.055(0.002)	9.531(0.023)
Food and tobacco	3+2	0.033(0.857)	1.812(0.128)	1.193(0.316)	2.496(0.002)	0.654(0.884)
Clothing	2+2	0.747(0.389)	0.891(0.471)	1.583(0.181)	5.696(0.000)	2.531(0.470)
Chemical products	2+3	2.308(0.131)	1.337(0.259)	0.581(0.677)	3.842(0.000)	6.251(0.100)
Paper products	4+2	0.021(0.884)	0.437(0.782)	0.707(0.588)	3.209(0.000)	4.535(0.209)
Energy products	4	2.079(0.151)	1.586(0.181)	0.783(0.538)	7.055(0.000)	19.665(0.000)
Fuels	2	0.020(0.888)	0.855(0.493)	1.988(0.099)	2.640(0.018)	16.194(0.001)

[1] Order selected by SC, possibly extended with extra lags to capture (non-)periodic serial correlation.

[2] F-type versions of LM-tests for first-order and first-to-fourth-order residual serial correlation, LM-test for first-order periodic serial correlation.

[3] F-test for periodicity in the AR parameters and an LR-test for seasonal heteroskedasticity.

Table 3.3
Specifying and analyzing a periodic autoregression

Step	Action
1	Estimate a PAR model of order $p = 1$ to $p = p_{\max}$.
2	Determine the order using SC and LM-tests.
3	Test for periodicity in AR parameters.
4	Test for seasonal heteroskedasticity.
5	Test for unit roots in PAR model or in VQ framework.

Continued in Table 4.3

from there. Also, if one were to generate seasonal ARMA-type models of high order and fit low-order periodic models, tests for periodicity would suggest that there is such variation, while in reality there is not, see Proietti (1998). This finding of spurious periodicity is, of course, due to dynamic misspecification, which is a well-known driving force behind finding many spurious outcomes, see, for example, Boswijk and Franses (1992) in the context of cointegration models. In summary, one should first get the dynamics right before one can rely on tests for parameter restrictions.

Returning to Table 3.2, we see from the last four columns that there is substantial evidence of periodic variation in the parameters of a periodic model. The ninth column of Table 3.2 shows the F-test for periodicity in the autoregressive parameters, that is, we test the hypothesis given in (3.48). The F_{per}-tests turn out to be significant at the 5 per cent level for all series. The final two columns concern the test results for the presence of seasonal heteroskedasticity. We test the hypothesis (3.46) using the $\mathrm{LR}_{\mathrm{sh}}$-test. It occurs that for eight out of the fourteen series we can reject equal variances across the seasons at the 5 per cent level of significance. This suggests that we can perhaps analyze these series better in the VQ representation, as in that model one can allow for seasonal heteroskedasticity.

To summarize, we collect the sequence of practical steps in Table 3.3. The first four steps are dealt with in this chapter, and step 5 will be expanded in Chapter 4.

3.4   Forecasting

Forecasting with PAR models proceeds roughly in the same way as with standard AR models. To illustrate this, we consider the PAR(1) model in (3.32). The 1-step ahead forecast made at the origin $t = n$ (where n can be thought of as 'now') is simply

$$\hat{y}_{n+1} = \mathrm{E}_n[y_{n+1}] = \mathrm{E}_n[\alpha_s y_n + \varepsilon_{n+1}] = \alpha_s y_n, \qquad (3.52)$$

where E denotes the expectation operator and it is assumed that the time $n+1$ corresponds to season s. We leave a derivation of similar expressions for other seasons to the reader, see below in (3.53). Assuming knowledge of the parameters, the forecast error $y_{n+1} - \hat{y}_{n+1}$ is ε_{n+1} and hence the variance of the 1-step ahead forecast equals σ^2. Likewise, we can generate the corresponding next three forecasts as

$$\hat{y}_{n+2} = \mathrm{E}_n[y_{n+2}] = \mathrm{E}_n[\alpha_{s+1}\alpha_s y_n + \varepsilon_{n+2} + \alpha_{s+1}\varepsilon_n] = \alpha_{s+1}\alpha_s y_n,$$
$$\hat{y}_{n+3} = \mathrm{E}_n[y_{n+3}] = \mathrm{E}_n[\alpha_{s+2}y_{n+2} + \varepsilon_{n+1}] = \alpha_{s+2}\alpha_{s+1}\alpha_s y_n, \qquad (3.53)$$
$$\hat{y}_{n+4} = \mathrm{E}_n[y_{n+4}] = \mathrm{E}_n[\alpha_{s+3}y_{n+3} + \varepsilon_{n+3}] = \alpha_{s+3}\alpha_{s+2}\alpha_{s+1}\alpha_s y_n.$$

These expressions show that the forecasts depend on the season in which one starts to forecast. In the case of periodic integration, when defined as requiring the product of the four α parameters to be equal to 1, the 4-steps ahead forecast simplifies to $\hat{y}_{n+4} = y_n$, as then $\alpha_{s+3}\alpha_{s+2}\alpha_{s+1}\alpha_s = 1$.

The forecast errors associated with the above forecasts are

$$\hat{y}_{n+2} - y_{n+2} = \varepsilon_{n+2} + \alpha_{s+1}\varepsilon_{n+1},$$
$$\hat{y}_{n+3} - y_{n+3} = \varepsilon_{n+3} + \alpha_{s+2}\varepsilon_{n+2} + \alpha_{s+2}\alpha_{s+1}\varepsilon_{n+1},$$
$$\hat{y}_{n+4} - y_{n+4} = \varepsilon_{n+4} + \alpha_{s+3}\varepsilon_{n+3} + \alpha_{s+3}\alpha_{s+2}\varepsilon_{n+2} + \alpha_{s+3}\alpha_{s+2}\alpha_{s+1}\varepsilon_{n+1},$$
$$(3.54)$$

and hence the variances of the forecast errors equal $\sigma^2(1 + \alpha_{s+1}^2)$, $\sigma^2(1 + \alpha_{s+2}^2 + \alpha_{s+2}^2\alpha_{s+1}^2)$, and $\sigma^2(1 + \alpha_{s+3}^2 + \alpha_{s+3}^2\alpha_{s+2}^2 + \alpha_{s+3}^2\alpha_{s+2}^2\alpha_{s+1}^2)$, respectively, as the error terms are assumed to be uncorrelated. These forecast error variances obviously also depend on the season from which one generates the forecasts. The variances can be used to construct forecast intervals in the standard way.

For PAR models with higher values of the order p, it is more convenient to use the VQ representation to compute forecasts and forecast error variances, see Franses (1996a). Forecasts can then be generated in a similar manner as for VAR models, see Lütkepohl (1991). For example, consider again the PAR(1) model in (3.32). The VQ representation is given by (3.33) and (3.34). The forecasts made at $t = n = 4N$ for the next year, where we thus assume that the forecasting origin is quarter 4 in year N, based on the VQ representation are

$$\hat{Y}_{N+1} = \mathrm{E}_N[Y_{N+1}] = \mathrm{E}_N[\Phi_0^{-1}\Phi_1 Y_N + \Phi_0^{-1}\varepsilon_{N+1}] = \Phi_0^{-1}\Phi_1 Y_N. \qquad (3.55)$$

The forecast errors equal $\hat{Y}_N - Y_N = \Phi_0^{-1}\varepsilon_{N+1}$ and hence the covariance matrix of the forecast errors is simply $\sigma^2(\Phi_0^{-1}(\Phi_0^{-1})')$. It is easy to show that the diagonal elements of this matrix are equal to the forecast error variances derived above, and we leave this as an exercise for the reader.

Likewise, the forecast for two years ahead, that is 5-steps to 8-steps ahead for the quarterly series y_t, is given by

$$
\begin{aligned}
\hat{Y}_{N+2} &= \mathrm{E}_N[Y_{N+2}] \\
&= \mathrm{E}_N[(\Phi_0^{-1}\Phi_1)^2 Y_N + \Phi_0^{-1}\varepsilon_{N+2} + (\Phi_0^{-1}\Phi_1)\Phi_0^{-1}\varepsilon_{N+1}] = (\Phi_0^{-1}\Phi_1)^2 Y_N,
\end{aligned}
\tag{3.56}
$$

where the corresponding covariance matrix for the forecast errors is given by $\sigma^2(\Phi_0^{-1}(\Phi_0^{-1})' + (\Phi_0^{-1}\Phi_1\Phi_0^{-1})(\Phi_0^{-1}\Phi_1\Phi_0^{-1})')$. In the next chapter we will see that these expressions become much simpler in the case of periodic integration. The covariances between 1-year ahead and 2-years ahead forecasts follow directly from $\mathrm{E}_N[(\hat{Y}_{N+2} - Y_{N+2})(\hat{Y}_{N+1} - Y_{N+1})'] = \sigma^2(\Phi_0^{-1}(\Phi_0^{-1})'\Phi_1'(\Phi_0^{-1})')$.

In general, if one wishes to forecast H-years ahead one may use

$$
Y_{N+H} = (\Phi_0^{-1}\Phi_1)^H Y_N + \sum_{i=1}^{H} (\Phi_0^{-1}\Phi_1)^{i-1}\Phi_0^{-1}\varepsilon_{N+i},
\tag{3.57}
$$

so that the H-year ahead forecast is given by

$$
\hat{Y}_{N+H} = \mathrm{E}_N[Y_{N+H}] = (\Phi_0^{-1}\Phi_1)^H Y_N,
\tag{3.58}
$$

and the corresponding covariance matrix of the forecast errors is equal to

$$
\begin{aligned}
&\mathrm{E}_N[(\hat{Y}_{N+H} - Y_{N+H})(\hat{Y}_{N+H} - Y_{N+H})'] \\
&= \sigma^2 \sum_{i=1}^{H} ((\Phi_0^{-1}\Phi_1)^{i-1}\Phi_0^{-1})((\Phi_1\Phi_0^{-1})^{i-1}\Phi_0^{-1})'.
\end{aligned}
\tag{3.59}
$$

Note that forecasting formulas also apply for PAR(p) models with $p \leq 4$ as these models can also be written in the VQ(1) representation. For higher-order PAR models, these expressions become a little more complicated.

3.5   Effects of neglecting periodicity

As outlined in Chapter 1, we believe that periodic time series models can be useful in practice when it comes to modeling and forecasting economic data. The tools outlined above can be used to find an appropriate model, and the outcomes of many simulation experiments suggest that the proposed strategy works well in practice. Upon application of the various tests, we have found thus far that there is substantial periodic variation in the fourteen US industrial production series. In the next chapter, we will take these outcomes into account when focusing on the trends in these data, and in Chapter 5 we will examine if there are common properties across the series, in terms of trends and periodicity.

We also noted in the introductory chapter that one does not have to use periodic models if one does not want to. There are many other models for seasonal data around, and it is also our personal experience that, in some circumstances or for some series, the out-of-sample forecasts are not dramatically different or that forecasts for non-periodic models are better, see, for example, Franses and Paap (2002). However, we believe that if there is evidence of periodicity, and one does have the intention to neglect it, it is important to have some understanding of the consequences.

A first consequence of fitting non-periodic models to otherwise periodic data concerns the lag order. Indeed, if there is seasonal variation that can best be captured by periodic parameters in a model with only one lag, then such seasonal variation must stand out in the lag structure of a non-periodic model. As there is genuine seasonal variation, the only way it can emerge in a non-periodic model is through relevant parameters at seasonal lags. Hence, one might expect to need higher-order lags in non-periodic models when the data are truly periodic. This can also be formally understood from deriving the implied univariate models for the annual time series $Y_{s,T}$, which follow from the VQ representation, see also Osborn (1991) for detailed derivations. Implied univariate models follow from pre-multiplying the multivariate model with the inverse of the autoregressive polynomial matrix and, next, from pre-multiplying with the determinant of this matrix, see also Franses (1998: ch. 9). This procedure is useful in order to understand what a multivariate model implies in terms of properties of the individual series. For simple PAR models it is also possible to see this when using the quarterly notation. For example, a PAR(1) model can be written as

$$
y_t = \alpha_{s+3}\alpha_{s+2}\alpha_{s+1}\alpha_s y_{t-4} + \varepsilon_t + \alpha_{s+3}\varepsilon_{t-1} + \alpha_{s+3}\alpha_{s+2}\varepsilon_{t-2}
$$
$$
+ \alpha_{s+3}\alpha_{s+2}\alpha_{s+1}\varepsilon_{t-3}. \tag{3.60}
$$

As $\alpha_{s+3}\alpha_{s+2}\alpha_{s+1}\alpha_s$ is equal for all seasons, the AR parameter at lag 4 in a non-periodic model is truly non-periodic. The MA part of this model is of order 3. If one estimates a non-periodic model for these data, that is also including a non-periodic MA part, the MA parameter estimates will attain some kind of an average value of α_{s+3}, $\alpha_{s+3}\alpha_{s+2}$, and $\alpha_{s+3}\alpha_{s+2}\alpha_{s+1}$ across the seasons. In other words, one might end up considering an ARMA(4,3) model for PAR(1) data. And, if one decides not to include an MA part in the model, one usually needs to increase the order of the autoregression so as to whiten the errors. This suggests that higher-order AR models might fit to low-order periodic data. Note that when $\alpha_{s+3}\alpha_{s+2}\alpha_{s+1}\alpha_s = 1$, this implies a higher-order AR model for the Δ_4 transformed time series.

Hence, there seems to be a trade-off between seasonality in parameters and short lags, and no seasonality in parameters and longer lags. It is evident though that, if one wants to diagnose the number of unit roots, it is better to start off with a periodic autoregressive model (which includes the possibility of

Table 3.4
The data generating processes in the
simulations

DGP	α_1	α_2	α_3	α_4	$\alpha_1\alpha_2\alpha_3\alpha_4$
A	0.40	1.20	0.80	1.60	0.614
B	0.60	0.80	1.00	1.20	0.576
C	1.30	0.30	1.50	1.30	0.761
D	0.70	0.95	1.20	1.00	0.798

The DGP is given by $y_t = \alpha_s y_{t-1} + \varepsilon_t$ with
$\varepsilon_t \sim N(0,1)$. The starting values are all equal
to zero.

having three seasonal unit roots), instead of filtering the data first with, say, Δ_4, as this already assumes a certain number of unit roots.

Next, it can be interesting to see what happens with the parameters in nonperiodic models for periodic data. For this purpose, many simulation experiments were run and reported in Franses (1995*b*). These simulations were based on 1000 replications for data of sample size 100. There were four data generating processes (DGPs), and these are displayed in Table 3.4. The four DGPs differ in the value of $\alpha_1\alpha_2\alpha_3\alpha_4$ and the average value of the individual parameters.

First, we examine the consequences of neglecting periodicity on the estimated autocorrelation functions of y_t, $\Delta_1 y_t$, $\Delta_4 y_t$, and $\hat{y}_t$. The variable $\hat{y}_t$ amounts to an estimated seasonally-adjusted series, using the linearization of the Census X-11 method. This linearization concerns the application of a two-sided symmetric 57-point moving-average filter, with weights as given in Laroque (1977) and Franses (1996*b*: Table 4.1) (where we thank Marius Ooms for the detailed computations). Table 3.5 gives the values of the estimated autocorrelations up to and including lag 5, when averaged over 1000 replications. It is evident that the y_t series has autocorrelations that seem to match with a high-order autoregression. The $\Delta_1 y_t$ series shows alternating patterns in the estimated autocorrelation function (ACF). The estimated ACF of $\Delta_4 y_t$ looks like that of an AR(1) model, as the values decay exponentially and rapidly to zero. Note that this result is remarkably close to some of the autocorrelations displayed in Table 2.3 for the fourteen production series. Finally, the seasonally-adjusted series $\hat{y}_t$ also seem to correspond with an AR(1) model. When comparing the top and bottom panel of this table, one can see that seasonal adjustment seems to increase the estimated ACF values. Hence, there might be more evidence of unit roots for seasonally-adjusted series, if we compare the first-order autocorrelation of y_t with that of $\hat{y}_t$.

Next, we examine what happens with the periodic patterns in the data when the data are filtered by the linearized Census X-11 procedure. First, we

Table 3.5
The first five non-periodic autocorrelations for
(transformed) periodic simulated series

Variable	Lag	DGP A	DGP B	DGP C	DGP D
y_t	1	0.73	0.80	0.74	0.87
	2	0.65	0.64	0.60	0.75
	3	0.50	0.53	0.56	0.68
	4	0.49	0.45	0.62	0.63
	5	0.34	0.35	0.44	0.54
$\Delta_1 y_t$	1	−0.31	−0.07	−0.19	−0.01
	2	0.12	−0.10	−0.15	−0.14
	3	−0.22	−0.08	−0.20	−0.04
	4	0.19	0.00	0.37	0.05
	5	−0.16	−0.03	−0.12	−0.00
$\Delta_4 y_t$	1	0.61	0.65	0.65	0.70
	2	0.36	0.34	0.34	0.41
	3	0.08	0.06	0.08	0.15
	4	−0.18	−0.22	−0.12	−0.11
	5	−0.14	−0.17	−0.10	−0.09
$\hat{y}_t$	1	0.82	0.84	0.87	0.90
	2	0.70	0.69	0.75	0.80
	3	0.57	0.56	0.65	0.70
	4	0.45	0.43	0.57	0.61
	5	0.39	0.37	0.51	0.55

The DGPs are given in Table 3.4.

fit PAR(1) models to the adjusted data for the four DGPs, and we test for
periodic variation in the autoregressive parameters. The rejection frequencies
for DGP A to DGP D are 99.2, 62.7, 99.6, and 29.2, respectively. This suggests
that periodicity does not disappear, at least not according to this test. This is of
course not unexpected, as the linearization treats each quarter in the same way,
and hence does not touch upon the intrinsic periodic pattern in the parameters.

The first row of Table 3.6 gives the average estimate of the parameter in a
non-periodic AR(1) model. Clearly, seasonal adjustment gives a value which is
much closer to unity than the true product $\alpha_1\alpha_2\alpha_3\alpha_4$. Hence, due to smoothing
the time series, it seems that one might get more evidence of unit roots as the
first-order autocorrelation gets closer to unity. In general, seasonal adjustment
introduces a higher persistence of shocks.

If one were to consider a PAR(1) model for the seasonally-adjusted data,
then one would on average find the parameter estimates as given in the last four

Table 3.6

AR parameter estimates of periodic and non-periodic models
for Census X-11 adjusted periodic data

Model	Parameter	DGP A	DGP B	DGP C	DGP D
AR(1)	α	0.856	0.873	0.907	0.937
PAR(1)	α_1	0.566	0.707	1.088	0.837
	α_2	1.013	0.843	0.593	0.941
	α_3	0.872	0.961	1.053	1.026
	α_4	1.219	1.061	1.089	0.965

The DGPs are given in Table 3.4.

rows of Table 3.6. Comparing these values with the values in the DGP shows that seasonal adjustment causes the parameters to converge towards each other as well as to unity.

Illustration

It is now perhaps interesting to see how these findings carry over to our actual seasonally-adjusted US production series. These data have been seasonally adjusted using the Census X-11 or X-12 program. Of course, these series concern estimated data, that is, they differ from the unadjusted data as there is one round of additional uncertainty, but for the moment we do not deal explicitly with the confidence intervals around the adjusted data. In fact, Koopman and Franses (2002) show that for structural models it is possible to assign confidence bounds around adjusted data, but for Census X-11 (or X-12) filtered data this is not possible.

The exercise in Table 3.2 is repeated for the adjusted data, and the results are summarized in Table 3.7. The results in the last four columns suggest that there is still much periodicity in the adjusted data. For nine of the fourteen series there is periodic parameter variation, while there is seasonal heteroskedasticity in seven series, where all tests have been evaluated against the 5 per cent level. Hence, indeed, periodicity does not get removed by seasonal adjustment programs. In other words, for the above series the data still display seasonality, which in fact is periodicity in the parameters, even after the application of the Census programs. This emphasizes that perhaps periodic models would be useful for describing the unadjusted original data.

It should be stressed though that, in principle, seasonally-adjusted data are not constructed for modeling and forecasting. They are, in fact, intended to allow better interpretation of the currently released observation on a macroeconomic variable. However, if the data are periodic, this interpretation might

Table 3.7

Lag order selection, diagnostics tests and test for periodicity for seasonally-adjusted series

Variable	Order[1]	Serial correlation tests[2]			Periodicity tests[3]	
		$F_{ser}(1)$	$F_{ser}(4)$	$F_{pser}(1)$	F_{per}	LR_{sh}
Total	5+1	1.281(0.259)	0.970(0.424)	1.849(0.120)	2.589(0.001)	32.306(0.000)
Products	2+3	0.165(0.685)	1.722(0.146)	1.206(0.309)	2.472(0.000)	8.199(0.042)
Final products	2+2	0.468(0.494)	1.322(0.263)	2.132(0.078)	3.073(0.000)	5.631(0.131)
Consumer goods	2+5	0.261(0.610)	1.538(0.193)	0.194(0.941)	1.917(0.012)	15.848(0.001)
Durable consumer goods	2	0.244(0.622)	1.012(0.403)	1.178(0.322)	2.224(0.042)	16.825(0.001)
Automotive products	1	2.423(0.121)	1.197(0.314)	1.518(0.199)	2.221(0.087)	31.934(0.000)
Auto parts	1+1	0.048(0.828)	1.319(0.264)	0.665(0.617)	1.646(0.136)	13.559(0.004)
Other durable goods	2	0.099(0.754)	2.049(0.089)	1.744(0.142)	3.136(0.006)	2.962(0.397)
Food and tobacco	1+1	0.515(0.474)	0.441(0.779)	0.746(0.561)	2.148(0.050)	0.180(0.180)
Clothing	2+3	0.411(0.522)	0.270(0.897)	0.425(0.791)	3.555(0.000)	1.913(0.591)
Chemical products	1+1	0.288(0.592)	2.295(0.061)	0.340(0.851)	0.369(0.898)	7.674(0.053)
Paper products	1+1	0.024(0.877)	0.531(0.713)	1.010(0.404)	1.174(0.322)	1.486(0.686)
Energy products	2+1	1.180(0.279)	0.801(0.526)	0.573(0.683)	2.070(0.059)	4.315(0.229)
Fuels	2	0.125(0.386)	0.125(0.724)	0.683(0.605)	2.894(0.010)	18.060(0.000)

[1] Order selected by SC with extra added lags if needed to capture (non-)periodic serial correlation.

[2] F-type versions of LM-tests for first-order and first-to-fourth-order residual serial correlation, LM-test for first-order periodic serial correlation.

[3] F-test for periodicity in the AR parameters and an LR-test for seasonal heteroskedasticity.

also be cumbersome. Ooms and Franses (1997) illustrate that for unemployment data in the US and Germany more seasonal variation is assigned to the seasonal component in recessions than in expansions. This finding makes interpretation of seasonally-adjusted data questionable, particularly when it really matters.

To summarize, to some extent it can be predicted what happens if the data are periodic and non-periodic models are considered for the original data, or periodic models for seasonally-adjusted data. Non-periodic models for otherwise small periodic autoregressive models will require a large lag length, in order to mop up the apparent seasonality in the data. If the data are seasonally adjusted using linearized Census filters, then periodic parameter variation does not vanish. This observation can be made for simulated data as well as for our fourteen production series. In the next section, we discuss how periodicity may also appear in the conditional second moment.

3.6 Periodic conditional heteroskedasticity

So far, we have only considered periodicity in the mean of a time series. As we have already seen from the forecasting exercise in Section 3.4, a periodic autoregression with the same variance in all seasons implies that the variance of the time series is different across seasons. Hence, periodic models might also be quite useful to model financial time series. They can be used not only to describe the so-called day-of-the-week effects in daily observed stock returns, see French (1980), Keim and Stambaugh (1984), French and Roll (1986), and Smirlock and Starks (1986), among others, but also to describe the differences in volatility across the day of the week. Foster and Viswanathan (1990) provide evidence that volatility on Mondays tends to be larger than on other days. Additionally, the correlations between daily volatilities also display a day-of-the-week effect. The latter empirical observation has led Bollerslev and Ghysels (1996) to advocate a so-called periodic generalized autoregressive conditional heteroskedasticity (PGARCH) model. In this section we discuss this periodic time series model which allows for the description of day-of-the-week seasonality in daily returns and volatility. There is substantial evidence that a GARCH(1,1) model suffices to describe volatility dynamics, see Bollerslev *et al.* (1992), and hence we limit our focus to a similar model.

A PAR(p)–PGARCH(1,1) model for a daily observed financial time series y_t, $t = 1, \ldots, n = 5N$, can be represented by

$$x_t = y_t - \sum_{s=1}^{5} \left(\mu_s + \sum_{i=1}^{p} \phi_{is} y_{t-i} \right) D_{s,t} = \sqrt{h_t} \eta_t \quad \text{with } \eta_t \sim \text{N}(0,1), \quad (3.61)$$

and

$$h_t = \sum_{s=1}^{5} (\omega_s + \psi_s x_{t-1}^2) D_{s,t} + \gamma h_{t-1}, \quad (3.62)$$

where the x_t denote the residual of the PAR model for y_t, and where $D_{s,t}$ denote the usual seasonal dummies but now for the days of the week, that is, $s = 1, 2, 3, 4, 5$. The key differences between the model in (3.61) and (3.62) and the standard AR–GARCH model are that (i) the AR parameters are allowed to vary with the day of the week, that is, ϕ_{is} instead of ϕ_i, and (ii) part of the parameters in the GARCH(1,1) model can also vary across the days. Our specification in (3.62), with only ψ_s varying with the day of the week and not γ, follows the approach taken in Bollerslev and Ghysels (1996) as it is convenient from an estimation point of view. Also, as PARMA models can be written as multivariate ARMA models for the VQ-type data (here vector of days (VD) data), one might run into identification problems by allowing too much flexibility. There are no general restrictions on the parameters to ensure positive conditional variances. Positiveness has to be verified on a case-by-case basis, see also Nelson and Cao (1992).

When we set $\psi_s = \psi$ and $p = 1$, we obtain the model used in Bessembinder and Hertzel (1993) and Abraham and Ikenberry (1994). When we set $\phi_{is} = \phi_i$ for all $s = 1, 2, 3, 4, 5$, we obtain the model used in Bollerslev and Ghysels (1996). Note that when $\phi_{is} \neq \phi_i$ and periodic variation such as in (3.61) is neglected, the results in Osborn (1991) indicate that spurious heteroskedastic effects can be obtained. Hence, it makes sense to consider (3.61) with (3.62) and not a non-periodic version of (3.61).

In order to investigate the properties of the conditional variance model in (3.62), it is useful to define $z_t = x_t^2 - h_t$, and to write (3.62) as a PARMA process

$$x_t^2 = \sum_{s=1}^{5} (\omega_s + (\psi_s + \gamma) x_{t-1}^2) D_{s,t} + z_t - \gamma z_{t-1}. \tag{3.63}$$

This ARMA process for x_t^2 contains time-varying parameters $\psi_s + \gamma$ and hence, strictly speaking, it is not a stationary process. To investigate the stationarity properties of x_t^2, it is more convenient to write (3.63) in a parameter time-invariant VD representation.

Let $X_T^2 = (X_{1,T}^2, X_{2,T}^2, X_{3,T}^2, X_{4,T}^2, X_{5,T}^2)'$ consist of the daily observations stacked in a weekly vector, that is, $X_{s,T}^2$ is the observation in day s of week T. Then model (3.63) can be written as

$$\Lambda_0 X_T^2 = \Omega + \Lambda_1 X_{T-1}^2 + \Gamma_0 Z_T + \Gamma_1 Z_{T-1}, \tag{3.64}$$

where $\Omega = (\omega_1, \omega_2, \omega_3, \omega_4, \omega_5)'$, $Z_T = (Z_{1,T}, Z_{2,T}, Z_{3,T}, Z_{4,T}, Z_{5,T})'$ represents a vector of stacked z_t, and where

$$\Lambda_0 = \begin{pmatrix} 1 & 0 & 0 & 0 & 0 \\ -\lambda_2 & 1 & 0 & 0 & 0 \\ 0 & -\lambda_3 & 1 & 0 & 0 \\ 0 & 0 & -\lambda_4 & 1 & 0 \\ 0 & 0 & 0 & -\lambda_5 & 1 \end{pmatrix}, \quad \Lambda_1 = \begin{pmatrix} 0 & 0 & 0 & 0 & \lambda_1 \\ 0 & 0 & 0 & 0 & 0 \\ 0 & 0 & 0 & 0 & 0 \\ 0 & 0 & 0 & 0 & 0 \\ 0 & 0 & 0 & 0 & 0 \end{pmatrix}, \tag{3.65}$$

with $\lambda_s = \psi_s + \gamma$, $s = 1, 2, 3, 4, 5$, and

$$\Gamma_0 = \begin{pmatrix} 1 & 0 & 0 & 0 & 0 \\ -\gamma & 1 & 0 & 0 & 0 \\ 0 & -\gamma & 1 & 0 & 0 \\ 0 & 0 & -\gamma & 1 & 0 \\ 0 & 0 & 0 & -\gamma & 1 \end{pmatrix}, \quad \Gamma_1 = \begin{pmatrix} 0 & 0 & 0 & 0 & -\gamma \\ 0 & 0 & 0 & 0 & 0 \\ 0 & 0 & 0 & 0 & 0 \\ 0 & 0 & 0 & 0 & 0 \\ 0 & 0 & 0 & 0 & 0 \end{pmatrix}. \quad (3.66)$$

To check the stationarity properties of x_t^2 it is now convenient to consider the solution to the characteristic equation of the autoregressive part of (3.64), which is

$$|\Lambda_0 - \Lambda_1 z| = 1 - \lambda_1 \lambda_2 \lambda_3 \lambda_4 \lambda_5 z = 0. \quad (3.67)$$

When $\lambda_1 \lambda_2 \lambda_3 \lambda_4 \lambda_5 < 1$ the x_t^2 process is, of course, periodically stationary. Obviously, X_T^2 and thus x_t^2 contain a unit root if $\lambda_1 \lambda_2 \lambda_3 \lambda_4 \lambda_5 = 1$. When not all λ_s are equal to λ, this restriction implies that x_t^2 is a periodically-integrated process. When all $\lambda_s = 1$, it is evident that $\lambda_1 \lambda_2 \lambda_3 \lambda_4 \lambda_5 = 1$, and hence that the usual integrated process is nested within the periodically-integrated process (PI). This implies that one can consider two restrictions on the parameters of (3.62) to allow for an integrated GARCH (IGARCH) equivalent of (3.62). The first is

$$\psi_s + \gamma = 1 \quad \text{for all } s = 1, 2, 3, 4, 5. \quad (3.68)$$

Notice, however, that this implies that $\psi_s = \psi$ for all s, and hence that the model in (3.62) reduces to the standard non-periodic GARCH model. The second and more sensible parameter restriction is

$$\prod_{s=1}^{5} (\psi_s + \gamma) = 1. \quad (3.69)$$

Model (3.62) with restriction (3.69) is called periodically-integrated GARCH (PIGARCH), as it is similar to the notion of periodic integration in an auto-regression. The nonlinear restriction in (3.69) is interesting, as it allows for at least one of the $\phi_s + \gamma$ values (for one of the days) to exceed 1, see Franses and Paap (2000) for a discussion.

Illustration

To illustrate the PAR–PGARCH model (3.61) and (3.62), we consider daily Standard and Poor's 500 Composite Index (S&P 500) for 1 January 1980 to 28 September 1994. The data are taken from Datastream. As we have 3847 observations, we test at a significance level of 1 per cent. We find that the order of the PAR model in (3.61) can be set equal to 1. In Table 3.8 we present the parameter estimates for (3.61) and (3.62) with $p = 1$. The parameters have

Table 3.8

Estimation results for a PAR(1)–PGARCH(1,1) model for daily
S&P 500 series

Day	Parameter					
	$\hat{\mu}_s$	$\hat{\phi}_{1s}$	$\hat{\omega}_s$	$\hat{\psi}_s$	$\hat{\gamma}$	$\hat{\psi}_s + \hat{\gamma}$
Monday	0.009	0.159***	−0.116***	0.090***	0.926***	1.016
	(0.029)	(0.040)	(0.047)	(0.015)	(0.009)	
Tuesday	0.057	−0.114***	0.073	0.028***	0.926***	0.954
	(0.029)	(0.037)	(0.045)	(0.009)	(0.009)	
Wednesday	0.088***	0.046	−0.102***	0.067***	0.926***	0.993
	(0.027)	(0.036)	(0.040)	(0.013)	(0.009)	
Thursday	0.047	0.055	0.037	0.074***	0.926***	1.000
	(0.028)	(0.041)	(0.037)	(0.016)	(0.009)	
Friday	0.022	0.049	0.168***	0.061***	0.926***	0.987
	(0.031)	(0.041)	(0.044)	(0.017)	(0.009)	

***denotes significant at the 0.01 level.
The estimated standard errors are given in parentheses.

been estimated using maximum likelihood techniques which were programed in Gauss, and details can be obtained from the authors.

We find that amongst the μ_s parameters only μ_3 (Wednesday) is significant. For the ϕ_{1s} parameters, we find that there is significant first-order autocorrelation on Monday and Tuesday. This confirms the findings in Bessembinder and Hertzel (1993) and Abraham and Ikenberry (1994). The Wald test statistic for $\phi_{1s} = \phi_1$ equals 26.092, which is significant at the 1 per cent level. The same is true for the Wald statistic for $\phi_{1s} = \phi_1$ and $\mu_s = \mu$ which equals 30.626. Furthermore, we find that ω_1, ω_3, and ω_5 are significant, where ω_1 and ω_3 take negative values.

Despite these negative values, the conditional variance h_t does not become negative, given a proper initial value for h_t. We now show that $h_t > k$ implies that h_{t+1}, h_{t+2}, h_{t+3}, and h_{t+4} are all > 0, that $h_{t+5} > k$, and hence that $h_{t+i} > 0$, $i = 6, 7, \ldots$. The value of k depends on the day of the week that corresponds to time t.

Suppose that the conditional variance $h_t > 0$ on Wednesday. The conditional variance h_{t+1} on Thursday is given by

$$h_{t+1} = \hat{\omega}_4 + \hat{\alpha}_4 x_t^2 + \hat{\beta} h_t. \tag{3.70}$$

As $x_t^2 > 0$ and $h_t > 0$ for the conditional variance on Thursday, it holds that

$$h_{t+1} > \hat{\omega}_4 = 0.037. \tag{3.71}$$

Hence, using the same arguments, the conditional variances on Friday, Monday, Tuesday, and the next Wednesday are positive as

$$
\begin{aligned}
h_{t+2} &> \hat{\omega}_5 + \hat{\gamma} h_{t+1} = 0.168 + 0.926 \times 0.037 = 0.202, \\
h_{t+3} &> \hat{\omega}_1 + \hat{\gamma} h_{t+2} = -0.116 + 0.926 \times 0.202 = 0.07, \\
h_{t+4} &> \hat{\omega}_2 + \hat{\gamma} h_{t+3} = 0.073 + 0.926 \times 0.07 = 0.139, \\
h_{t+5} &> \hat{\omega}_3 + \hat{\gamma} h_{t+4} = -0.102 + 0.926 \times 0.139 = 0.03.
\end{aligned}
\tag{3.72}
$$

For reasons of simplicity, we started with the assumption of a positive variance on Wednesday. However, in the same way we can prove that a conditional variance on Monday that is larger than 0.041 implies positive conditional variances in the future, and so on.

The ψ_s and γ parameters are all significant at the 1 per cent level, thereby rejecting the constant variance model used in Bessembinder and Hertzel (1993), among others. The Wald test statistic for $\psi_s = \psi$ equals 20.725, which is significant at the 1 per cent level. The Wald test statistic for $\psi_s = \psi$ and $\mu_s = \mu$ equals 45.360, which is also significant at the same level. In the last column of Table 3.8 we give the values of $\hat{\psi}_s + \hat{\gamma}$. Additionally, $\prod_{s=1}^{5}(\hat{\psi}_s + \hat{\gamma}) = 0.950$, and hence a PIGARCH model may yield an adequate description of the conditional variance of the S&P 500 index. The Wald test for periodic integration in (3.62) equals 4.589, which is not significant at the 1 per cent level.

In summary, we reject each restriction that leads to non-periodic dynamics in returns and in conditional heteroskedasticity. We do not reject the periodic integration hypothesis, though, and therefore we find that a statistically adequate empirical model for the S&P 500 index is a PAR(1)–PIGARCH(1,1) model. When we estimate the parameters in the PAR(1)–PIGARCH(1,1) model, that is, when we impose the restriction in (3.69) on (3.62), we find $\hat{\gamma} = 0.936$, $\hat{\psi}_1 + \hat{\gamma} = 1.023$, $\hat{\psi}_2 + \hat{\gamma} = 0.960$, $\hat{\psi}_3 + \hat{\gamma} = 1.007$, $\hat{\psi}_4 + \hat{\gamma} = 1.011$, and $\hat{\psi}_5 + \hat{\gamma} = 1.000$. More details can be found in Franses and Paap (2000). This illustration shows that sometimes one can usefully consider periodic models for describing the conditional second moment of financial returns data.

3.7 Discussion

Before we turn to a more formal examination of the fascinating case of periodic models for trending data in Chapter 4, we end this chapter with a brief discussion of two topics of further interest. These topics concern nonlinear models for periodic data and possible sources which can suggest periodicity which in reality is not there.

So far, we have only discussed linear models for periodic data. When we turn to periodic integration in the next chapter, we will have to impose nonlinear restrictions on the parameters. However, it is also conceivable that the data themselves are nonlinear, in addition to being periodic. Indeed, it has been widely documented that series like industrial production, and notably unemployment, display nonlinear features. These features usually amount to the possibility that there are two or more regimes in the data which require distinct descriptive and forecasting models. Examples are the threshold autoregressive model of Tong (1990), the smooth transition autoregression of Granger and Teräsvirta (1993), and the Markov switching regime model of Hamilton (1989). A survey of a range of nonlinear time series models appears in Franses and van Dijk (2000).

It is not trivial to decide how one should best incorporate seasonality or periodicity in nonlinear models. One way can be motivated by the empirical findings of Ghysels (1994), in which he documents that there is seasonality in the business cycle. That is, it turns out to be more likely to enter or exit recessions in some seasons than in others. If this is the case, one way to model this amounts to a Markov switching regime model in which the probabilities of entering a recession from an expansion, or exiting a recession into an expansion, depend on the month or quarter of the year. These so-called periodic regime-switching models have been analyzed in considerable detail in Ghysels (2000) and Bac et al. (2001), while estimation issues are discussed extensively in Ghysels et al. (1998).

In the recent work by Lewis and Ray (2002) the authors consider nonparametric methods for periodic data. It can be expected that future research will bring forward other models and methods for periodic and nonlinear data. It should be borne in mind though that nonlinear features in economic data are scarce, in the sense that there are only a few recessions and expansions in a few decades. Hence, new models need to be parsimonious but still informative.

A final issue we should mention is the possibility that apparent periodicity in economic data is spurious. There are a few possible reasons for finding periodicity, while this feature is not intrinsic to the data. One example is given in Dezhbakhsh and Levy (1994), who show that interpolation of annual data to get quarterly data can create data that have periodic autocorrelation structures. Another possible cause of spurious periodicity is neglecting level shifts in the seasonal intercepts. If there are seasonal mean shifts and, in particular, in only one or a few seasons, then the data may also display periodic autocorrelation, see Franses (1995c). Given that measurements on certain economic variables originate from various data sources, which are combined somewhere in time, these level shifts may not be rare. In any case, it can be important to test for structural breaks in periodic models.

4

Periodic models for trending data

Many economic data, and, in particular, many macroeconomic data, display a trend, which is usually moving upwards. Obviously, when one aims to forecast, one needs to decide on the type of model for the trend, as the ultimate forecast will very much depend on this model. One might also be interested in examining whether two or more time series share the same trend, which might be likely if economic variables are somehow related. Hence, it is important to study the trend properties of economic data. To do so for data which show seasonal fluctuations, one can construct time series models which include descriptions of a trend and of seasonality at the same time. This chapter deals with such models for the case in which the data display periodic characteristics.

There are two types of trends which are commonly associated with macroeconomic data. The first is what is called the deterministic trend, which, in words, entails that the observed trend line will persist in the future, and hence forecasts can easily be made. That is, a variable y_t can partly be explained by the variable t, with $t = 1, 2, 3, \ldots$. The second is the so-called stochastic trend, which means that the data display a dominant trending pattern, but it seems that the direction of this trend changes once in a while. An exemplary expression is the random walk with drift model $y_t = \mu + y_{t-1} + \varepsilon_t$, which, upon backward substitution, can be written such that y_t is a function of t and of $\sum_{i=1}^{t} \varepsilon_i$. As expected, data with a stochastic trend tend to be more difficult to forecast, and one is more uncertain about the quality of out-of-sample forecasts, which is, of course, due to the summation of innovations.

As it is also important to know what type of trend model describes the data best when it comes to considering more than one time series, one can imagine that a first important step in empirical time series analysis is to decide whether the trend in the data can be characterized by a deterministic trend or by a stochastic trend. As a stochastic trend can be associated with a unit root in the autoregressive polynomial of a time series model, one tends to rely on tests for unit roots to make a choice. If there is evidence of such a unit root, then there is a stochastic trend, and if not, there is most likely a deterministic trend, or some other type of trend one allows for in the test regression. Alternatively, one can also consider the deterministic trend as the starting point, and usually the associated tests are called tests for stationarity. In this book, we focus on tests for unit roots, as is most common in applied studies.

Before we turn to analyzing how unit roots can be represented and tested for in periodic time series models, we first discuss a few general topics. These will become very relevant later on, as the model specification, which is to be used as a vehicle to test for one or more unit roots, is very important.

Consider a univariate time series y_t, $t = 1, 2, \ldots, n$, and assume that it can be described by a first-order autoregression, that is,

$$y_t - \mu - \delta t = \phi(y_{t-1} - \mu - \delta(t-1)) + \varepsilon_t, \tag{4.1}$$

where ε_t is assumed to be a standard white noise process. The behavior of y_t, when generated by (4.1), depends on the values of ϕ, μ, and δ. When $|\phi| < 1$, y_t is what is called a trend-stationary series, and the out-of-sample forecasts will be dominated by the deterministic trend term δt. Indeed, when both μ and δ are not equal to zero, the y_t series always returns to the trending level $\mu + \delta t$. In other words, when forecasting y_{n+h} at time y_n, with h large, the forecast will be approximately equal to $y_{n+h} = \mu + \delta(n + h)$. If $\delta = 0$, this long-run forecast is μ. This indicates that longer horizon forecasts from time series models converge to a mean, which can be fixed or can be trending.

When $\phi = 1$ in (4.1), matters become different as the model reduces to

$$y_t = \delta + y_{t-1} + \varepsilon_t. \tag{4.2}$$

Notice that the parameter μ in (4.1) is not identified when $\phi = 1$. Hence, under the null hypothesis of interest later, that is, that $\phi = 1$, the parameter μ is not identified, while it is identified under the alternative hypothesis that $\phi < 1$. Recursive backward substitution of (4.2) results in

$$y_t = y_0 + \delta t + \sum_{i=1}^{t} \varepsilon_i, \tag{4.3}$$

where y_0 is a starting value. The $\sum_{i=1}^{t} \varepsilon_i$ component is sometimes called the stochastic trend component. Notice from (4.3) that the long-run forecast of y_t equals $y_0 + \delta t$. In other words, a nonzero drift δ in (4.2) implies that this forecast is a function of an intercept and a linear deterministic trend, even though there is no such deterministic trend included explicitly in (4.2).

The above shows that it is not straightforward to separate out the stochastic trend part from the deterministic trend part. One way to make this distinction as clear as possible is by writing (4.1) in an alternative way. This concerns separating the long-run forecast (for both cases $|\phi| < 1$ and $\phi = 1$) and the drift (for $\phi = 1$), which results in

$$\Delta_1 y_t = \delta + \rho(y_{t-1} - \mu - \delta(t-1)) + \varepsilon_t, \qquad (4.4)$$

where $\rho = \phi - 1$. This expression immediately shows that, when $\rho = 0$, y_t has a stochastic trend with drift δ. It also indicates that, when $\rho < 0$, which occurs when $\phi < 1$, (4.4) can be viewed as a univariate error correction equation and y_t is a stationary AR(1) series with attractor $\mu + \delta t$.

In the univariate case it can be easy to test for $\phi = 1$ in yet another version of (4.1), which is

$$\Delta_1 y_t = \mu^* + \delta^* t + \rho y_{t-1} + \varepsilon_t, \qquad (4.5)$$

with

$$\mu^* = (1 - \phi)\mu + \phi\delta, \qquad (4.6)$$

$$\delta^* = (1 - \phi)\delta. \qquad (4.7)$$

This representation shows that the test regression includes the deterministic trend variable, even though it disappears under the null hypothesis of $\phi = 1$, as the associated parameter δ^* disappears under the null hypothesis. However, setting δ^* equal to zero implies that one imposes, *before* any test is carried out, that $\phi = 1$ (which is what one aims to test) or that $\delta = 0$ (which means that the data have no trend), or both. If the data do have a trend, setting $\delta = 0$ might not be plausible. Hence, from this point of view it is better to perform a joint test for $\rho = 0$ and $\delta^* = 0$, see Dickey and Fuller (1981). It is our experience that this approach is rarely used in practice, although we did so in Chapter 2 when applying the tests for seasonal unit roots, see Table 2.7. We are convinced though that it matters a great deal in practice, and in particular for multivariate models. Hence, the use of the proper model representation for testing unit roots is very important. This is indeed even more relevant when considering multivariate time series. As periodic data can be represented as a vector series, the above discussion is relevant for such data, as we will discuss in Section 4.2.

The remainder of this chapter commences with a discussion on the representation of unit roots in PAR models. Utilizing the familiar concepts of integration, we discuss the concept of periodic integration, which is specific only to periodic models. In Section 4.2 we discuss the inclusion of trends and intercepts in periodic models which allows for sensible testing strategies for unit roots. Here we will see that the above discussion carries over to periodic models, albeit that the notation is a bit more involved. In Section 4.3 we discuss the statistical theory of testing for unit roots in periodic models. Proofs and additional details can be found in the indicated references. Section 4.4 deals with fore-casting periodically-integrated autoregressions and how one can understand the propagation of shocks through periodic models. Section 4.5 discusses what happens when periodic data with unit roots are analyzed by non-periodic models and by periodic models for seasonally-adjusted series. Section 4.6 concludes this chapter.

4.1 Representation of unit roots

Consider again the periodic autoregression of order p [PAR(p)] for a quarterly observed time series y_t, that is,

$$y_t = \mu_s + \tau_s T_t + \phi_{1s} y_{t-1} + \cdots + \phi_{ps} y_{t-p} + \varepsilon_t, \tag{4.8}$$

where $T_t = [(t-1)/4] + 1$ represents an annual linear deterministic trend and μ_s and τ_s, $s = 1, 2, 3, 4$, are seasonal dummy and trend parameters, respectively. This model can be written in multivariate format as

$$\Phi_0 Y_T = \mu + \tau T + \Phi_1 Y_{T-1} + \cdots + \Phi_P Y_{T-P} + \varepsilon_T, \tag{4.9}$$

where $\Phi_0, \Phi_1, \ldots, \Phi_P$ are 4×4 matrices containing the ϕ_{is} parameters. See Section 3.1 for more details on this notation. The number of unit roots in y_t can be checked by solving the characteristic equation

$$|\Phi_0 - \Phi_1 z - \cdots - \Phi_P z^P| = 0. \tag{4.10}$$

Given these expressions it is clear that unit roots in y_t correspond to unit roots in the 4×1 vector process Y_T. When there are not as many unit roots as there are variables, there must be cointegration relations between the elements of Y_T, see Engle and Granger (1987) and Johansen (1991). To discuss the role of unit roots, we first consider the case of a single unit root in (4.10).

Single unit root

As is well known from the cointegration literature, a single unit root in a quarterly y_t series corresponds to three cointegrating relations in the Y_T vector process, that is, there are three stable relations between the four elements of Y_T and there is a single stochastic trend driving the total vector process. This can be illustrated by the simple PAR(1) process

$$y_t = \alpha_s y_{t-1} + \varepsilon_t, \tag{4.11}$$

where we again use the notation α_s for convenience. This can be written as (3.33) and (3.34), or as

$$Y_T = \Phi_0^{-1} \Phi_1 Y_{T-1} + \Phi_0^{-1} \varepsilon_T, \tag{4.12}$$

with

$$\Phi_0^{-1}\Phi_1 = \begin{pmatrix} 0 & 0 & 0 & \alpha_1 \\ 0 & 0 & 0 & \alpha_1\alpha_2 \\ 0 & 0 & 0 & \alpha_1\alpha_2\alpha_3 \\ 0 & 0 & 0 & \alpha_1\alpha_2\alpha_3\alpha_4 \end{pmatrix}, \tag{4.13}$$

because

$$\Phi_0^{-1} = \begin{pmatrix} 1 & 0 & 0 & 0 \\ \alpha_2 & 1 & 0 & 0 \\ \alpha_2\alpha_3 & \alpha_3 & 1 & 0 \\ \alpha_2\alpha_3\alpha_4 & \alpha_3\alpha_4 & \alpha_4 & 1 \end{pmatrix}. \tag{4.14}$$

In turn, (4.12) can be written in error correction form as

$$\Delta_1 Y_T = (\Phi_0^{-1}\Phi_1 - I_4)Y_{T-1} + \Phi_0^{-1}\varepsilon_T, \tag{4.15}$$

where Δ_1 is the first-differencing filter for the annual vector series, that is, $1 - L$ operating on the annual Y_T data. Hence, $\Delta_1 Y_T$ corresponds to $\Delta_4 y_t$. Furthermore,

$$\Phi_0^{-1}\Phi_1 - I_4 = \begin{pmatrix} -1 & 0 & 0 & \alpha_1 \\ 0 & -1 & 0 & \alpha_1\alpha_2 \\ 0 & 0 & -1 & \alpha_1\alpha_2\alpha_3 \\ 0 & 0 & 0 & \alpha_1\alpha_2\alpha_3\alpha_4 - 1 \end{pmatrix}. \tag{4.16}$$

Obviously, when $\alpha_1\alpha_2\alpha_3\alpha_4 = 1$ and when it is assumed that the $Y_{s,T}$ have at most one unit root, the rank of the matrix $\Phi_0^{-1}\Phi_1 - I_4$ equals 3, and this implies three cointegrating relationships between the $Y_{s,T}$ series. This link between the rank of a matrix and the number of cointegration relations as well as with the error correction format is called the Granger representation theorem, see Engle and Granger (1987) and Johansen (1995).

In general, it applies that the VQ(P) representation of (4.8) can be written in error (or equilibrium) correction form as

$$\Delta_1 Y_T = \Phi_0^{-1}\mu + \Phi_0^{-1}\tau T + \Pi Y_{T-1} + \Gamma_1\Delta_1 Y_{T-1} + \cdots + \Gamma_{P-1}\Delta_1 Y_{T-(P-1)} \\ + \Phi_0^{-1}\varepsilon_T, \tag{4.17}$$

where

$$\Gamma_i = -\Phi_0^{-1}\sum_{j=i+1}^{P}\Phi_j \quad \text{for } i = 1, 2, \ldots, P-1,$$

$$\Pi = \Phi_0^{-1}\sum_{j=1}^{P}\Phi_j - I_4. \tag{4.18}$$

It is this matrix Π which is relevant for the analysis of cointegration relations.

When there are r cointegration relations between the $Y_{s,T}$ elements, the matrix Π has rank r, with $0 < r < 4$, and it can be written as

$$\Pi = \gamma \alpha', \qquad (4.19)$$

where γ and α are $4 \times r$ matrices. In the case of three cointegration relations in (4.17), it is clear that the cointegration space can, for example, be spanned by

$$\alpha = \begin{pmatrix} -\alpha_2 & 0 & 0 \\ 1 & -\alpha_3 & 0 \\ 0 & 1 & -\alpha_4 \\ 0 & 0 & 1 \end{pmatrix} \qquad (4.20)$$

such that

$$\begin{aligned} Y_{2,T} - \alpha_1 Y_{1,T}, \\ Y_{3,T} - \alpha_2 Y_{2,T}, \\ Y_{4,T} - \alpha_3 Y_{3,T} \end{aligned} \qquad (4.21)$$

are the three cointegrating relations. Note that (4.16) also suggests other relations which are obviously linear combinations of those in (4.20). Given these relations, it can be understood that $Y_{4,T} - \alpha_4 \alpha_3 \alpha_2 Y_{1,T}$ is stationary, and hence that $Y_{1,T} - \alpha_1 Y_{4,T-1}$ with $\alpha_1 = (\alpha_2 \alpha_3 \alpha_4)^{-1}$ is a stationary variable. This implies that, in the case of a single unit root in the Y_T process, the quarterly y_t series can be transformed to a process that does not contain a stochastic trend upon using the differencing filter $1 - \alpha_s L$. Imposing such a differencing filter, the PAR(p) model in (4.8) can also be written as

$$\begin{aligned} y_t - \alpha_s y_{t-1} = \mu_s + \tau_s T_t + \beta_{1s}(y_{t-1} - \alpha_{s-1} y_{t-2}) + \cdots \\ + \beta_{(p-1)s}(y_{t-(p-1)} - \alpha_{s-(p-1)} y_{t-p}) + \varepsilon_t, \qquad (4.22) \end{aligned}$$

where $\alpha_{s-4k} = \alpha_s$ and $\beta_{s-4k} = \beta_s$ for $k \in \mathbb{N}$ and $s \in \{1, 2, 3, 4\}$. When there is periodic variation in the α_s parameters, we can call (4.22) the periodically-differenced form of (4.8).

The periodic differencing filter $1 - \alpha_s L$ was first defined in Osborn *et al.* (1988). They defined periodic integration of order 1 by the property that there exists a set of α_s such that $(1 - \alpha_s L)y_t$ does not contain a unit root. This definition is an example of the time-varying parameter definition introduced by Granger (1986). Notice that this definition also nests the usual filter $1 - L$, for which all α_s equal unity. In order to avoid confusion, and also as periodic integration is a key concept in this chapter, we define periodic integration as follows.

Definition *A quarterly time series y_t is said to be periodically integrated of order 1 (PI), when the differencing filter $1 - \alpha_s L$ is needed to remove the stochastic trend from y_t, where α_s are seasonally-varying parameters with the property that $\alpha_1 \alpha_2 \alpha_3 \alpha_4 = 1$ and $\alpha_s \neq \alpha$ for all $s = 1, 2, 3, 4$.*

The definition of periodic integration indicates that PI nests the usual $1 - L$ filter, for which all α_s are equal to 1, as well as the filter $1 + L$, where all α_s equal -1, which corresponds to the seasonal unit root -1. This immediately suggests that a useful empirical strategy would amount to first checking if there are three cointegrating relations in Y_T, that is, whether $\alpha_1 \alpha_2 \alpha_3 \alpha_4 = 1$, and then checking whether $\alpha_s = 1$ or $\alpha_s = -1$ in a second step, see Boswijk and Franses (1995b) for a discussion for simple PAR models. It turns out that this strategy is also convenient from a statistical perspective, as we will discuss below. For comparison purposes we will, however, also discuss a method which tests whether $1 - L$ or $1 + L$ are useful filters in PAR(p) processes immediately. Finally, note that the α_s parameters in the periodic differencing filter have to be estimated from the data. Boswijk and Franses (1996) show that, under the null hypothesis that $\alpha_1 \alpha_2 \alpha_3 \alpha_4 = 1$, these α_s parameters can be estimated super-consistently.

Multiple unit roots

It can happen that there is more than one unit root in the data, where examples are seasonal unit roots or two non-seasonal unit roots. The series y_t contains more than a single unit root if the rank of the matrix Π is smaller than 3. If the rank of Π equals 2, there are two unit roots in the time series Y_T (and y_t) and two cointegration relations between the elements of Y_T, which look like

$$
\begin{aligned}
Y_{4,T} - \alpha_{14} Y_{3,T} - \alpha_{24} Y_{2,T}, \\
Y_{3,T} - \alpha_{13} Y_{2,T} - \alpha_{23} Y_{1,T}.
\end{aligned}
\tag{4.23}
$$

These two cointegration relations imply the two other cointegration relationships

$$
\begin{aligned}
Y_{2,T} - \alpha_{12} Y_{1,T} - \alpha_{22} Y_{4,T-1}, \\
Y_{1,T} - \alpha_{11} Y_{4,T-1} - \alpha_{21} Y_{3,T-1}.
\end{aligned}
\tag{4.24}
$$

As the rank of Π is 2, these cointegration relations have to be linear combinations of the relations in (4.23). This implies the following restrictions on the α_{is} parameters in (4.24):

$$
\begin{aligned}
\alpha_{11} &= -\alpha_{13}/\alpha_{23}\alpha_{24}, \\
\alpha_{21} &= (1/\alpha_{23}) - \alpha_{13}\alpha_{14}/\alpha_{23}\alpha_{24}, \\
\alpha_{12} &= -\alpha_{14}\alpha_{23}/(\alpha_{13}\alpha_{14} + \alpha_{24}), \\
\alpha_{22} &= 1/(\alpha_{13}\alpha_{14} + \alpha_{24}),
\end{aligned}
\tag{4.25}
$$

see Boswijk *et al.* (1997) for full derivations and more details. The relations (4.23) and (4.24) imply the following differencing filter for y_t:

$$
1 - \alpha_{1s} L - \alpha_{2s} L^2,
\tag{4.26}
$$

where the α_{is} parameters obey the restrictions in (4.25), $i = 1, 2$, and $s = 1, 2, 3, 4$. In practice, these restrictions can be imposed on the parameters, and their validity can be tested.

The differencing filter (4.26) nests several non-periodic differencing filters. If $\alpha_{1s} = 0$ and $\alpha_{2s} = 1$ for all s, we obtain the filter $1 - L^2$, which corresponds to the presence of the roots 1 and -1 in y_t. If $\alpha_{1s} = 0$ and $\alpha_{2s} = -1$ for all s, the differencing filter simplifies to $1 + L^2$, in which case the series y_t contains the roots i and $-$i.

Note that when $\alpha_{12} = 2$ and $\alpha_{2s} = -1$ for all s, the double filter $(1 - L)^2$ is needed. However, in this case the restrictions in (4.25) are violated, which may be checked by the reader, and hence this I(2) case with two unit roots 1 is excluded automatically. For the same reason, the filter $(1 - \alpha_s L)(1 - \beta_s L)$ with $\alpha_1 \alpha_2 \alpha_3 \alpha_4 = 1$ and $\beta_1 \beta_2 \beta_3 \beta_4 = 1$ is not nested in (4.26) with the restrictions (4.25). We will deal with these cases below. Note that the combination of a periodic unit root and the seasonal unit root -1, corresponding to the filter $(1 - \alpha_s L)(1 + L)$ with $\alpha_1 \alpha_2 \alpha_3 \alpha_4 = 1$, does not violate the restrictions (4.25), so this case is allowed.

The case of three unit roots in the Y_T process corresponds to a single cointegration relation between the $Y_{s,T}$ elements. This relation can be written as

$$Y_{4,T} - \alpha_{14} Y_{3,T} - \alpha_{24} Y_{2,T} - \alpha_{34} Y_{1,T}. \tag{4.27}$$

Again, this cointegration relation implies the three other cointegration relations

$$
\begin{aligned}
Y_{3,T} - \alpha_{13} Y_{2,T} - \alpha_{23} Y_{1,T} - \alpha_{33} Y_{4,T-1}, \\
Y_{2,T} - \alpha_{12} Y_{1,T} - \alpha_{22} Y_{4,T-1} - \alpha_{32} Y_{3,T-1}, \\
Y_{1,T} - \alpha_{11} Y_{4,T-1} - \alpha_{21} Y_{3,T-1} - \alpha_{31} Y_{2,T-1},
\end{aligned}
\tag{4.28}
$$

with the following restrictions on the α_{is} parameters:

$$
\begin{array}{lll}
\alpha_{11} = 1/\alpha_{34}, & \alpha_{12} = -\alpha_{34}/\alpha_{24}, & \alpha_{13} = -\alpha_{24}/\alpha_{14}, \\
\alpha_{21} = -\alpha_{14}/\alpha_{34}, & \alpha_{22} = 1/\alpha_{24}, & \alpha_{23} = -\alpha_{34}/\alpha_{14}, \\
\alpha_{31} = -\alpha_{24}/\alpha_{34}, & \alpha_{32} = -\alpha_{14}/\alpha_{24}, & \alpha_{33} = 1/\alpha_{14},
\end{array}
\tag{4.29}
$$

see again Boswijk *et al.* (1997). This leads to the following differencing filter for y_t:

$$1 - \alpha_{1s} L - \alpha_{2s} L^2 - \alpha_{3s} L^3, \tag{4.30}$$

with the restrictions on the α_{is} parameters given in (4.29). In principle, these restrictions can easily be included in estimation routines in, for example, EViews. The validity of these restrictions can then be tested.

A non-periodic version of (4.30), while allowing for another type of seasonal variation in the data, appears when $\alpha_{1s} = 1$, $\alpha_{2s} = -1$, and $\alpha_{3s} = 1$ for all s. In this case the differencing filter equals $(1 - L)(1 + L^2)$. The differencing filter $(1 + L)(1 + L^2)$ is obtained by putting $\alpha_{1s} = -1$, $\alpha_{2s} = -1$, and $\alpha_{3s} = -1$ for all s.

Evidently, a sensible strategy for testing for seasonal unit roots in periodic data amounts to first imposing the parameter restrictions given above and, in the case that these cannot be rejected by the data, imposing the restrictions corresponding to the seasonal unit roots of interest. Boswijk *et al.* (1997) show that this strategy is also very convenient from a statistical testing point of view, as no new asymptotic theory needs to be developed. Indeed, a direct test for seasonal unit roots in periodic models involves new asymptotic theory and new critical values, as it mixes parameter restrictions and unit roots, which is in fact completely unnecessary. Also, we believe that the number of tables with additional critical values in time series books should be limited, and we should try to avoid having to present new tables.

Finally, there can also be four unit roots in Y_T and hence no cointegration relations between the elements $Y_{s,T}$. Then, the rank of the matrix Π is zero. The differencing filter in this case is $\Delta_4 = 1 - L^4$, and hence the y_t series contains one non-seasonal unit root and three seasonal unit roots $(-1, i, -i)$.

Other types of integration

As we already have seen, the double-differencing filter $(1 - L)^2$ does not result from a simplification of the second-order periodic differencing filter (4.26), where the restrictions (4.25) are imposed. This is due to the fact that the $\Delta_1 Y_{s,T}$ are still I(1) processes. Another example of a periodic I(2) model concerns the case where the differencing filter equals $(1 - \alpha_s L)(1 - \beta_s L)$, where $\alpha_1 \alpha_2 \alpha_3 \alpha_4 = 1$ and $\beta_1 \beta_2 \beta_3 \beta_4 = 1$. To analyze the stationarity conditions of such series one has to use second differences of Y_T in the VQ representation, see Boswijk *et al.* (1997, section 3) for more elaborate discussions. It is our empirical experience that the validity of these restrictions is quite rare for macroeconomic data, see Franses and Paap (1994) and Boswijk *et al.* (1997) for examples.

Another type of integration, that might be relevant for certain specific macroeconomic data, is called fractional integration. This concept was introduced in Granger and Joyeux (1980) and Hosking (1981), and it starts from the idea that models imply different trajectories of the impact of innovations (shocks). It amounts to the notion that there might be something in between I(1) and I(0), where the first type of integration assumes that shocks have a permanent effect, and the second type assumes they only have a transitory effect. Actually, this transitory effect typically takes a very short time. It might be that shocks do not have a permanent effect, but that they have a very long-lasting effect. One way to describe this is to allow fractional integration, usually denoted as I(d), where d is between 0 and 1. There is an enormous amount of literature on this type of integration, also as it is commonly found that neglected (or difficult to detect) level shifts cause the data to have long-memory properties, see Granger and Hyung (1999), Diebold and Inoue (2001), and Franses *et al.* (2002), among others.

It might also be that shocks in only particular seasons have long-lasting effects, while shocks in others do not. Hence, it may be relevant to consider periodic fractional integration. Franses and Ooms (1997) consider the model

$$(1 - L)^{d_s} y_t = \varepsilon_t \tag{4.31}$$

for quarterly UK inflation, where d_s can take values between 0 and 1, which may differ across the quarters. Upon application of this model, it turns out that its dynamic properties are not that easy to analyze. Therefore, Ooms and Franses (2001) consider

$$(1 - L^S)^{d_s} y_t = \varepsilon_t \tag{4.32}$$

instead, where the application concerns the well-known Fraser river flow data. Due to the annual cycle in this model, captured by the annual differencing filter $1 - L^S$, the dynamic properties of this fractional integration model are easier to analyze.

Illustration

Before one starts with formally testing how many roots there are in empirical data, which may involve imposing complicated restrictions on model

Table 4.1
Estimated roots of series in unrestricted VQ models

Variable	Lag order	Roots
Total	2	$0.732, -0.325 \pm 0.450i, 0.499 \pm 0.103i,$ $-0.172 \pm 0.397i, -0.120$
Products	1	$0.563 \pm 0.156i, -0.277, 0.178$
Final products	1	$0.529 \pm 0.164i, -0.285, 0.229$
Consumer goods	1	$0.876, 0.550, -0.280, -0.091$
Durable consumer goods	1	$0.593 \pm 0.116i, -0.265, 0.122$
Automotive products	1	$0.803, 0.304 \pm 0.219i, -0.166$
Auto parts	1	$0.733, 0.170, -0.138, -0.108$
Other durable goods	1	$0.538 \pm 0.141i, -0.401, 0.274$
Food and tobacco	2	$0.922, 0.892, 0.575, -0.288 \pm 0.472i,$ $0.116 \pm 0.201i, -0.233$
Clothing	1	$0.971, -0.485, 0.445, 0.045$
Chemical products	2	$0.893, 0.636 \pm 0.169i, 0.638, -0.595,$ $-0.270 \pm 0.403i, -0.258$
Paper products	2	$0.838 \pm 0.018i, 0.338 \pm 0.363i, 0.386,$ $-0.270 \pm 0.226i, -0.249$
Energy products	1	$0.930, 0.644, -0.263, -0.116$
Fuels	1	$0.920, 0.291, -0.291, 0.173$

parameters, it seems wise to first get an impression of what one might expect. It may then be useful to fit periodic models, be it in VQ format or in the univariate representation, and to see what the roots of the autoregressive polynomials are. As seasonal unit roots also appear as regular unit roots in VQ models, one can see whether one might expect to use sequential testing strategies.

To illustrate this, we fit VQ(P) models for the fourteen production series under scrutiny, where we include equation-specific intercepts and trends, and we compute the roots of

$$|\hat{\Phi}_0 - \hat{\Phi}_1 z - \cdots - \hat{\Phi}_P z^P| = 0. \tag{4.33}$$

Note that this means that a VQ(1) model has four roots, and that a VQ(2) model has eight roots, as the model parameters are unrestricted. The results appear in Table 4.1. It is obvious from these outcomes that if there are unit roots then their number seems to be restricted to just 1, and perhaps 2 in only one or two cases (see, for example, the row for food and tobacco). Clearly, we do not see four roots with norms close to unity.

The same exercise can be performed for periodic models when estimated in the univariate representation, where we include seasonal intercepts and seasonal

Table 4.2

Estimated roots of periodic polynomials in PAR models when translated into VQ models

Variable	Lag order	Roots
Total	6	0.831, $-0.096 \pm 0.299i$, $-0.013 \pm 0.134i$, -0.002
Products	4	0.568, 0.213, -0.068, -0.004
Final products	4	$0.400 \pm 0.129i$, -0.075, -0.013
Consumer goods	2	0.890, -0.001
Durable consumer goods	2	0.584, -0.001
Automotive products	2	0.475, 0.002
Auto parts	2	0.753, 0.000
Other durable goods	3	0.616, 0.022, -0.005
Food and tobacco	5	0.967, 0.529, 0.486, 0.096, -0.048
Clothing	4	0.960, -0.248, 0.224, -0.050
Chemical products	5	0.904, 0.787, -0.387, 0.219, 0.048
Paper products	6	0.886, 0.807, $0.180 \pm 0.027i$, $-0.078 \pm 0.054i$
Energy products	4	0.919, 0.657, 0.045, -0.005
Fuels	2	0.912, 0.006

Note that the corresponding VQ models have parameter matrices with occasional zeros.

trend terms. Note that these models differ essentially from the VQ models as the PAR(p) models assume that the error terms have a common variance, while the VQ models in principle allow for a seasonally-varying variance. In cases where this restriction is incorrectly imposed, one might perhaps find too much periodicity in the AR parameters. As the order p can be smaller than the maximum order implied by the VQ(P) model, the estimated roots of (4.33) can differ from those obtained earlier. The results appear in Table 4.2. Again, it is quite suggestive that we might expect only a single root to be present in the fourteen series, and hence there is not much effect of possible seasonal heteroskedasticity, if there is any at all.

These first results can be indicative for the application of subsequent more formal testing procedures. Before we turn to these tests, we need to discuss further the representation of trends and intercepts in the periodic model. This is important for the reasons outlined at the start of this chapter.

4.2   Intercepts and deterministic trends

So far we have not paid attention to the deterministic terms in the periodic autoregressions. We have simply added seasonal intercepts and seasonal linear trends to a periodic autoregression in a linear way, as in (4.8). In general, unrestricted periodic models like (4.8) can generate data with diverging seasonal trends. This is because the seasons have different parameters, and with different values of the intercepts the seasonal trends can diverge or converge. This may not be plausible in all practical cases, at least based on visual inspection of the data, and hence one may want to be careful about how intercepts and trends are included in the model. Common seasonal linear deterministic trends require restrictions on the seasonal trend parameters τ_s. Note that the simple restriction $\tau_1 = \tau_2 = \tau_3 = \tau_4$ does not correspond to common seasonal trends, because the τ_s parameters do not represent the slope of the trend in each season.

To illustrate the role of seasonal intercepts and seasonal linear deterministic trends, we consider two cases. The first case corresponds to the situation in which the roots of the multivariate representation of (4.10) are within the unit circle, implying periodic (trend-)stationarity. The second case deals with the situation of periodic integration.

Periodic trend-stationarity

To analyze the role of the linear trend under periodic trend-stationarity, we rewrite (4.10) as

$$y_t - \mu_s^* - \tau_s^* T_t = \sum_{i=1}^{p} \phi_{i,s}(y_{t-i} - \mu_{s-i}^* - \tau_{s-i}^* T_{t-i}) + \varepsilon_t, \qquad (4.34)$$

where μ_s^* and τ_s^* are nonlinear functions of the μ_s, τ_s, and $\phi_{i,s}$ parameters, and where $\mu_{s-4k}^* = \mu_s^*$ and $\tau_{s-4k}^* = \tau_s^*$. This model can easily be estimated using nonlinear least squares (NLS). The restriction for common linear seasonal deterministic trends is given by $\tau_1^* = \tau_2^* = \tau_3^* = \tau_4^*$. This restriction can be tested with a standard likelihood ratio test, which, in the case of quarterly data, is $\chi^2(3)$ distributed. The restriction for the absence of linear deterministic trends is, of course, simply $\tau_1^* = \tau_2^* = \tau_3^* = \tau_4^* = 0$.

Periodic integration

The presence of a linear deterministic trend in a (non-periodic) autoregression for y_t, with a unit root imposed, corresponds to the presence of a quadratic trend in y_t. Likewise, the inclusion of linear deterministic trends in a periodically-integrated autoregression (PIAR), that is, the autoregression where one needs to difference the data with $1 - \hat{\alpha}_s L$, assumes the presence of seasonal quadratic trends in y_t. To discuss the role of trends in a PIAR we distinguish three cases, that is, the presence of no quadratic trends (NQT), common (seasonal) linear trends (CLT) and no linear trends (NLT). Here we closely follow the discussion in Paap and Franses (1999).

To discuss these three cases it is convenient to write (4.8) using the periodic differencing filter, as in (4.22), that is a PIAR(p) model such as

$$y_t - \alpha_s y_{t-1} - \mu_s^{**} - \tau_s^{**} T_t = \sum_{i=1}^{p-1} \beta_{i,s}(y_{t-i} - \alpha_{s-i} y_{t-1-i} - \mu_{s-i}^{**} - \tau_{s-i}^{**} T_{t-i}) + \varepsilon_t.$$

$$(4.35)$$

Here $\alpha_1 \alpha_2 \alpha_3 \alpha_4 = 1$; μ_s^{**}, τ_s^{**}, and $\beta_{i,s}$ are again nonlinear functions of the parameters μ_s, τ_s, and $\phi_{i,s}$, and $\mu_{s-4k}^{**} = \mu_s^{**}$ and $\tau_{s-4k}^{**} = \tau_s^{**}$ for $k \in \mathbb{N}$ and $s = 1, 2, 3, 4$. To analyze the role of the deterministic terms, it is convenient to write (4.35) in VQ representation, that is,

$$(\Xi_0 - \Xi_1 L - \cdots - \Xi_{P-1} L^{P-1})(\Phi_0 Y_T - \Phi_1 Y_{T-1} - \mu - \tau T) = \varepsilon_T,$$
$$\Xi(L)(\Phi_0 Y_T - \Phi_1 Y_{T-1} - \mu - \tau T) = \varepsilon_T,$$

$$(4.36)$$

where Φ_0 and Φ_1 are the same as in (3.34), and Ξ_i, $i = 0, \ldots, P - 1$, are 4×4 matrices. The matrix Ξ_0 is lower triangular with unit elements on the diagonal and its (s, j)th element is $-\beta_{s-j,s}$ for $j < s$. The (s, j)th element of Ξ_i equals $\beta_{4i+s-j,s}$ for $i = 1, \ldots, P - 1$.

If the PIAR(p) model contains only one unit root, such that the roots of the polynomial $|\Xi_0 - \Xi_1 z - \cdots - \Xi_{P-1} z^{P-1}|$ are outside the unit circle, we can write

$$\Delta_1 Y_T = \Phi_0^{-1} \mu + \tau T + (\Phi_0^{-1} \Phi_1 - I_4) Y_{T-1} + \eta_T,$$

$$(4.37)$$

where $\eta_T = \Xi(L)^{-1} \varepsilon_T$ is a possibly-infinite invertible vector moving average process. The rank of the matrix $\Pi = \Phi_0^{-1} \Phi_1 - I_4$ equals 3 and can be written as $\gamma\alpha'$, where α is given in (4.20) and

$$
\gamma = \begin{pmatrix} 1/\alpha_2 & 1/(\alpha_2\alpha_3) & \alpha_1 \\ 0 & 1/\alpha_3 & \alpha_1\alpha_2 \\ 0 & 0 & \alpha_1\alpha_2\alpha_3 \\ 0 & 0 & 0 \end{pmatrix}. \tag{4.38}
$$

Applying the Granger representation theorem to (4.37) results in

$$
Y_T = C\sum_{i=0}^{T-1}\Phi_0^{-1}(\mu + \tau(T-i) + \eta_{T-i}) + C^*(L)\Phi_0^{-1}(\mu + \tau T + \eta_T) + Y_0,
$$
$$\tag{4.39}$$

where $C = \gamma_\perp(\alpha'_\perp\gamma_\perp)^{-1}\alpha'_\perp$ with $\gamma_\perp = (1,\alpha_2,\alpha_2\alpha_3,\alpha_2\alpha_3\alpha_4)'$ and $\alpha_\perp = (0,0,0,1)'$, and where the coefficients of the lag polynomial $C^*(L)$ decrease exponentially, see Johansen (1991, Theorem 4.1). This last feature means that this concerns the stationary part of the model. Notice that $C = \gamma_\perp(\alpha'_\perp\gamma_\perp)^{-1}\alpha'_\perp = \Phi_0^{-1}\Phi_1$. The matrix $C\Phi_0^{-1} = (\Phi_0^{-1}\Phi_1)\Phi_0^{-1}$ displays the impact of the accumulated shocks $\sum_{i=0}^{T-1}\eta_{T-i}$. This matrix is

$$
(\Phi_0^{-1}\Phi_1)\Phi_0^{-1} = \begin{pmatrix} 1 & \alpha_1\alpha_3\alpha_4 & \alpha_1\alpha_4 & \alpha_1 \\ \alpha_2 & 1 & \alpha_1\alpha_2\alpha_4 & \alpha_1\alpha_2 \\ \alpha_2\alpha_3 & \alpha_3 & 1 & \alpha_1\alpha_2\alpha_3 \\ \alpha_2\alpha_3\alpha_4 & \alpha_3\alpha_4 & \alpha_4 & 1 \end{pmatrix} \tag{4.40}
$$

and it has rank 1. This matrix is also of importance for computing the impulse response function, see Breitung and Franses (1997). The rank of 1 follows from the fact that the matrix can be written as ab', where a and b are two 4×1 vectors defined as

$$
a = \begin{pmatrix} 1 \\ \alpha_2 \\ \alpha_2\alpha_3 \\ \alpha_2\alpha_3\alpha_4 \end{pmatrix} \quad \text{and} \quad b' = \begin{pmatrix} 1 & \alpha_1\alpha_3\alpha_4 & \alpha_1\alpha_4 & \alpha_1 \end{pmatrix}. \tag{4.41}
$$

Collecting the deterministic components in (4.39) results in

$$
Y_T = \kappa T^2 + \delta T + \theta + C\Phi_0^{-1}\sum_{i=0}^{T-1}\eta_{T-i} + C^*(L)\Phi_0^{-1}\eta_T + Y_0, \tag{4.42}
$$

where

$$
\begin{aligned}
\kappa &= \tfrac{1}{2}C\tau = \tfrac{1}{2}ab'\tau, \\
\delta &= C\left(\tfrac{1}{2}\tau + \mu\right) + C^*(1)\Phi_0^{-1}\tau = ab'\left(\tfrac{1}{2}\tau + \mu\right) + \Phi_0^{-1}\tau,
\end{aligned} \tag{4.43}
$$

and θ represents the initial value of the trend component, see also Johansen (1991). This representation is quite crucial for understanding how trends and intercepts in a model imply properties of the data that can be generated from the model.

No quadratic trends First of all, the quadratic trend disappears from (4.42) if $\kappa = 0$. This corresponds to the restriction $b'\tau = 0$, that is,

$$\tau_1 + \alpha_1\alpha_3\alpha_4\tau_2 + \alpha_1\alpha_4\tau_3 + \alpha_1\tau_4 = 0, \tag{4.44}$$

which is again highly nonlinear in the parameters. Of course, a special case is the trivial solution $\tau = 0$.

Common linear deterministic trends Next, under the restriction $b'\tau = 0$, Y_T contains a linear deterministic trend, see (4.42). The slope of this linear deterministic trend is given by

$$\delta = ab'\mu + \Phi_0^{-1}\tau, \tag{4.45}$$

see (4.43), such that $\delta = (\delta_1, \delta_2, \delta_3, \delta_4)'$ can be shown to be equal to

$$\begin{pmatrix} \delta_1 \\ \delta_2 \\ \delta_3 \\ \delta_4 \end{pmatrix} = \begin{pmatrix} d_1 \\ d_2 \\ d_3 \\ d_4 \end{pmatrix} + \begin{pmatrix} 1 & 0 & 0 & 0 \\ \alpha_2 & 1 & 0 & 0 \\ \alpha_2\alpha_3 & \alpha_3 & 1 & 0 \\ \alpha_2\alpha_3\alpha_4 & \alpha_3\alpha_4 & \alpha_4 & 1 \end{pmatrix} \begin{pmatrix} \tau_1 \\ \tau_2 \\ \tau_3 \\ \tau_4 \end{pmatrix}, \tag{4.46}$$

with

$$\begin{pmatrix} d_1 \\ d_2 \\ d_3 \\ d_4 \end{pmatrix} = \begin{pmatrix} 1 & \alpha_1\alpha_3\alpha_4 & \alpha_1\alpha_4 & \alpha_1 \\ \alpha_2 & 1 & \alpha_1\alpha_2\alpha_4 & \alpha_1\alpha_2 \\ \alpha_2\alpha_3 & \alpha_3 & 1 & \alpha_1\alpha_2\alpha_3 \\ \alpha_2\alpha_3\alpha_4 & \alpha_3\alpha_4 & \alpha_4 & 1 \end{pmatrix} \begin{pmatrix} \mu_1 \\ \mu_2 \\ \mu_3 \\ \mu_4 \end{pmatrix}. \tag{4.47}$$

It is obvious that we generally have different deterministic trends in the elements of Y_T, and therefore for each season in y_t. The same linear deterministic trend for each component in Y_T corresponds to the restriction $\delta_1 = \delta_2 = \delta_3 = \delta_4$.

There are in turn two cases of interest. The first case is $\tau = 0$. If $\tau = 0$ the slope of the deterministic trend equals $d = (d_1, d_2, d_3, d_4)'$. As $d = ab'\mu$, it holds that $d_s = \alpha_s d_{s-1}$ with $d_0 = d_4$. It is therefore not possible to have an equal linear deterministic trend due to $d_1 = d_2 = d_3 = d_4$ in Y_T unless $\mu = 0$, which corresponds to the absence of a linear deterministic trend.

The second case is $b'\tau = 0$. Note that, due to this restriction, the slope of the deterministic trend in the fourth quarter equals d_4, which can be seen by substituting (4.44) into the last row of (4.46). The restriction for equal slopes is therefore obtained by setting the slope of the first three quarters equal to the slope in the fourth quarter d_4, or

$$\begin{pmatrix} d_1 \\ d_2 \\ d_3 \end{pmatrix} + \begin{pmatrix} 1 & 0 & 0 \\ \alpha_2 & 1 & 0 \\ \alpha_2\alpha_3 & \alpha_3 & 1 \end{pmatrix} \begin{pmatrix} \tau_1 \\ \tau_2 \\ \tau_3 \end{pmatrix} = \begin{pmatrix} d_4 \\ d_4 \\ d_4 \end{pmatrix}. \tag{4.48}$$

Using the fact that $d_s = \alpha_s d_{s-1}$ with $d_0 = d_4$, the restrictions on τ_1, τ_2, and τ_3 for a common deterministic trend are given by the solution of (4.48), that is,

$$\tau_1 = (1 - \alpha_1)d_4, \quad \tau_2 = (1 - \alpha_2)d_4, \quad \tau_3 = (1 - \alpha_3)d_4, \tag{4.49}$$

and the restriction (4.44) (or $\tau_4 = (1 - \alpha_4)d_4$), where d_4 is given by

$$d_4 = \mu_4 + \alpha_4\mu_3 + \alpha_3\alpha_4\mu_2 + \alpha_2\alpha_3\alpha_4\mu_1. \tag{4.50}$$

Notice that, to obtain common seasonal linear deterministic trends, we only need four instead of six restrictions.

No linear deterministic trends Finally, under the restrictions in (4.49) and (4.44), y_t contains the same deterministic trend in every season. The restriction for the absence of a deterministic trend is equivalent to $\delta_s = 0$, $s = 1, 2, 3, 4$. As the matrix Φ_0^{-1} has full rank, it follows from (4.42) and (4.45) that the condition for no deterministic trends is equivalent to $\tau = 0$ and $b'\mu = 0$. The latter restriction corresponds to $d_4 = 0$, where d_4 is given in (4.50). In summary, the restrictions equal

$$\mu_4 + \alpha_4\mu_3 + \alpha_3\alpha_4\mu_2 + \alpha_2\alpha_3\alpha_4\mu_1 = 0 \quad \text{and} \quad \tau_1 = \tau_2 = \tau_3 = \tau_4 = 0. \tag{4.51}$$

Of course, a special case is the trivial solution $\mu = \tau = 0$.

All of the above restrictions can be tested with standard likelihood ratio tests. Under the restriction of periodic integration, these tests are asymptotically $\chi^2(\nu)$ distributed, where ν denotes the number of restrictions, see Johansen (1994, Theorem 3) for a similar result. Finally, these restrictions are also valid in non-periodic AR models or PAR models for the first differences of a time series.

Later, in Table 4.3, we summarize the steps one can sequentially follow in practice. These steps involve decisions on the inclusion of intercepts and deterministic trends in the test regression. We discuss this table in more detail once we have presented the relevant statistical theory.

4.3 Testing for unit roots

In this section we discuss how one can formally examine whether a periodic model has one or more unit roots. We start with the univariate representation, and after that we turn to the VQ representation. We also examine the fourteen production series for their unit root properties. In the appendix to this chapter (Section 4.A) we give some exemplary EViews code that one can use in specific empirical situations.

A single unit root

We start by considering the simple periodic first-order autoregressive model in (3.32). Define $\alpha = (\alpha_1, \alpha_2, \alpha_3, \alpha_4)$. The vector process Y_T is stationary if the root of the characteristic equation

$$|\Phi_0 - \Phi_1 z| = 1 - \alpha_1 \alpha_2 \alpha_3 \alpha_4 z = 0 \tag{4.52}$$

is outside the unit circle, that is, if $|g(\alpha)| < 1$, where $g(\alpha) = \alpha_1 \alpha_2 \alpha_3 \alpha_4$. Note again that the values of some α_s are allowed to exceed unity. The vector process Y_T is integrated if (4.52) has a unit root, so that

$$H_0 : g(\alpha) = \prod_{s=1}^{4} \alpha_s = 1 \tag{4.53}$$

holds. We aim to test the hypothesis (4.53) against the alternative that $|g(\alpha)| < 1$, in which case the process y_t is said to be periodically (trend-)stationary. Note that the maximum number of unit roots for the Y_T process in (4.52) is one. Assuming that the errors ε_t in (4.8) are normally distributed, the maximum likelihood (ML) estimators of α_s are given by the OLS estimators in the regression

$$y_t = \sum_{s=1}^{4} \alpha_s D_{s,t} y_{t-1} + \varepsilon_t. \tag{4.54}$$

Because of the orthogonality of the regressors in (4.54), we have

$$\hat{\alpha}_s = \left(\sum_{t=2}^{n} D_{s,t} y_{t-1}^2 \right)^{-1} \left(\sum_{t=2}^{n} D_{s,t} y_{t-1} y_t \right), \tag{4.55}$$

for $s = 1, 2, 3, 4$. Imposing H_0 leads to the restricted regression

$$y_t = \alpha_1 D_{1,t} y_{t-1} + \alpha_2 D_{2,t} y_{t-1} + \alpha_3 D_{3,t} y_{t-1} + (\alpha_1 \alpha_2 \alpha_3)^{-1} D_{4,t} y_{t-1} + \varepsilon_t,$$

$$\tag{4.56}$$

which can be estimated by NLS. A likelihood ratio test statistic may be constructed as

$$\text{LR}_1^1 = n \log \left(\frac{\text{RSS}_{01}}{\text{RSS}_{11}} \right), \tag{4.57}$$

where RSS_{01} and RSS_{11} denote the residual sums of squares from (4.54) and (4.56), respectively. A one-sided test is given by

$$\text{LR}_{1\tau}^1 = \text{sign}(g(\hat{\alpha}) - 1)\sqrt{\text{LR}_1^1}, \tag{4.58}$$

where $g(\hat{\alpha})$ is evaluated under the alternative hypothesis.

Boswijk and Franses (1996) show that under the H_0 in (4.53) we have, as $n \to \infty$,

$$N(g(\hat{\alpha}) - 1) \to \left(\int_0^1 W(r)^2 \, dr \right)^{-1} \int_0^1 W(r) \, dW(r),$$

$$\text{LR}_{1\tau}^1, \to \left(\int_0^1 W(r) \, dr \right)^{-1/2} \int_0^1 W(r) \, dW(r), \tag{4.59}$$

$$\text{LR}_1^1, \to \left(\int_0^1 W(r) \, dr \right)^{-1} \left(\int_0^1 W(r) \, dW(r) \right)^2,$$

where $W(r)$ is a standard Brownian motion process. The asymptotic distributions of the first two statistics are the same as those tabulated in the first panel of Tables 8.5.1 and 8.5.2, respectively, of Fuller (1976). In practice, the first statistic is hardly used, and hence we only replicate Table 8.5.2 in Table A.1. We see that $N(g(\hat{\alpha}) - 1)$ already has an asymptotic distribution under the null hypothesis that does not depend upon nuisance parameters. So, it can be used as a test statistic alternative to $\text{LR}_{1\tau}^1$, just like the $n(\hat{\rho} - 1)$ statistic in the non-periodic case, see Dickey and Fuller (1979). Observe that $g(\hat{\alpha}) - 1$ should be scaled by N if it is to be compared with the critical values in Fuller (1976). The final asymptotic distribution in (4.59) is the same as the distribution of the Johansen's trace statistic tabulated in the first row of Table B.1.

To generalize the likelihood ratio test for a unit root to higher-order periodic autoregressions with seasonal dummies and seasonal trends, consider the linear regression

$$y_t = \sum_{s=1}^4 \mu_s D_{s,t} + \sum_{s=1}^4 \tau_s D_{s,t} T_t + \sum_{i=1}^p \sum_{s=1}^4 \phi_{is} D_{s,t} y_{t-i} + \varepsilon_t, \tag{4.60}$$

the parameters of which can be estimated using OLS. Let RSS_{13} denote the residual sum of squares of (4.60) in the case where $\tau_s = 0$ for all s, and RSS_{15}

in the case where only the four trend parameters are included. Next, consider the nonlinear regression

$$y_t = \sum_{s=1}^{4} \alpha_s y_{t-1} + \sum_{s=1}^{4} \mu_s D_{s,t} + \sum_{s=1}^{4} \tau_s D_{s,t} T_t$$

$$+ \sum_{i=1}^{p-1} \sum_{s=1}^{4} \beta_{is} D_{s,t}(y_{t-i} - \alpha_{s-i} y_{t-i-1}) + \varepsilon_t, \qquad (4.61)$$

which can be estimated using NLS under the restriction $\alpha_1 \alpha_2 \alpha_3 \alpha_4 = 1$. Denote the residual sum of squares of (4.61) as RSS_{05}, and RSS_{03} in the case $\tau_s = 0$ for all s. The relevant LR-test statistics for (4.61) versus (4.60) are equal to

$$\text{LR}_i^1 = n \log \left(\frac{\text{RSS}_{0i}}{\text{RSS}_{1i}} \right), \qquad (4.62)$$

for $i = 3, 5$.

Boswijk and Franses (1996) show that, under the H_0 in (4.53) and as $n \rightarrow \infty$, one has

$$\text{LR}_i^1 \rightarrow \left(\left(\int_0^1 W_i(r)^2 \, dr \right)^{-1/2} \int_0^1 W_i(r) \, dW(r) \right)^2 \qquad (4.63)$$

for $i = 3, 5$. Here $W(r)$ is a standard Brownian motion process and

$$W_3(r) = W(r) - \int_0^1 W(t) \, dt,$$

$$W_5(r) = W_3(r) - \left(\left(r - \frac{1}{2} \right) 12 \right) \int_0^1 \left(t - \frac{1}{2} \right) W_3(t) \, dt, \qquad (4.64)$$

where the processes W_3 and W_5 may be interpreted as 'demeaned' and 'detrended' Brownian motions, respectively, see Park and Phillips (1988).

The distributions (4.63) appear as special cases of the Johansen (1991) cointegration analysis. Hence, for the LR_3^1-test the critical values are given in the first row of Table B.3. The critical values for the LR_5^1-test are given in the first row of Table B.5. Similar to (4.58), one may construct the one-sided LR-tests $\text{LR}_{3\tau}^1$ and $\text{LR}_{5\tau}^1$. The corresponding distributions can be found in the second and third panel of Table 8.5.2 of Fuller (1976), see also Table A.1. The application of these one-sided tests may be less useful in the case of $\text{PAR}(p)$ models with $p > 1$, as the α_s parameters are not identified under the alternative hypothesis, see equation (4.60).

Following on from the discussion of the implications of trends and intercepts in periodic models, one might consider alternative versions of the above unit root test statistics. We have already seen that the asymptotic distribution of the test statistics for periodic integration depends on the deterministic components in the test regression. We take this issue seriously, as the alternative hypothesis should allow for plausible patterns of the data under scrutiny. For example, if the data do not display quadratic types of patterns, one should also not allow for this under the alternative hypothesis.

To account for the possibility of periodic trend-stationarity under the alternative hypothesis, one usually includes a deterministic trend in the test equation. This implies that under $|\alpha_1\alpha_2\alpha_3\alpha_4| < 1$ one assumes that the series contains a linear deterministic trend, while under the restriction $\alpha_1\alpha_2\alpha_3\alpha_4 = 1$ one allows the series to contain a quadratic trend. In practice, it would be convenient to test which deterministic trends have to be included in the test regression. Unfortunately, however, a pre-test for the significance of deterministic components in the test equation is not very convenient as the distributions of these tests depend on whether the series has a unit root or not. A better strategy therefore, as also indicated at the start of this chapter, is to consider the joint test of periodic integration and the absence of a quadratic trend by using the null hypothesis

$$H_{04} : \alpha_1\alpha_2\alpha_3\alpha_4 = 1 \wedge \tau_1 + \alpha_1\alpha_3\alpha_4\tau_2 + \alpha_1\alpha_4\tau_3 + \alpha_1\tau_4 = 0, \qquad (4.65)$$

which leads to the periodic analog of the Φ_3-test proposed by Dickey and Fuller (1979). Likewise, under $\tau_s = 0$ for all s, we can test the joint null hypothesis

$$H_{02} : \alpha_1\alpha_2\alpha_3\alpha_4 = 1 \wedge \mu_4 + \alpha_4\mu_3 + \alpha_3\alpha_4\mu_2 + \alpha_2\alpha_3\alpha_4\mu_1 = 0 \qquad (4.66)$$

to compare periodic stationarity versus periodic integration with no deterministic trend in the series. To construct likelihood ratio tests for both hypotheses we define the residual sum of squares of (4.61) as RSS_{04} under the restriction given in (4.65), and as RSS_{02} under the restriction (4.65) with $\tau_s = 0$ for all s. The residual sum of squares RSS_{14} and RSS_{12} follow from the residuals of (4.60), where we make the restriction $\tau_s = 0$ for all s for the latter residual sum. The likelihood ratio statistics to test the hypotheses H_{04} (4.65) and H_{02} (4.66) are now defined as

$$LR_i^1 = n \log \left(\frac{RSS_{0i}}{RSS_{1i}} \right) \qquad (4.67)$$

for $i = 2, 4$. The asymptotic distribution of the LR_2^1 statistic is given in Johansen (1991, Theorem 4.1) and tabulated in the first row of Table B.2 in Appendix B, while the asymptotic distribution of the LR_4^1 statistic is given in Johansen (1991, Theorem 1) and tabulated in the first row of Table B.4.

Testing for a non-periodic differencing filter   Once it has been established that the hypothesis of $\alpha_1\alpha_2\alpha_3\alpha_4 = 1$ cannot be rejected using either of the LR_i^1-test statistics in (4.63), the next possible step is to investigate whether the hypotheses

$$H_0 : \alpha_s = 1 \quad \text{for } s = 1, 2, 3, \tag{4.68}$$

$$H_0 : \alpha_s = -1 \quad \text{for } s = 1, 2, 3 \tag{4.69}$$

are valid, which would imply that either $\alpha_4 = 1$ or $\alpha_4 = -1$. In PAR models of order 2 or higher, this would mean that any periodicity does not appear in the differencing filter but in the other autoregressive parameters. The first H_0 reduces the periodic differencing filter to $1 - L$, while the second H_0 reduces it to the differencing filter that corresponds to a seasonal unit root -1. In the case when H_0 in (4.68) cannot be rejected, it is said that the PAR(p) process contains a non-seasonal unit root. Otherwise formulated, this H_0 results in a PAR process for an I(1) time series. In Boswijk and Franses (1996) it is shown that, conditional on the restriction $\alpha_1 \alpha_2 \alpha_3 \alpha_4 = 1$, the likelihood ratio test statistics for the hypotheses (4.68) and (4.69) are asymptotically $\chi^2(3)$ distributed under the null hypotheses. Simulation experiments in Franses and Paap (1994) confirm this result. Hence, the sequential strategy of first testing for unit roots and then for parameter restrictions does not involve new asymptotic theory, and also no new simulated critical values are needed.

A final step in our model selection strategy, see Table 4.3, can involve a test for the significance of the β_{is} parameters in (4.61). Given that $(1 - \alpha_s L)y_t$ is a periodically-stationary process, the t-tests for the significance of the β_{is} parameters asymptotically follow a standard normal distribution under the null hypothesis. However, as the α_s have to be estimated, one may expect biased distributions in small samples. The simulation results in Franses and Paap (1996) indicate that this bias is very small for regularly sized samples of quarterly data, which are like the samples we analyze in this book.

A joint test for a non-periodic differencing filter In the case where one is only interested in testing whether the $1 - L$ filter is adequate for a PAR(p) process, one may rewrite the PAR(p) model as

$$\Delta_1 y_t = \mu_s + \tau_s T_t + \delta_s y_{t-1} + \sum_{i=1}^{p-1} \psi_{is} \Delta_1 y_{t-i} + \varepsilon_t. \tag{4.70}$$

The presence of a non-seasonal unit root in y_t corresponds to

$$H_0 : \delta_s = 0 \quad \text{for } s = 1, 2, 3, 4. \tag{4.71}$$

This null hypothesis is tested against

$$H_1 : \delta_s \neq 0 \quad \text{for at least one } s = 1, 2, 3, 4, \tag{4.72}$$

see Ghysels *et al.* (1996). Notice that under the alternative hypothesis the y_t process can be either periodically integrated or periodically stationary, which might be viewed as rather inconvenient. So, in a sense, one would only be interested in finding evidence in favor of the null hypothesis, as under the alternative one still does not know the trend properties of the time series. Furthermore, notice that $(\delta_1 + 1)(\delta_2 + 1)(\delta_3 + 1)(\delta_4 + 1) = 1$ in (4.70) only implies periodic integration when $p = 1$. The restriction for PI in (4.70) is much more complicated for larger values of p.

The hypothesis in (4.71) can be tested using a Wald test, which can be expressed as

$$W_i = \frac{N}{n-k} \sum_{s=1}^{4} t(\delta_s)^2, \qquad (4.73)$$

where $t(\delta_s)$ represents the t value for the test $\delta_s = 0$, k is the number of regressors in (4.70), and $i = 1, 3$, and 5 when (4.70) contains, respectively, no seasonal dummies and no trends, only four seasonal constants, and four seasonal constants and four seasonal trends. Boswijk and Franses (1996) prove that the asymptotic distribution of the W_i-test in (4.73) is the sum of the square of the Dickey–Fuller distribution and a $\chi^2(3)$ distribution. Using this approach, one needs to tabulate new critical values, while this is not needed for our preferred sequential approach.

In order to test for the validity of the $1 - L$ filter in a PAR(p) model, another possibility is to modify the Dickey–Fuller t-test for PAR models, that is,

$$\Delta_1 y_t = \mu_s + \tau t + \delta y_{t-1} + \sum_{i=1}^{p-1} \psi_{is} \Delta_1 y_{t-i} + \varepsilon_t, \qquad (4.74)$$

and to test the significance of δ using the t-test. Ghysels *et al.* (1996) show that, under the null hypothesis, this periodic augmented DF test (PADF) follows a standard Dickey–Fuller distribution. Note that the deterministic trend in the auxiliary regression (4.74) enters the equation without seasonally-varying parameters, but an extension should not be too difficult.

To compare the two-step and joint test methods for investigating the adequacy of the $1 - L$ filter, Franses and Paap (1996) consider a small simulation experiment. They conclude that the empirical performance of the test procedures is similar when the DGP is indeed a PAR model for a $(1-L)$-transformed time series. On the other hand, when the DGP is a PI process, only the two-step method is able to detect this, while the other methods often select the $1 - L$ filter, especially when the PADF is used. For practical purposes, we therefore advocate the use of the two-step method.

It should be noted that we follow the commonly-used approach that the null hypothesis corresponds to a unit root, and the alternative to stationarity. Of course, one can also reverse this order and test periodic stationarity against unit roots in periodic models. This is pursued in Kurozumi (2002), who adapts the approach of Kwiatkowski *et al.* (1992). It should be stressed though that there is no indication in the literature that one strategy is preferred over the other, see, for example, Hylleberg (1995). One might be tempted to consider both approaches, and if they both point towards the same conclusion then one gains more confidence in the outcome.

Multiple unit roots

The analysis above is concerned with the case when one has some indication that there can be at most one unit root in the PAR(p) process, as we seem to have for our exemplary fourteen production series. In some applications it may, however, be useful to allow for the possible presence of more than one unit root. For the moment we will exclude the possibility of I(2)-type processes and consider cases in which the multiple unit roots concern seasonal unit roots. Again, one may directly test for seasonal unit roots in PAR(p) processes along similar lines as in (4.70), see Ghysels *et al.* (1996). A drawback of this method is that one has to assume that the $1 - L$ filter can remove a non-seasonal unit root, as one needs to impose this differencing filter. A second drawback is that the tests have to be done for each type of seasonal unit root at a time. Indeed, the HEGY approach discussed in Chapter 2 cannot be straightforwardly extended to periodic models, as the resultant and relevant regressors are no longer orthogonal, see also Ghysels and Osborn (2001, p. 158). Given the results in the literature, like, for example, Franses and Romijn (1993) and Franses and Paap (1994), where it is often found that the $1 - L$ filter can be rejected against a periodic differencing filter, it is unclear what the effect is on test results for seasonal unit roots when the inappropriate $1 - L$ filter is assumed. This suggests that it may be useful to test for seasonal unit roots while allowing for the possibility of having a periodically-integrated time series, and to follow the method in Boswijk *et al.* (1997).

Tests for the presence of more than a single unit root can be done in a similar manner as for the single unit root case. As a starting point, we consider a PAR(p) model (without deterministic elements to save notation)

$$y_t = \sum_{i=1}^{p} \phi_{is} y_{t-i} + \varepsilon_t. \tag{4.75}$$

As we have already seen in Section 4.1, the presence of two unit roots corresponds to the periodic differencing filter $1 - \alpha_{1s} L - \alpha_{2s} L^2$ with the restrictions (4.25) imposed. This implies that (4.75) in the case of two unit roots can be written as

$$y_t - \alpha_{1s} y_{t-1} - \alpha_{2s} y_{t-2} = \sum_{i=1}^{p-2} \beta_{is}(y_{t-i} - \alpha_{1,s-i} y_{t-1-i} - \alpha_{2,s-i} y_{t-2-i}) + \varepsilon_t,$$

$$\tag{4.76}$$

with the restrictions (4.25). The validity of this differencing filter, that is, the presence of two unit roots, can be tested using a likelihood ratio test defined as

$$\mathrm{LR}_1^2 = n \log \left(\frac{\mathrm{RSS}_{01}}{\mathrm{RSS}_{11}} \right), \qquad (4.77)$$

where RSS_{11} denotes the residual sum of squares of (4.75) after parameter estimation with OLS, and RSS_{01} denotes the residual sum of squares of (4.76). The parameters of the latter model can be estimated with NLS.

Similarly, we can define a likelihood ratio test for the presence of three unit roots, in which case the model under the null hypothesis is

$$y_t - \alpha_{1s} y_{t-1} - \alpha_{2s} y_{t-2} - \alpha_{3s} y_{t-3}$$
$$= \sum_{i=1}^{p-3} \beta_{is} (y_{t-i} - \alpha_{1,s-i} y_{t-1-i} - \alpha_{2,s-i} y_{t-2-i} - \alpha_{3,s-i} y_{t-3-i}) + \varepsilon_t, \quad (4.78)$$

with the restrictions (4.29). In other words, one can examine unit roots by imposing cointegration restrictions and checking their validity. The likelihood ratio test for the presence of three unit roots, denoted by LR_1^3, is defined as in (4.77), where RSS_{01} is now the residual sum of squares of (4.78). Finally, to test for the presence of four unit roots we have to consider

$$\Delta_4 y_t = \sum_{i=1}^{p-4} \beta_{is} \Delta_4 y_{t-i} + \varepsilon_t. \qquad (4.79)$$

The corresponding likelihood ratio test to analyze the validity of this seasonal differencing filter is denoted by LR_1^4.

Boswijk *et al.* (1997) show that, under the presence of q unit roots, we have as $n \to \infty$

$$\mathrm{LR}_1^q \to \mathrm{tr} \left(\int_0^1 \mathrm{d}\bar{W}(r) \, \bar{W}(r)' \left(\int_0^1 \bar{W}(r) \bar{W}(r)' \, \mathrm{d}r \right)^{-1} \int_0^1 \bar{W}(r) \, \mathrm{d}\bar{W}(r)' \right),$$
$$(4.80)$$

where $\bar{W}(r)$ is a standard q-dimensional vector Brownian motion process. The limiting distribution is the same as the trace statistic of the Johansen cointegration tests for $4 - q$ cointegration relations. Asymptotic fractiles of this distribution are given in Table B.1, for the case of no deterministics. Just as in the single unit root case, we can extend the PAR(p) model (4.75) with seasonal dummies and seasonal linear trends. In the case the asymptotic distribution consists of demeaned and detrended vector Brownian motions, as in (4.64). The fractiles of the distributions are presented in Tables B.3 and B.5.

The maximum number of unit roots in a series is determined by the order of the periodic autoregression. Boswijk *et al.* (1997) propose to use a sequential testing procedure in which one starts with testing the maximum number of unit roots, and only proceed to testing q unit roots if the hypothesis of $q + 1$ unit roots is rejected, as in Pantula (1989). Johansen (1992b) shows that this procedure has an asymptotically controllable size.

If the number of unit roots in the PAR(p) model is determined, one may again test whether the periodic differencing filters correspond to seasonal unit roots, as discussed in Section 4.1. For example, one may want to test whether the $1 - \alpha_{1s}L - \alpha_{2s}L^2$ filter with restrictions (4.25) can be simplified to the $1 - L^2$ filter. This corresponds to the parameter restrictions $\alpha_{1s} = 0$ and $\alpha_{2s} = 1$ for all s. Note that the number of restrictions equals four and not eight due to the validity of (4.25). These restrictions can be tested with a likelihood ratio test, which is, under the null hypothesis, asymptotically χ^2 distributed. So, once again, no new tables with critical values are needed.

The VQ approach   So far, we have discussed tests for unit roots based on univariate periodic models. It can be seen that these tests may involve cumbersome nonlinear restrictions which have to be programed in, say, EViews. In practice, it may therefore be convenient to exploit the link between univariate models and the VQ representation. Indeed, as we have demonstrated previously, the number of unit roots in y_t is linked to the number of cointegration relations between the elements of Y_T.

Before we elaborate further on unit root tests based on the VQ model, we should again say a few words about the impact of intercepts and trends. We therefore consider the VAR(1) model

$$Y_t = \Phi Y_{t-1} + e_t, \tag{4.81}$$

for an $m \times 1$ time series Y_t containing $y_{1t}, \ldots, y_{mt}$, where e_t is an $m \times 1$ vector white noise series for $t = 1, \ldots, N$. Here we employ a slightly more general notation in terms of m, but of course one may think of $m = 4$. For cointegration analysis it is convenient to write (4.81) in error correction format, that is,

$$\Delta_1 Y_t = \Pi Y_{t-1} + e_t, \tag{4.82}$$

where $\Pi = \Phi - I_m$. The matrix Π contains information on cointegrating relations between the m elements of Y_t. In cointegration analysis it is common to write (4.82) as

$$\Delta_1 Y_t = \gamma \alpha' Y_{t-1} + e_t, \tag{4.83}$$

where γ and α are $m \times r$ full rank matrices. When $0 < r < m$, there are r cointegrating relations between the m variables, see Engle and Granger (1987) and Johansen (1995).

The likelihood-based cointegration test method, developed in Johansen (1988), tests the rank of the matrix Π using the reduced rank regression technique based on canonical correlations. For model (4.83) this amounts to calculating the canonical correlations between $\Delta_1 Y_t$ and Y_{t-1}. This gives the eigenvalues $\hat{\lambda}_1 \geq \cdots \geq \hat{\lambda}_m$ and the corresponding eigenvectors $\hat{\alpha}_1, \ldots, \hat{\alpha}_m$. The most reliable test for the rank of Π is the likelihood ratio test statistic Q, namely,

$$Q(r|m) = -N \sum_{i=r+1}^{m} \log(1 - \hat{\lambda}_i), \qquad (4.84)$$

which is usually called the trace statistic. The null hypothesis is that there are at most r cointegration relations. Asymptotic theory for $Q(r|m)$ is given in Johansen (1995), and the critical values for this Q for the model (4.83) are replicated in Table B.1 where $q = m - r$.

Notice that the model in (4.83) assumes that the m time series do not have a trend, and that the cointegrating relations $\alpha' Y_t$ have zero equilibrium values. We now discuss two extensions of (4.83) which are often more useful.

The imposed restriction that the cointegrating relations $\alpha' Y_t$ in (4.83) all have an attractor which is exactly equal to zero does not seem plausible for many economic data. Hence, it is more appropriate to extend (4.83) as follows:

$$\Delta_1 Y_t = \gamma(\alpha' Y_{t-1} - \mu_1) + e_t. \qquad (4.85)$$

To compute the LR statistic, one should now calculate the canonical correlations between $\Delta_1 Y_t$ and $(Y_{t-1}, 1)'$. The relevant asymptotic theory is given in Johansen (1995). The critical values of the corresponding LR-test appear in Table B.2. This case corresponds to Option 2 in the relevant routine in EViews.

When (some or all) series display trending patterns, one should consider a multivariate version of (4.4), which is

$$\Delta_1 Y_t = \mu_0 + \gamma(\alpha' Y_{t-1} - \mu_1 - \delta_1 t) + e_t. \qquad (4.86)$$

In other words, this model allows the individual time series to have trends by not restricting μ_0 to zero, while the cointegrating relations attain their equilibrium values at $\mu_0 + \delta_1 t$. In very special cases all of the parameters in δ_1 may equal 0, but it is safe not to assume this beforehand.

To compute the LR statistic, one should calculate the canonical correlations between demeaned first-differenced series and demeaned $(Y_{t-1}, 1, t)'$. The relevant asymptotic theory is again given in Johansen (1995). The critical values of the LR-test appear in Table B.4. This second case corresponds to Option 4 in the relevant routine in EViews.

We now return to a discussion of testing for unit roots in the multivariate representation of periodic models, still for a univariate series. This alternative approach to test for the presence of unit roots which allows for periodic and seasonal integration is given by the application of the Johansen maximum likelihood cointegration method, see Franses (1994) and Boswijk *et al.* (1997).

Consider the VQ(1) process as in (4.15),

$$\Delta_1 Y_T = \tilde{\mu} + \tilde{\tau}T + \Pi Y_{T-1} + \omega_T, \tag{4.87}$$

with $\omega_T = \Phi_0^{-1}\varepsilon_T$ and $\Pi = \Phi_0^{-1}\Phi_1 - I_4$. The rank r of the matrix Π conveys the information on the cointegration properties of the Y_T vector series. The Y_T process is stationary when r equals 4. There is no cointegration between the elements of Y_T when r is equal to 0. When $0 < r < 4$, one can write $\Pi = \gamma\alpha'$, where γ and α are $4 \times r$ matrices and the matrix α contains the cointegration vectors.

We use the Johansen procedure described above to test for the value of r which determines the number of unit roots in the y_t series. For (4.87), the method amounts to the choice of the r linear combinations of the elements of Y_T which have the largest correlation with $\Delta_1 Y_T$ after correcting for a vector of intercepts and linear deterministic trends. The corresponding eigenvalues $\hat{\lambda}_i$, where $\hat{\lambda}_i \geq \hat{\lambda}_{i+1}$, are used to construct the trace statistic, which is in this case given by

$$Q(r|4) = -N \sum_{i=r+1}^{4} \log(1 - \hat{\lambda}_i). \tag{4.88}$$

This trace test statistic is used to test for the number of cointegration vectors. Asymptotic fractiles for these statistics are displayed in Tables B.1–B.5 with $q = 4 - r$.

To test for linear restrictions on the cointegrating vectors α, define a $4 \times q$ matrix H, where $r \leq q \leq 4$, which reduces α to the parameters φ, or $\alpha = H\varphi$. For brevity, we shall denote these restrictions by their matrix H. Assuming the validity of the restrictions H, one compares the corresponding eigenvalues $\hat{\xi}$ of the canonical correlation matrix with the $\hat{\lambda}_i$ via the test statistic

$$N \sum_{i=1}^{r} \log\left(\frac{1 - \hat{\xi}_i}{1 - \hat{\lambda}_i}\right). \tag{4.89}$$

Under the null hypothesis, this test statistic asymptotically follows a $\chi^2(r(4 - q))$ distribution.

An application of the Johansen cointegration method to the VQ model in (4.87) gives an opportunity to gain insights into the properties of the univariate quarterly y_t series. No differencing filter is needed for y_t when r is equal to four, see also Osborn (1993). When $r = 0$, the Δ_4 filter for y_t may be appropriate. If r is 3, and pairs of successive Y_T are cointegrated with the parameters $(1, -1)$, a transformation Δ_1 for y_t is required. This Δ_1 filter assumes the cointegration relations $Y_{2,T} - Y_{1,T}$, $Y_{3,T} - Y_{2,T}$, and $Y_{4,T} - Y_{3,T}$. In terms of the model (4.87), this means that the restrictions on the columns of α given by

$$H_{31} = \begin{pmatrix} -1 & 0 & 0 \\ 1 & -1 & 0 \\ 0 & 1 & -1 \\ 0 & 0 & 1 \end{pmatrix} \tag{4.90}$$

cannot be rejected, which implies that y_t has a non-seasonal unit root. It is also possible to test for the presence of seasonal unit roots. When $r = 3$, one can check for the presence of the root -1 by testing the restrictions

$$H_{32} = \begin{pmatrix} 1 & 0 & 0 \\ 1 & 1 & 0 \\ 0 & 1 & 1 \\ 0 & 0 & 1 \end{pmatrix}. \tag{4.91}$$

If both hypotheses H_{31} and H_{32} are rejected, one has encountered three general cointegration relationships between the elements of Y_T. This implies the appropriateness of the periodic differencing filter $1 - \alpha_s L$ with $\alpha_1 \alpha_2 \alpha_3 \alpha_4 = 1$ and not all $\alpha_s = \alpha$.

When r is equal to 1 or 2, one can proceed along similar lines to test for the presence of non-seasonal and/or specific seasonal unit roots. When r is 2, and one wants to test for the unit roots ± 1 or $\pm i$, the H matrices are given by

$$H_{21} = \begin{pmatrix} -1 & 0 \\ 0 & -1 \\ 1 & 0 \\ 0 & 1 \end{pmatrix} \quad \text{and} \quad H_{22} = \begin{pmatrix} 1 & 0 \\ 0 & 1 \\ 1 & 0 \\ 0 & 1 \end{pmatrix}. \tag{4.92}$$

When $r = 1$ and the focus is on the unit roots $(1, \pm i)$ or $(-1, \pm i)$, the matrices are

$$H_{11} = \begin{pmatrix} -1 \\ 1 \\ -1 \\ 1 \end{pmatrix} \quad \text{and} \quad H_{12} = \begin{pmatrix} 1 \\ 1 \\ 1 \\ 1 \end{pmatrix}. \tag{4.93}$$

As stated, when r is found to be equal to 0, the $1 - L^4$ filter is useful.

In summary, an application of the Johansen cointegration method to a VAR model for the Y_T vector truly generalizes the HEGY approach, see also Osborn and Rodrigues (2002), as it allows for the presence of periodically-varying parameters. One possible model that follows from the above is a univariate periodic error correction model where Π is replaced by $\gamma \alpha'$. The 'error' of over-differencing is then corrected by $\alpha' Y_{T-1}$, which represents linear relationships between the annual series.

Table 4.3
Examining unit roots in a periodic autoregression

Step	Action
1	Compute the roots of the estimated PAR model.
2	Inspect if the series contains a linear trend (visual).
3	Test the restrictions (4.65) (in the case of a linear trend) or (4.66) (in the case of no linear trend).
4	Impose restriction for unit root if necessary.
5	Test the relevant restrictions on the deterministic elements, see Section 4.2.
6	In the case of periodic integration, test for $\alpha_s = 1$ or -1 for all s.

As a final remark, if one thinks that the series at hand might be I(2), one can apply the same approaches as above, but then for the series $\Delta_4 y_t$ in the univariate case and $\Delta_1 Y_T$ in the VQ case. Hence, this strategy follows that advocated by Pantula (1989).

Before we turn to illustrations, we summarize the relevant steps to analyze the presence of unit roots in Table 4.3. These steps are useful for most applications. In some rare cases one may want to test for the presence of more than one unit root. In this case one has to replace step 3 by a multiple unit root analysis.

Illustration

In Table 4.4, we report on the unit root-related inference for univariate periodic models. The third column of this table contains the test statistic values for the hypothesis that there is a unit root, jointly with the absence of quadratic trends. We see that the null hypothesis gets rejected in five of the fourteen cases. Hence, these five series only contain deterministic trends. The next column concerns the test for the absence of quadratic trends. The absence is confirmed for nine of the fourteen series, at the 10 per cent significance level. Next, we see that, for most series, we reject that the linear deterministic trends are common across the quarters. The last column suggests that we find the adequacy of the first-differencing filter for only one series, that is, chemical products. In summary, we observe evidence of periodic integration with seasonally-varying trends.

In Table 4.5 we consider unit root inference for VQ models. For nine of the fourteen series we find that there are three cointegrating relations between the elements of Y_T. The final column of this table shows that, for almost all of these nine cases, we reject the adequacy of the $1 - L$ or $1 + L$ filters, except for the series other durable goods. Next, we find that products and final products are stationary, and that paper products obey a seasonal random walk process, with periodic short-run dynamics.

Table 4.4

Testing for periodic integration, restrictions on the deterministic components, and the appropriate differencing filter

Variable	Order	LR_4^1	LR_{NQT}	$LR_{\tau=0}$	LR_{CLT}	LR_{Δ_1}
Total	6	7.428	0.015(0.903)	4.483(0.214)	14.402(0.006)	15.148(0.002)
Products	4	15.494**	–	30.794(0.000)	29.757(0.000)	–
Final products	4	17.735***	–	33.753(0.000)	12.137(0.007)	–
Consumer goods	2	6.750	2.833(0.092)	21.486(0.000)	15.719(0.003)	19.533(0.000)
Durable consumer goods	2	14.124**	–	21.616(0.000)	20.006(0.000)	–
Automotive products	2	17.344***	–	24.974(0.000)	1.462(0.691)	–
Auto parts	2	6.840	0.002(0.964)	6.653(0.084)	10.563(0.032)	13.038(0.005)
Other durable goods	3	11.041*	0.004(0.950)	5.649(0.130)	2.942(0.568)	7.375(0.061)
Food and tobacco	5	7.486	7.078(0.008)	21.517(0.000)	15.274(0.004)	8.838(0.032)
Clothing	4	5.717	5.257(0.022)	21.964(0.000)	61.306(0.000)	40.452(0.000)
Chemical products	4	9.885	0.413(0.511)	8.448(0.076)	11.132(0.025)	3.272(0.352)
Paper products	6	3.645	0.712(0.399)	0.743(0.863)	10.767(0.029)	11.767(0.008)
Energy products	4	8.610	4.262(0.039)	14.648(0.002)	17.819(0.001)	18.683(0.000)
Fuels	2	7.236	4.051(0.044)	33.311(0.000)	17.371(0.002)	7.855(0.049)

LR_4^1 denotes the test statistic for periodic integration and the absence of quadratic deterministic trends. Critical values are given in Table B.4.

LR-tests for the absence of quadratic deterministic trends (NQT), $\tau_s = 0$ for all s, common linear deterministic trends (CLT), and for the presence of a Δ_1 filter. These tests are performed in a PIAR model without restrictions on the deterministic components for the periodically-integrated series and in a PAR model without restrictions on the deterministic components for the periodically-stationary series.

***Significant at the 0.01 level, **at the 0.05 level, *at the 0.10 level.

Table 4.5

Johansen cointegration analysis applied to the VQ representation

Variable	Order[1]	Trace test statistics[2]				Rank	Restrictions[3]	
		$r=3$	$r=2$	$r=1$	$r=0$	r	H_{r1}	H_{r2}
Total	2	8.099	33.790	92.295	167.836	3	20.267 (0.000)	45.557 (0.000)
Products	1	12.445	40.006	98.868	275.032	4	11.682 (0.000)	26.585 (0.000)
Final products	1	12.542	42.719	101.939	290.990	4	15.634 (0.000)	33.921 (0.000)
Consumer goods	1	5.275	30.443	82.560	212.599	3	20.276 (0.000)	47.606 (0.000)
Durable consumer goods	1	8.883	30.694	60.856	160.870	3	10.997 (0.012)	16.494 (0.001)
Automotive products	1	6.297	26.378	60.600	119.160	3	14.638 (0.002)	24.821 (0.000)
Auto parts	1	7.430	39.687	87.125	190.225	3	10.016 (0.018)	38.440 (0.000)
Other durable goods	1	9.268	31.639	74.491	224.742	3	5.422 (0.143)	51.630 (0.000)
Food and tobacco	2	6.733	16.909	34.150	65.819	1	15.249 (0.002)	22.862 (0.000)
Clothing	1	5.918	29.621	72.551	199.505	3	14.017 (0.003)	49.435 (0.000)
Chemical products	2	3.460	17.412	40.830	98.879	2	34.227 (0.000)	43.247 (0.000)
Paper products	2	2.762	12.531	30.360	54.859	0		
Energy products	1	8.205	38.800	74.574	155.196	3	25.038 (0.000)	34.895 (0.000)
Fuels	1	7.225	27.635	55.671	126.980	3	8.148 (0.043)	22.550 (0.000)

[1]VAR order based on univariate lag orders.

[2]Johansen trace statistics. All tests are performed in a VAR model with a constant and a linear trend restricted in the cointegrating space. Critical values are given in Table B.4.

[3]Likelihood ratio test statistics for restrictions on the cointegrating space.

4.4   Forecasting trending time series

One may use periodically-integrated AR models for forecasting in the same way as non-integrated PAR models in Section 3.4. It should be mentioned, though, that PIAR models have a feature which can appear attractive for forecasting. This feature is that the out-of-sample forecasts allow for changing seasonal patterns. The periodic differencing filter $1 - \alpha_s L$ establishes that the differences between $\hat{Y}_{s,N+H}$ and $\hat{Y}_{s-1,N+H}$ are not constant for $s = 2, 3, 4$ and for increasing H. Hence, the slowly changing seasonal patterns which can be observed within the sample will also appear in the out-of-sample forecasts. So, if a process of changing seasonality has started in the data immediately before the forecast origin, the periodically-integrated model will pick it up and extend it to the out-of-sample period. Notice that this is not the case for the seasonally-integrated model, that is, $\Delta_4 y_t = \varepsilon_t$, for which the differences between $\hat{Y}_{s,N+H}$ and $\hat{Y}_{s-1,N+H}$ remain constant. Hence, the seasonal integration model can describe changing seasonal patterns within the sample, but it does not extract information from the time series that can be used to generate such patterns out of sample.

Consider again the PIAR(1) process $y_t = \alpha_s y_{t-1} + \varepsilon_t$ with $\alpha_1 \alpha_2 \alpha_3 \alpha_4 = 1$. As we have already seen in Section 3.4, the one-step to four-step ahead forecasts are given by

$$
\begin{aligned}
\hat{y}_{n+1} &= \mathrm{E}_n[y_{n+1}] = \mathrm{E}_n[\alpha_s y_n + \varepsilon_{n+1}] = \alpha_s y_n, \\
\hat{y}_{n+2} &= \mathrm{E}_n[y_{n+2}] = \mathrm{E}_n[\alpha_{s+1}\alpha_s y_n + \varepsilon_{n+2} + \alpha_{s+1}\varepsilon_n] = \alpha_{s+1}\alpha_s y_n, \\
\hat{y}_{n+3} &= \mathrm{E}_n[y_{n+3}] = \mathrm{E}_n[\alpha_{s+2} y_{n+2} + \varepsilon_{n+1}] = \alpha_{s+2}\alpha_{s+1}\alpha_s y_n, \\
\hat{y}_{n+4} &= \mathrm{E}_n[y_{n+4}] = \mathrm{E}_n[\alpha_{s+3} y_{n+3} + \varepsilon_{n+3}] = \alpha_{s+3}\alpha_{s+2}\alpha_{s+1}\alpha_s y_n = y_n,
\end{aligned}
\tag{4.94}
$$

while the corresponding variances of the forecast and hence the variances of the forecast errors equal σ^2, $\sigma^2(1 + \alpha_{s+1}^2)$, $\sigma^2(1 + \alpha_{s+2}^2 + \alpha_{s+2}^2\alpha_{s+1}^2)$, and $\sigma^2(1 + \alpha_{s+3}^2 + \alpha_{s+3}^2\alpha_{s+2}^2 + \alpha_{s+3}^2\alpha_{s+2}^2\alpha_{s+1}^2)$, respectively. Comparing these variances with those of a non-periodic random walk process $y_t = y_{t-1} + \varepsilon_t$, which are σ^2, $2\sigma^2$, $3\sigma^2$, and $4\sigma^2$, it is clear that a periodically-integrated process allows the forecast intervals to vary with the seasons. This property reflects the seasonal heteroskedasticity in the PIAR process that is present within the sample.

Note that the PIAR(1) model generates the same four-step ahead forecast as the seasonally-integrated model $\Delta_4 y_t = \varepsilon_t$. The variance of the latter four-step ahead forecast is, however, equal to σ^2.

Again, it is simpler to use the VQ representation for forecasting several years ahead. One may apply the same formulas as in Section 3.4. To forecast H-years ahead, one uses that

$$
Y_{N+H} = (\Phi_0^{-1}\Phi_1)^H Y_N + \sum_{i=1}^{H} (\Phi_0^{-1}\Phi_1)^{i-1}\Phi_0^{-1}\varepsilon_{N+i}.
\tag{4.95}
$$

Note that, under the restriction of periodic integration, the matrix $\Phi_0^{-1}\Phi_1$ is idempotent and hence the H-year ahead forecasts are given by

$$\hat{Y}_{N+H} = \mathrm{E}_N[Y_{N+H}] = (\Phi_0^{-1}\Phi_1)^H Y_N = (\Phi_0^{-1}\Phi_1)Y_N. \qquad (4.96)$$

The vector of H-year ahead forecasts is therefore equal for each horizon. This is, however, not true for the associated forecast uncertainty. The corresponding covariance matrix of the forecast errors (3.59) simplifies to

$$\mathrm{E}_N[(\hat{Y}_{N+H} - Y_{N+H})(\hat{Y}_{N+H} - Y_{N+H})']$$

$$= \sigma^2\left(\Phi_0^{-1}(\Phi_0^{-1})' + (H-1)((\Phi_0^{-1}\Phi_1)\Phi_0^{-1})((\Phi_1\Phi_0^{-1})\Phi_0^{-1})'\right). \quad (4.97)$$

Hence, the variances of the H-year ahead forecasts are given by

$$\sigma^2 + (H-1)(1 + \alpha_1^2 + \alpha_1^2\alpha_4^2 + \alpha_1^2\alpha_3^2\alpha_4^2)\sigma^2,$$

$$(1 + \alpha_2^2)\sigma^2 + (H-1)(1 + \alpha_2^2 + \alpha_1^2\alpha_2^2 + \alpha_1^2\alpha_2^2\alpha_4^2)\sigma^2,$$

$$(1 + \alpha_3^2 + \alpha_2^2\alpha_3^2)\sigma^2 + (H-1)(1 + \alpha_3^2 + \alpha_2^2\alpha_3^2 + \alpha_1^2\alpha_2^2\alpha_3^2)\sigma^2,$$

$$(1 + \alpha_4^2 + \alpha_3^2\alpha_4^2 + \alpha_2^2\alpha_3^2\alpha_4^2)\sigma^2 + (H-1)(1 + \alpha_4^2 + \alpha_3^2\alpha_4^2 + \alpha_2^2\alpha_3^2\alpha_4^2)\sigma^2. \tag{4.98}$$

The derivation of the variances of the multi-step ahead forecasts for higher-order periodically-integrated time series is slightly more complicated. For example, consider the PIAR(2) model $y_t - \alpha_s y_{t-1} = \beta_s(y_{t-1} - \alpha_{s-1}y_{t-2}) + \varepsilon_t$, with $\alpha_1\alpha_2\alpha_3\alpha_4 = 1$. This model can be written in VQ representation as

$$\Xi(L)(\Phi_0 Y_T - \Phi_1 Y_{T-1}) = \varepsilon_T, \qquad (4.99)$$

where Φ_0 and Φ_1 are given in (3.34) and

$$\Xi(L) = \begin{pmatrix} 1 & 0 & 0 & -\beta_1 L \\ -\beta_2 & 1 & 0 & 0 \\ 0 & -\beta_3 & 1 & 0 \\ 0 & 0 & -\beta_4 & 1 \end{pmatrix}. \qquad (4.100)$$

The VAR model (4.99) can be written as the VARMA model

$$Y_T = \Phi_0^{-1}\Phi_1 Y_{T-1} + \Phi_0^{-1}\Xi(L)^{-1}\varepsilon_T, \qquad (4.101)$$

where

$$\Xi(L)^{-1} = (1 - \tilde{\beta}L)^{-1}(\Gamma_0 + \Gamma_1 L), \qquad (4.102)$$

with $\tilde{\beta} = \beta_1\beta_2\beta_3\beta_4$ and

$$\Gamma_0 = \begin{pmatrix} 1 & 0 & 0 & 0 \\ \beta_2 & 1 & 0 & 0 \\ \beta_2\beta_3 & \beta_3 & 1 & 0 \\ \beta_2\beta_3\beta_4 & \beta_3\beta_4 & \beta_4 & 1 \end{pmatrix} \quad \text{and} \quad \Gamma_1 = \begin{pmatrix} 0 & \beta_1\beta_3\beta_4 & \beta_1\beta_4 & \beta_1 \\ 0 & 0 & \beta_1\beta_2\beta_4 & \beta_1\beta_4 \\ 0 & 0 & 0 & \beta_1\beta_2\beta_3 \\ 0 & 0 & 0 & 0 \end{pmatrix}.$$

$$\tag{4.103}$$

The moving average part of (4.101) is of infinite order, as can be observed by rewriting that part as

$$
\begin{aligned}
\Phi_0^{-1}(1 - \tilde{\beta}L)^{-1}&(\Gamma_0\varepsilon_T + \Gamma_1\varepsilon_{T-1}) \\
&= (1 + \tilde{\beta}L + \tilde{\beta}^2 L^2 + \tilde{\beta}^3 L^3 + \cdots)\Phi_0^{-1}(\Gamma_0\varepsilon_T + \Gamma_1\varepsilon_{T-1}) \\
&= \Phi_0^{-1}(\Gamma_0\varepsilon_T + \Gamma_1\varepsilon_{T-1}) + \tilde{\beta}\Phi_0^{-1}(\Gamma_0\varepsilon_{T-1} + \Gamma_1\varepsilon_{T-2}) \\
&\quad + \tilde{\beta}^2\Phi_0^{-1}(\Gamma_0\varepsilon_{T-2} + \Gamma_1\varepsilon_{T-3}) + \tilde{\beta}^3\Phi_0^{-1}(\Gamma_0\varepsilon_{T-3} + \Gamma_1\varepsilon_{T-4}) + \cdots \\
&= G_0\varepsilon_T + G_1\varepsilon_{T-1} + \tilde{\beta}G_1\varepsilon_{T-2} + \tilde{\beta}^2 G_1\varepsilon_{T-3} + \tilde{\beta}^3 G_1\varepsilon_{T-4} + \cdots ,
\end{aligned}
\tag{4.104}
$$

with $G_0 = \Phi_0^{-1}\Gamma_0$ and $G_1 = \Phi_0^{-1}\Gamma_1 + \tilde{\beta}\Phi_0^{-1}\Gamma_0$, where G_0 is a lower triangular matrix. In the PIAR(1) case it holds that $G_0 = \Phi_0^{-1}$ and $G_1 = 0$. When we combine (4.101) and (4.104), the PIAR(2) process can be written as

$$
Y_T = \Phi_0^{-1}\Phi_1 Y_{T-1} + G_0\varepsilon_T + G_1\varepsilon_{T-1} + \tilde{\beta}G_1\varepsilon_{T-2} + \tilde{\beta}^2 G_1\varepsilon_{T-3} + \tilde{\beta}^3 G_1\varepsilon_{T-4} + \cdots .
\tag{4.105}
$$

This expression can easily be used to derive the infinite VMA representation for the Y_T vector process, which is useful for computing the impulse response functions. In fact, recursively substituting lagged Y_T in (4.105), while taking account of the fact that $(\Phi_0^{-1}\Phi_1)^m = \Phi_0^{-1}\Phi_1$ for $m = 1, 2, 3, \ldots$, yields

$$
Y_T = \Phi_0^{-1}\Phi_1 Y_0 + \sum_{i=0}^{T-1} F_i\varepsilon_{T-i},
\tag{4.106}
$$

where

$$
\begin{aligned}
F_0 &= G_0, \\
F_1 &= \Phi_0^{-1}\Phi_1 G_0 + G_1 = \Phi_0^{-1}\Phi_1 F_1 + G_1, \\
F_2 &= \Phi_0^{-1}\Phi_1 G_0 + \Phi_0^{-1}\Phi_1 G_1 + \tilde{\beta}G_1 = \Phi_0^{-1}\Phi_1 F_3 + \tilde{\beta}G_1, \\
&\vdots \\
F_i &= \Phi_0^{-1}\Phi_1 F_{i-1} + \tilde{\beta}^{i-1}G_1,
\end{aligned}
\tag{4.107}
$$

where Y_0 is the starting value of the Y_T process.

The infinite VMA representation (4.106) allows us to compute the multi-step ahead forecast errors. If we opt for unbiased forecasts

$$E_N[Y_{N+H}] = \hat{Y}_{N+H},\tag{4.108}$$

which follow directly from (4.105), it follows that

$$
\begin{aligned}
\hat{Y}_{N+1} - Y_{N+1} &= F_0\varepsilon_{N+1}, \\
\hat{Y}_{N+2} - Y_{N+2} &= F_0\varepsilon_{N+2} + F_1\varepsilon_{N+1}, \\
&\;\;\vdots \\
\hat{Y}_{N+H} - Y_{N+H} &= F_0\varepsilon_{N+H} + F_1\varepsilon_{N+H-1} + \cdots + F_{H-1}\varepsilon_{N+1}.
\end{aligned}
\tag{4.109}
$$

As ε_T is independent from ε_{T+k} for any k not equal to 0, we easily arrive at

$$
\begin{aligned}
E_N[(\hat{Y}_{N+1} - Y_{N+1})^2] &= \sigma^2 F_0 F_0', \\
E_N[(\hat{Y}_{N+2} - Y_{N+2})^2] &= \sigma^2 (F_0 F_0' + F_1 F_1'), \\
&\;\;\vdots \\
E_N[(\hat{Y}_{N+H} - Y_{N+H})^2] &= \sigma^2 \sum_{i=0}^{H-1} F_i F_i'.
\end{aligned}
\tag{4.110}
$$

The diagonal elements of the matrices in (4.110) can now be used to calculate the forecast error variances of y_t.

Illustration

To illustrate this, we re-estimate the PAR(p) models for all observations except for the last three years. We impose the restrictions as found in Table 4.4, and we generate twelve one-step ahead forecasts and nine four-step ahead forecasts for each series. We also generate the same forecasts for the non-periodic models that would follow from the HEGY analysis, and from periodic models for the first-order differenced series. The lag structure of the models is based on an LM-test for first-order and first-to-fourth-order serial correlation. The root mean squared errors (RMSE) and the mean absolute percentage errors (MAPE) appear in Table 4.6 and we summarize these results in Table 4.7.

There are various conclusions to be drawn from Table 4.7. Firstly, for larger horizons the periodic models do better than non-periodic models, while for one-step ahead forecasting the HEGY models show competitive forecast performance. Secondly, when evaluating the periodic models only, imposing the improper restriction Δ_1 leads to better one-step ahead forecasts, while for the larger horizon the forecasts are about equally as good.

Table 4.6
Out-of-sample forecasting. The estimation period ends at 1997.4; the
forecasting period is 1998.1–2000.4

		HEGY		PAR Δ_1		PAR	
		RMSE	MAPE	RMSE	MAPE	RMSE	MAPE
Total	1 step	1.062	0.183	1.533	0.256	0.769	0.131
	4 step	1.080	0.149	2.134	0.346	0.976	0.167
Products	1 step	0.958	0.165	0.882	0.142	1.253	0.222
	4 step	2.275	0.530	1.489	0.279	3.733	0.730
Final products	1 step	0.978	0.166	0.990	0.173	1.230	0.209
	4 step	2.178	0.375	1.289	0.194	3.505	0.654
Consumer goods	1 step	1.496	0.257	0.990	0.318	2.188	0.422
	4 step	2.350	0.400	1.289	0.446	3.296	0.581
Durable	1 step	3.487	0.601	1.797	0.579	3.667	0.647
consumer goods	4 step	4.198	0.713	2.734	0.956	4.723	0.837
Automotive	1 step	3.671	0.621	6.235	1.010	5.689	0.953
products	4 step	5.436	0.962	7.044	1.097	5.357	0.797
Auto parts	1 step	1.751	0.323	1.157	0.332	2.670	0.492
	4 step	0.784	0.111	1.054	0.118	3.247	0.631
Other durable	1 step	3.381	0.537	3.919	0.648	3.557	0.603
goods	4 step	5.598	0.914	7.872	1.361	4.819	0.799
Food and tobacco	1 step	1.023	0.181	1.434	0.256	1.394	0.263
	4 step	2.674	0.578	2.552	0.509	2.253	0.421
Clothing	1 step	2.706	0.569	2.126	0.380	4.303	0.814
	4 step	11.604	2.582	8.637	1.923	9.908	2.152
Chemical products	1 step	3.393	0.545	3.268	0.538	7.007	1.063
	4 step	3.091	0.536	4.187	0.771	6.133	1.043
Paper products	1 step	1.807	0.295	1.923	0.357	3.030	0.613
	4 step	5.782	1.082	6.317	1.209	4.699	0.906
Energy products	1 step	3.753	0.623	3.868	0.674	3.642	0.653
	4 step	3.403	0.521	3.629	0.486	2.967	0.457
Fuels	1 step	0.926	0.147	1.942	0.349	1.466	0.257
	4 step	1.739	0.334	0.971	0.196	1.191	0.205

Table 4.7
Number of times a model is best in
terms of forecasting

Model	Horizon	Criterion	
		RMSE	MAPE
HEGY	1	6	9
	4	2	5
PAR Δ_1	1	6	4
	4	6	4
PAR	1	2	1
	4	6	5

4.5   Effects of neglecting periodicity

As we did in Chapter 3, it is of interest to see what happens if one considers non-periodic models for periodically-integrated data, or periodic models for seasonally-adjusted periodically-integrated data. Again, we report on some simulation experiments, and the results are drawn from the tables in Franses (1995b). The data generating processes are given in Table 4.8.

In Table 4.9 we report on the first five estimated autocorrelations of various series. Similar to Table 3.5, we see the same kinds of general patterns, that is, low-order AR models seem useful for $\Delta_4 y_t$, and the ACF of the seasonally-adjusted series $\hat{y}_t$ takes larger values than that of y_t.

Next, we examine what happens with the periodic patterns in the data when the data are filtered by the linearized Census X-11 procedure. Firstly, we fit periodic AR(1) models to the adjusted data for the two DGPs, and we test for periodic variation in the autoregressive parameters. The rejection frequencies for DGP E and DGP F are 41.9 and 0.0, respectively. This suggests that periodicity can disappear somewhat. Table 4.10 shows that the estimated parameter in a non-periodic AR(1) model is around 0.99. We again see that the periodic parameters get smoothed towards unity.

As seasonally-adjusted data are proclaimed to be useful for interpreting data (instead of modeling them), it is of interest to see what happens if periodic data get seasonally adjusted. Ooms and Franses (1997) analyze unemployment data for the US and Germany, and find that these can best be characterized as periodically-integrated data. Using simulations, they show that seasonally adjusting these data leads to an over-estimation of seasonality in specific quarters in times of recession. In fact, one tended to be too optimistic in the first quarter in terms of rising unemployment.

Finally, and similar to the related discussion in Chapter 3, it might be that the true data are not periodic, but that neglected level shifts make us think

Table 4.8

The data generating processes in the simulations

DGP	α_1	α_2	α_3	α_4	$\alpha_1\alpha_2\alpha_3\alpha_4$
E	0.50	0.90	1.50	$1/(\alpha_1\alpha_2\alpha_3)$	1
F	1.10	0.91	1.05	$1/(\alpha_1\alpha_2\alpha_3)$	1

The DGP is $y_t = \alpha_s y_{t-1} + \varepsilon_t$ with $\varepsilon_t \sim \mathrm{N}(0,1)$.

Table 4.9

The first five estimated non-periodic
autocorrelations for (transformed) periodic
simulated series

Variable	Lag	DGP E	DGP F
y_t	1	0.59	0.91
	2	0.33	0.86
	3	0.51	0.79
	4	0.81	0.75
	5	0.44	0.68
$\Delta_1 y_t$	1	-0.11	-0.07
	2	-0.42	-0.06
	3	-0.13	-0.07
	4	0.59	0.03
	5	-0.09	-0.06
$\Delta_4 y_t$	1	0.67	0.72
	2	0.37	0.46
	3	0.15	0.20
	4	-0.04	-0.05
	5	-0.03	-0.04
$\hat{y}_t$	1	0.92	0.94
	2	0.84	0.88
	3	0.78	0.81
	4	0.72	0.74
	5	0.68	0.70

The DGPs are given in Table 4.8.

that they are. In fact, if one had data with a unit root 1, requiring the regular
differencing filter Δ_1, and there were shifts in the seasonal intercepts, then one
could find spurious evidence of periodic integration. When one suspects this
then one can proceed with the nested or non-nested test strategies, as proposed
in Franses and McAleer (1997).

Table 4.10
Parameter estimates for periodic and
non-periodic models for simulated Census
X-11 adjusted periodic series

Model	Parameter	DGP E	DGP F
AR(1)	α	0.983	0.989
PAR(1)	α_1	0.902	0.999
	α_2	0.982	0.979
	α_3	1.031	0.993
	α_4	1.040	0.985

The DGPs are given in Table 4.8.

4.6 Conclusion

This chapter dealt with the analysis of periodic time series which display trends. The analysis of such data is already quite complicated for non-periodic data, and even more so for periodic data. The main cause of this is that periodic models allow for subtle interplays between seasonality and trends. As diagnosing unit roots, and imposing these in subsequent forecasting and multivariate analysis, is important, we proposed a sequence of steps along which one can proceed. The relevant critical values are all given in Appendix A and B, in order to make this self-contained. Our forecasting illustration did not demonstrate the superiority of the periodic models, but we did not have this intention in the first place. We showed that this model can be an interesting competitor for other models for seasonal and trending data. In the next chapter we will examine multivariate periodic models, including models for data with stochastic trends.

4.A EViews code

In this section we give the EViews code for estimating the parameters in the PAR(1) model, which include seasonally-varying intercepts and trends. We focus on the unrestricted model, the model with the periodic integration restriction, the model with the $1 - L$ restriction imposed, the model with the $1 + L$ restriction imposed, the model with the additional restriction of common linear trends, and with the absence of quadratic trends.

```
' load workfile
load c:\iproq.wf1

' give begin date and end date of series
!byr=1947.1
!eyr=2000.4
```

```
smpl !byr !eyr

'assign series to y
genr y=log(nsa1)

'generate seasonal dummies and annual trend
genr d1=@seas(1)
genr d2=@seas(2)
genr d3=@seas(3)
genr d4=@seas(4)
smpl !byr !byr+3
genr tr=1
smpl !byr+4 !eyr
genr tr=tr(-4)+1

'set estimation sample
smpl !byr !eyr

' PAR(1) model with seasonal dummies and seasonal deterministic trends
equation parsdst.ls(c=0.0000001,m=2500)
y=c(1)*d1+c(2)*d2+c(3)*d3+c(4)*d4+(c(5)*d1+c(6)*d2+c(7)*d3+c(8)*d4)*tr
+(c(9)*d1+c(10)*d2+c(11)*d3+c(12)*d4)*y(-1)

' PAR(1) model with seasonal dummies and common linear deterministic trends
equation parsdclt.ls(c=0.0000001,m=2500)
y=c(1)*d1+c(2)*d2+c(3)*d3+c(4)*d4+c(5)*tr
+(c(9)*d1+c(10)*d2+c(11)*d3+c(12)*d4)*(y(-1)-c(1)*d1(-1)-c(2)*d2(-1)
-c(3)*d3(-1)-c(4)*d4(-1)-c(5)*tr(-1))

' PAR(1) model with seasonal dummies
equation parsd.ls(c=0.0000001,m=2500)
y=c(1)*d1+c(2)*d2+c(3)*d3+c(4)*d4+(c(9)*d1+c(10)*d2+c(11)*d3
  +c(12)*d4)*y(-1)

' PIAR(1) with seasonal dummies and seasonal deterministic trends
equation piarsdst.ls(c=0.0000001,m=2500)
y=c(1)*d1+c(2)*d2+c(3)*d3+c(4)*d4
+(c(5)*d1+c(6)*d2+c(7)*d3+c(8)*d4)*tr
+(c(9)*d1+c(10)*d2+c(11)*d3+(1/(c(9)*c(10)*c(11)))*d4)*y(-1)

' PIAR(1) with seasonal dummies and seasonal deterministic trends
' under the restriction of no quadratic trends
equation piarsdstnqt.ls(c=0.0000001,m=2500)
y=c(1)*d1+c(2)*d2+c(3)*d3+c(4)*d4
+(-((c(6)/c(10))+(c(7)/(c(10)*c(11)))+c(8)*c(9))*d1+c(6)*d2+c(7)*d3
+c(8)*d4)*tr+(c(9)*d1+c(10)*d2+c(11)*d3+(1/(c(9)*c(10)*c(11)))*d4)*y(-1)
```

```
' PIAR(1) with seasonal dummies and seasonal deterministic trends
' under the restriction of common linear deterministic trends
equation piarsdstclt.ls(c=0.0000001,m=2500)
y=c(1)*d1+c(2)*d2+c(3)*d3+c(4)*d4
+(c(4)+(c(3)/(c(9)*c(10)*c(11)))+(c(2)/(c(9)*c(10)))+(c(1)/c(9)))
*((1-c(9))*d1+(1-c(10))*d2+(1-c(11))*d3+(1-(1/(c(9)*c(10)*c(11))))*d4)*tr
+(c(9)*d1+c(10)*d2+c(11)*d3+(1/(c(9)*c(10)*c(11)))*d4)*y(-1)

' PIAR(1) with seasonal dummies
equation piarsd.ls(c=0.0000001,m=2500)
y=c(1)*d1+c(2)*d2+c(3)*d3+c(4)*d4
+(c(9)*d1+c(10)*d2+c(11)*d3+(1/(c(9)*c(10)*c(11)))*d4)*y(-1)

' PAR(0) for the first difference of y with seasonal dummies
' and seasonal deterministic trends
equation dparsdst.ls(c=0.0000001,m=2500)
d(y)=c(1)*d1+c(2)*d2+c(3)*d3+c(4)*d4+(c(5)*d1+c(6)*d2+c(7)*d3+c(8)*d4)*tr

' PAR(0) for the first difference of y with seasonal dummies and
' seasonal deterministic trends under the restriction of no quadratic trends
equation dparsdstnqt.ls(c=0.0000001,m=2500)
d(y)=c(1)*d1+c(2)*d2+c(3)*d3+c(4)*d4
+(c(5)*d1+c(6)*d2+c(7)*d3+(-c(5)-c(6)-c(7))*d4)*tr

' PAR(0) for the first difference of y with seasonal dummies
equation dparsd.ls(c=0.0000001,m=2500)
d(y)=c(1)*d1+c(2)*d2+c(3)*d3+c(4)*d4
```

5

Multivariate periodic time series models

In many cases in macroeconomics one is interested in linking together two or more time series variables. This can be done for descriptive purposes or for forecasting. For example, one can examine which variables are correlated with inflation and unemployment, and how these correlations can yield insights into business cycle fluctuations. One may also use these insights to see if one variable can be predicted using recent information from other variables. In these instances one can construct a multivariate time series model.

If it is found that one or more of the variables under scrutiny displays periodic properties, then it is relevant to incorporate these into a multivariate model. Obviously, the number of parameters in such a model can be rather large. Hence, in practice, one should pay specific attention to this phenomenon, in order to save enough degrees of freedom. This implies that one needs to pay close attention to the representation of a multivariate periodic time series model. So far, we have argued that periodic time series models for univariate data are most easily analyzed in the vector of quarters (VQ) form. This amounts to investigating the properties of a quarterly observed time series y_t via an analysis of the properties of the 4×1 vector process $Y_{s,T}$, which contains the annual observations in each of the quarters. For multivariate periodic data, matters are a little more complicated. In fact, as we will show below, it turns out that analysis of the stationarity property of a periodic VAR (PVAR) model can be quite involved, even for the PVAR(1) model. In this chapter we therefore propose two reasonably useful alternative approaches for analyzing a multivariate time series using a periodic model.

Next, as many macroeconomic data display trends, one has to worry about the way a multivariate model incorporates a description of these trends. Obviously, when it comes to forecasting, but also for business cycle analysis, it is

103

sensible to examine whether two or more series have the same type of trend. We have seen in the previous chapter, and one can also find similar results in the relevant literature, that it seems that the trend in many macroeconomic series is of a stochastic nature. Hence, in this chapter we also discuss the issue of common stochastic trends for periodic models. We will argue that sensible methods to examine such cointegration require specific representations of multivariate periodic time series models, and that cointegration analysis of unrestricted periodic models is cumbersome, if not impossible.

The outline of this chapter is as follows. In Section 5.1 we consider notation and representation issues of multivariate periodic models. We consider a particular VQ representation of multivariate periodic autoregressions. This VQ representation is used to derive stationarity conditions for periodic autoregressions. In Section 5.2 we show that several empirically useful models impose restrictions on the rank of the matrix containing the long-run relationships. As it does not seem tractable in practice to formally investigate this rank with methods as given in Chapter 4, we consider two alternative approaches to test for periodic cointegration.

In Section 5.3 we focus on a single-equation approach to test for the presence of periodic cointegration relations within the context of an error correction model. Part of the material is drawn from Boswijk and Franses (1995a). This approach starts with an analysis of a periodic error correction model, that is, an error correction model where the cointegrating parameters and the adjustment parameters are allowed to vary with the seasons. This model then involves so-called periodic cointegration relationships. We consider estimation methods and illustrate their practical usefulness by an analysis of two industrial production series, that is, total production and the production of other durables. In Section 5.4 we consider a full-system approach to test for periodic cointegration. This approach is based on Kleibergen and Franses (1999). Again, we illustrate this method for the same two series, and examine if these series share the same stochastic trend. The last section gives a discussion of miscellaneous topics.

5.1   Notation and representation

Consider a PVAR model of order p for the m-dimensional vector of seasonal time series $\bar{y}_t = (y_{1,t}, \ldots, y_{m,t})'$, for $t = 1, \ldots, n = 4N$, that is,

$$\bar{y}_t = \bar{\mu}_s + \bar{\tau}_s T_t + \bar{\phi}_{1s} y_{t-1} + \cdots + \bar{\phi}_{ps} + \bar{\varepsilon}_t, \tag{5.1}$$

where $\bar{\mu}_s = (\mu_{1,s}, \ldots, \mu_{m,s})'$ and $\bar{\tau}_s = (\tau_{1,s}, \ldots, \tau_{m,s})'$, for $s = 1, 2, 3, 4$, are m-dimensional parameter vectors containing seasonal intercept and seasonal trend parameters, respectively, and $\bar{\phi}_{is}$, $i = 1, \ldots, p$, $s = 1, 2, 3, 4$, are $m \times m$ matrices containing the autoregressive parameters. The m-dimensional vector process $\bar{\varepsilon}_t = (\varepsilon_{1,t}, \ldots, \varepsilon_{m,t})'$ is assumed to be a standard vector white noise process with constant covariance matrix Σ. This assumption may be relaxed, in which case we have a different covariance matrix across the seasons, to be denoted by Σ_s.

Periodic vector moving-average models can be defined in a similar way. For example, a vector moving-average model of order q [VMA(q)] for the m-dimensional vector of time series $\bar{y}_t$ is given by

$$\bar{y}_t = \bar{\mu}_s + \bar{\theta}_{q,s}(L)\varepsilon_t, \tag{5.2}$$

with

$$\bar{\theta}_{q,s}(L) = 1 + \bar{\theta}_{1s}L + \cdots + \bar{\theta}_{qs}L^q, \tag{5.3}$$

where $\bar{\theta}_{is}$, $i = 1, \ldots, p$, $s = 1, 2, 3, 4$, are $m \times m$ matrices containing the moving-average parameters. Also, periodic vector autoregressive moving-average models can be defined in a similar manner. Obviously, these models contain larger numbers of parameters. Also, the lag specification strategy and other model selection issues can be rather involved. This may explain why, at least at the time of writing, we have never seen applications of PMA or PARMA models for multivariate series.

Vector of quarters representation

Strictly speaking, periodic vector time series generated by (5.1) and (5.2) are non-stationary, as the parameters change with the season. To analyze the presence of stochastic trends, it is therefore more convenient to rewrite (5.1) in a time-invariant (VQ) form, like we did for the univariate PAR models.

In general, the PVAR(p) process in (5.1) can be rewritten as a VAR(P) model for the stacked $4m \times 1$ vector process $\bar{Y}_T$. There are now several possible ways to stack the individual $\bar{y}_t$, but not all of these result in easy-to-analyze representations. For example, one could consider stacking the vector of annual observations per individual time series, as was done in Franses (1995a). There, the vector first includes the four seasons of the first variable, then the four seasons of the second variable, and so on. This turns out to be inconvenient for the analysis of stochastic trends, and hence we think it is a better strategy to stack the vector of m time series observations into a vector $\bar{Y}_T$, for each of the seasons. So, firstly, one has the observations in the first quarter for all m variables, then for the second quarter, and finally for the fourth quarter.

Let the m-dimensional vector $\bar{Y}_{s,T}$ denote the vector of m observations of $\bar{y}_t$ which correspond to quarter s of year T, $s = 1, 2, 3, 4$ and $T = 1, \ldots, N$. The vector $\bar{Y}_T$ becomes $(\bar{Y}'_{1,T}, \bar{Y}'_{2,T}, \bar{Y}'_{3,T}, \bar{Y}'_{4,T})'$. As in the univariate case, we can write (5.1) using $\bar{Y}_T$ in its VQ representation, that is,

$$\bar{\Phi}_0\bar{Y}_T = \bar{\mu} + \bar{\tau}T + \bar{\Phi}_1\bar{Y}_{T-1} + \cdots + \bar{\Phi}_P\bar{Y}_{T-P} + \bar{\varepsilon}_T \qquad (5.4)$$

or

$$\bar{\Phi}(L)Y_T = \bar{\mu} + \bar{\tau}T + \bar{\varepsilon}_T, \qquad (5.5)$$

with

$$\bar{\Phi}(L) = \bar{\Phi}_0 - \bar{\Phi}_1 L - \cdots - \bar{\Phi}_P L^P, \qquad (5.6)$$

where $\bar{\mu} = (\bar{\mu}_1', \bar{\mu}_2', \bar{\mu}_3', \bar{\mu}_4')'$, $\bar{\tau} = (\bar{\tau}_1', \bar{\tau}_2', \bar{\tau}_3', \bar{\tau}_4')'$ and $\bar{\varepsilon}_T = (\bar{\varepsilon}_{1,T}', \bar{\varepsilon}_{2,T}', \bar{\varepsilon}_{3,T}', \bar{\varepsilon}_{4,T}')'$, with $\bar{\varepsilon}_{s,T}$ being the vector of m observations on the error process $\bar{\varepsilon}_t$ in season s of year T. The $\bar{\Phi}_0, \bar{\Phi}_1, \ldots, \bar{\Phi}_P$ are $4m \times 4m$ parameter matrices containing

$$\bar{\Phi}_0(4i-3:4i, 4j-3:4j) = \begin{cases} I_m & \text{if } i = j, \\ 0 & \text{if } j > i, \\ -\bar{\phi}_{i-j,i} & \text{if } i < j, \end{cases} \qquad (5.7)$$

$$\bar{\Phi}_k(4i-3:4i, 4j-3:4j) = \bar{\phi}_{i+4k-j,i},$$

for $i = 1, 2, 3, 4$, $j = 1, 2, 3, 4$, and $k = 1, 2, \ldots, P$. The model order P in (5.4) is equal to $P = 1 + [(p-1)/4]$, where $[\cdot]$ is again the integer function. As with the univariate case, when p is smaller or equal to 4, the value of P is only 1.

To illustrate the preferred notation of a periodic vector autoregression, consider a PVAR(1) model for a two-dimensional vector of time series $\bar{y}_t = (y_{1,t}, y_{2,t})'$, that is,

$$\begin{pmatrix} y_{1,t} \\ y_{2,t} \end{pmatrix} = \begin{pmatrix} \mu_{1,s} \\ \mu_{2,s} \end{pmatrix} + \begin{pmatrix} \tau_{1,s} \\ \tau_{2,s} \end{pmatrix} T_t + \begin{pmatrix} \phi_{11,1s} & \phi_{12,1s} \\ \phi_{21,1s} & \phi_{22,1s} \end{pmatrix} \begin{pmatrix} y_{1,t-1} \\ y_{2,t-1} \end{pmatrix} + \begin{pmatrix} \varepsilon_{1,t} \\ \varepsilon_{2,t} \end{pmatrix}. \qquad (5.8)$$

In VQ notation, this model looks like

$$\bar{\Phi}_0\bar{Y}_T = \bar{\mu} + \bar{\tau}T + \bar{\Phi}_1\bar{Y}_{T-1} + \bar{\varepsilon}_T, \qquad (5.9)$$

where the 8×8 matrices $\bar{\Phi}_0$ and $\bar{\Phi}_1$ are defined by

$$\bar{\Phi}_0 = \begin{pmatrix} I_2 & 0 & 0 & 0 \\ -\bar{\phi}_{12} & I_2 & 0 & 0 \\ 0 & -\bar{\phi}_{13} & I_2 & 0 \\ 0 & 0 & -\bar{\phi}_{14} & I_2 \end{pmatrix} \quad \text{and} \quad \bar{\Phi}_1 = \begin{pmatrix} 0 & 0 & 0 & \bar{\phi}_{11} \\ 0 & 0 & 0 & 0 \\ 0 & 0 & 0 & 0 \\ 0 & 0 & 0 & 0 \end{pmatrix}. \qquad (5.10)$$

As the matrix $\bar{\Phi}_0$ can easily be inverted, that is,

$$\bar{\Phi}_0^{-1} = \begin{pmatrix} I_2 & 0 & 0 & 0 \\ \bar{\phi}_{12} & I_2 & 0 & 0 \\ \bar{\phi}_{13}\bar{\phi}_{12} & \bar{\phi}_{13} & I_2 & 0 \\ \bar{\phi}_{14}\bar{\phi}_{13}\bar{\phi}_{12} & \bar{\phi}_{13}\bar{\phi}_{12} & \bar{\phi}_{14} & I_2 \end{pmatrix}, \qquad (5.11)$$

we can write (5.9) as

$$\bar{Y}_T = \bar{\Phi}_0^{-1}\bar{\mu} + \bar{\Phi}_0^{-1}\bar{\tau}T + \bar{\Phi}_0^{-1}\bar{\Phi}_1\bar{Y}_{T-1} + \bar{\Phi}_0^{-1}\bar{\varepsilon}_T, \qquad (5.12)$$

with

$$\bar{\Phi}_0^{-1}\bar{\Phi}_1 = \begin{pmatrix} 0 & 0 & 0 & \bar{\phi}_{11} \\ 0 & 0 & 0 & \bar{\phi}_{12}\bar{\phi}_{11} \\ 0 & 0 & 0 & \bar{\phi}_{13}\bar{\phi}_{12}\bar{\phi}_{11} \\ 0 & 0 & 0 & \bar{\phi}_{14}\bar{\phi}_{13}\bar{\phi}_{12}\bar{\phi}_{11} \end{pmatrix}. \qquad (5.13)$$

This last matrix bears strong similarities to the related matrix for a univariate periodic autoregression of order 1. As such, our preferred representation seems to amount to a natural extension of the univariate models. Note that this might seem a trivial matter, but we leave it to the reader to write down the VQ representation using the notation in Franses (1995a), to verify that the preferred notation definitively makes more sense.

Stationarity conditions

The PVAR(p) model in (5.1) is periodically stationary if the roots of the characteristic equation

$$|\bar{\Phi}_0 - \bar{\Phi}_1 z - \cdots - \bar{\Phi}_P z^P| = 0 \qquad (5.14)$$

are outside the unit circle. Given the complexity of the characteristic equation in a univariate setting for a PAR(2) model as given in (3.28), one can imagine that a restriction for stationarity is highly nonlinear and very complex. Deriving such restrictions is therefore not useful. However, given estimates of the parameters, one may use (5.14) to check whether the series are periodically stationary.

For the PVAR(1) model the restriction for stationarity amounts to a rather simple expression. Indeed, the characteristic equation can be simplified to

$$|I_{4m} - \bar{\Phi}_0^{-1}\bar{\Phi}_1 z| = |I_m - \bar{\phi}_{14}\bar{\phi}_{13}\bar{\phi}_{12}\bar{\phi}_{11} z| = 0. \qquad (5.15)$$

Hence, the series are periodically stationary if the roots of the matrix $\bar{\phi}_{14}\bar{\phi}_{13}\bar{\phi}_{12}\bar{\phi}_{11}$ are within the unit circle. Note that the number of roots in an m-dimensional PVAR(1) model is equal to m. Of course, this also holds for a univariate periodic model of order 1, but we are aware of potential confusion. Hence, note again that the number of roots is determined by the number of lags and the number of series and not by the number of seasons.

5.2   Useful representations in practice

When it comes to the analysis of common stochastic trends, it is often insightful to write a vector autoregressive model in error correction format. Here, the $VQ(P)$ process in (5.4) can be written in error correction form as

$$\Delta_1 \bar{Y}_T = \bar{\Phi}_0^{-1}\bar{\mu} + \bar{\Phi}_0^{-1}\bar{\tau}T + \bar{\Pi}\bar{Y}_{T-1} + \bar{\Gamma}_1\Delta_1\bar{Y}_{T-1} + \cdots + \bar{\Gamma}_{P-1}\Delta_1\bar{Y}_{T-(P-1)} + \bar{\Phi}_0^{-1}\bar{\varepsilon}_T,$$
(5.16)

where

$$\bar{\Gamma}_i = -\bar{\Phi}_0^{-1}\sum_{j=i+1}^{P}\bar{\Phi}_j \quad \text{for } i = 1, 2, \ldots, P-1,$$

$$\bar{\Pi} = \bar{\Phi}_0^{-1}\sum_{j=1}^{P}\bar{\Phi}_j - I_{4m}.$$
(5.17)

The rank of the matrix $\bar{\Pi}$ determines the number of stationary relations between the elements of $\bar{Y}_T$. The dimension of the matrix $\bar{\Pi}$ is $4m \times 4m$ and stationarity corresponds to $4m$ cointegration relations between the univariate series $y_{1,t}, \ldots, y_{m,t}$.

When all the univariate series $y_{1,t}, \ldots, y_{m,t}$ are at most integrated of order 1, that is, they need the $1 - L$ or $1 - \hat{\alpha}_s L$ differencing filter, there are already $3m$ cointegration relations, that is, those relations between the quarters of the individual series. Therefore, if the rank of $\bar{\Pi}$ is larger than $3m$ then this corresponds to stationary relations between quarters of different series.

Specific cases

To illustrate some possibilities, consider again the two-dimensional PVAR(1) model (5.8). The matrix $\bar{\Pi}$ is given by

$$\bar{\Pi} = \begin{pmatrix} -I_2 & 0 & 0 & \bar{\phi}_{11} \\ 0 & -I_2 & 0 & \bar{\phi}_{12}\bar{\phi}_{11} \\ 0 & 0 & -I_2 & \bar{\phi}_{13}\bar{\phi}_{12}\bar{\phi}_{11} \\ 0 & 0 & 0 & \bar{\phi}_{14}\bar{\phi}_{13}\bar{\phi}_{12}\bar{\phi}_{11} - I_2 \end{pmatrix}.$$
(5.18)

The rank is completely determined by the lower right 2×2 submatrix $\bar{\phi}_{14}\bar{\phi}_{13}\bar{\phi}_{12}$ $\bar{\phi}_{11} - I_2$. Hence, the rank of $\bar{\Pi}$ is at least $3m = 6$. If the series in $\bar{y}_t$ are periodically stationary, the rank equals $4m = 8$. The series contain two unit roots if the rank of $\bar{\Pi}$ is equal to $3m = 6$ (the rank of $\bar{\phi}_{14}\bar{\phi}_{13}\bar{\phi}_{12}\bar{\phi}_{11} - I_2$). This can occur, for example, when both series are periodically integrated, but there is no cointegration across all quarters of the two series. A special case appears when the rank of $\bar{\Pi}$ is $3m + 1 = 7$, which corresponds to the case when the rank of $\bar{\phi}_{14}\bar{\phi}_{13}\bar{\phi}_{12}\bar{\phi}_{11} - I_2$ equals 1. There are then seven cointegration relations between the elements of $\bar{Y}_T$ denoted by $\bar{Y}_{s,T}$. Several interesting situations may occur, and we now will describe a few of these, see also Osborn (2000) for an extensive discussion. To save notation, we continue to consider the case of a bivariate time series.

If $y_{1,t}$ and $y_{2,t}$ are I(1) then there are three cointegration relations between the quarters of $y_{1,t}$ and $y_{2,t}$, respectively. This already makes six cointegration relations. The seventh cointegration relation may correspond to $y_{1,t} - \kappa y_{2,t}$. As $\Delta_1 y_{1,t}$ and $\Delta_1 y_{2,t}$ are stationary, the cointegration relation has to hold for each quarter. This must result in the following error correction specification:

$$\begin{pmatrix} \Delta_1 y_{1,t} \\ \Delta_1 y_{2,t} \end{pmatrix} = \begin{pmatrix} \gamma_{1,s} \\ \gamma_{2,s} \end{pmatrix} (y_{1,t-1} - \kappa y_{2,t-1}) + \begin{pmatrix} \varepsilon_{1,t} \\ \varepsilon_{2,t} \end{pmatrix}. \tag{5.19}$$

In this model, the long-run link between the two variables is constant over time, but deviations from this equilibrium-type of variables get corrected differently across seasons. Note that, due to the fact that both series are I(1), it is not possible for the κ parameter to be different across the seasons.

If one wishes to allow for periodic variation in the κ, at least one of the two series should be periodically integrated. For example, if $y_{1,t}$ is periodically integrated and $y_{2,t}$ is I(1), we may have the cointegration relations $y_{1,t} - \kappa_s y_{2,t}$. This would result in the error correction specification given by

$$\begin{pmatrix} y_{1,t} - \alpha_{1s} y_{1,t-1} \\ \Delta_1 y_{2,t} \end{pmatrix} = \begin{pmatrix} \gamma_{1,s} \\ \gamma_{2,s} \end{pmatrix} (y_{1,t-1} - \kappa_{s-1} y_{2,t-1}) + \begin{pmatrix} \varepsilon_{1,t} \\ \varepsilon_{2,t} \end{pmatrix}, \tag{5.20}$$

with $\alpha_{11}\alpha_{12}\alpha_{13}\alpha_{14} = 1$. Note that there is only a single free κ_s parameter as the relation $\kappa_{s-1} = \alpha_{1s}\kappa_{s-2}$ has to hold, due to the fact that $y_{2,t}$ is not periodically integrated.

Finally, one may have that $y_{1,t}, y_{2,t} \sim$ PI(1), together with the cointegration relation $y_{1,t} - \kappa_s y_{2,t}$. The corresponding error correction specification is then

$$\begin{pmatrix} y_{1,t} - \alpha_{1s} y_{1,t-1} \\ y_{2,t} - \alpha_{2s} y_{2,t-1} \end{pmatrix} = \begin{pmatrix} \gamma_{1,s} \\ \gamma_{2,s} \end{pmatrix} (y_{1,t-1} - \kappa_{s-1} y_{2,t-1}) + \begin{pmatrix} \varepsilon_{1,t} \\ \varepsilon_{2,t} \end{pmatrix}, \tag{5.21}$$

with $\alpha_{i1}\alpha_{i2}\alpha_{i3}\alpha_{i4} = 1$ for $i = 1, 2$. Note that, again, only a single κ_s parameter is free as the relation between the κ parameters is now $\kappa_{s-1} = \alpha_{1s}\kappa_{s-2}/\alpha_{2s}$. It is also possible that the cointegration relations are the same across the seasons, that is, $\kappa_s = \kappa$. In that case it must hold that $\alpha_{1s} = \alpha_{2s}$ for all s, and hence the same periodic differencing filter applies for both series. This is an interesting example of a common feature across two series.

So far we have considered a PVAR model of order 1. The analysis can be extended to higher-order PVAR models. We then end up with the VQ error correction specification (5.16). When $m = 2$ and the rank of $\bar{\Pi}$ is 7, the above discussion is still valid. We only have to extend the error correction models with lagged stationary variables, that is, lagged $\Delta_1 y_{i,t}$ or lagged $y_{i,t} - \alpha_{is} y_{i,t-1}$ with $\alpha_{i1}\alpha_{i2}\alpha_{i3}\alpha_{i4} = 1$, the variables depending on the type of integration.

It is important to understand that if the order of the PVAR model is higher than one then the rank of Π may be less than 6, which is due to the fact that the number of lags determines the number of possible unit roots. Hence, the individual series may have seasonal unit roots. It is also possible that the series are seasonally cointegrated, see Hylleberg *et al.* (1990), Lee (1992), Engle *et al.* (1993), and Johansen and Shaumburg (1999). In this book we abstain from a discussion of seasonal cointegration within the context of periodic models. First of all, it is our experience that, once one allows for periodic parameters, evidence of seasonal unit roots quickly disappears, see also Boswijk *et al.* (1997). Also, the statistical analysis of seasonal cointegration relations in periodic models is expected to be rather complicated. Finally, as of yet, we are uncertain as to whether we can give a sensible economic interpretation to the resultant models. A review of cointegration possibilities can be found in Osborn (2000).

Instead, we investigate another form of periodic cointegration which is sometimes considered in practice. Assume that $y_{1,t}$ and $y_{2,t}$ are seasonally integrated, that is, $\Delta_4 y_{1,t}$ and $\Delta_4 y_{2,t}$ are stationary and that the rank of $\bar{\Pi}$ equals 4. The four cointegration relations between $y_{1,t}$ and $y_{2,t}$ may in this case be given by $y_{1,t} - \kappa_s y_{2,t}$, and the corresponding error correction specification is

$$\begin{pmatrix} \Delta_4 y_{1,t} \\ \Delta_4 y_{2,t} \end{pmatrix} = \begin{pmatrix} \gamma_{1s} \\ \gamma_{2s} \end{pmatrix} (y_{1,t-4} - \kappa_s y_{2,t-4}) + \begin{pmatrix} \varepsilon_{1,t} \\ \varepsilon_{2,t} \end{pmatrix}. \tag{5.22}$$

The error correction model can be extended with lagged $\Delta_4 y_{i,t}$, $i = 1, 2$, if necessary. Note that the restriction $\kappa_s = \kappa$ may also be imposed.

Finally, the restrictions for stationarity and cointegration in PVAR models of order $p > 1$ are highly nonlinear and complex. This complicates testing for periodic cointegration. Kleibergen and Franses (1999) therefore propose to extend the PVAR(1) model to higher orders by adding a special structure of lagged $\bar{y}_{t-4i-1}$, resulting in

$$\bar{y}_t = \bar{\mu}_s + \bar{\tau}_s T_t + \sum_{i=1}^{Q} \bar{\psi}_{is} \bar{y}_{t-4(i-1)-1} + \bar{\varepsilon}_t, \tag{5.23}$$

where $\bar{\psi}_{is}$ are $m \times m$ parameter matrices. This implies a PVAR$(4(Q-1)+1)$ for the $\bar{y}_t$ series. The advantage of this particular extension is that the restriction for periodic cointegration is still quite easy to analyze. We can write

$$\bar{y}_t = \bar{\mu}_s + \bar{\tau}_s T_t + \bar{\psi}_s(L^4) y_{t-1} + \bar{\varepsilon}_t, \tag{5.24}$$

where $\bar{\psi}_s = \sum_{i=1}^{Q} \bar{\psi}_{is} z^{i-1}$. The corresponding characteristic equation of the VQ representation is (5.15), where we have to replace $\bar{\phi}_{1s}$ by $\bar{\psi}_s(z)$, that is,

$$|I_m - \bar{\psi}_4(z) \bar{\psi}_3(z) \bar{\psi}_2(z) \bar{\psi}_1(z) z| = 0. \tag{5.25}$$

Periodic cointegration occurs if the matrix

$$\bar{\psi}_4(1) \bar{\psi}_3(1) \bar{\psi}_2(1) \bar{\psi}_1(1) - I_m \tag{5.26}$$

has reduced rank. A convenient representation of the PVAR($4(Q - 1) + 1$) model is therefore

$$\bar{y}_t = \mu_s + \tau_s T_t + \bar{\psi}_s(1)\bar{y}_{t-1} + \sum_{i=1}^{Q-1} \bar{\psi}_{is}^* \Delta_4 \bar{y}_{t-4(i-1)-1} + \bar{\varepsilon}_t, \qquad (5.27)$$

where $\bar{\psi}_{is}^* = -\sum_{j=i+1}^{Q} \bar{\psi}_{js}$.

A disadvantage of a test for periodic cointegration which is based on the rank of $\bar{\psi}_4(1)\bar{\psi}_3(1)\bar{\psi}_2(1)\bar{\psi}_1(1) - I_m$ is that one only considers cases where the rank of $\bar{\Pi}$ is at least $3m$, therefore excluding the possibility of more than one unit root in the individual time series contained in $\bar{y}_t$. On the other hand, the advantage is that it allows for a direct test for cointegration specifications like (5.21) if univariate analysis shows that the individual series are (periodically-) integrated of order 1.

5.3 Cointegration testing—single-equation approach

At present, there are two approaches to test for periodic cointegration. The first approach is the single-equation approach of Boswijk and Franses (1995a). There one tests for the significance of the error correction terms in the error correction model (5.22). This approach is discussed in this section. The second approach is a system approach, in which one tests for the rank of the matrix $\bar{\phi}_{14}\bar{\phi}_{13}\bar{\phi}_{12}\bar{\phi}_{11} - I_2$ in a PVAR. This approach is due to Kleibergen and Franses (1999) and is discussed in Section 5.4.

Single-equation statistical inference on periodic cointegration models is discussed in great detail in Boswijk and Franses (1995a). In this section we confine ourselves to presenting the main results which are necessary for a sensible empirical use of an error correction model like (5.22). We restrict our discussion to the case of only two variables $y_{1,t}$ and $y_{2,t}$. The results can easily be generalized to more dimensions by replacing the univariate series $y_{2,t}$ by a vector of series containing $y_{2,t}, \ldots, y_{m,t}$.

To be more specific, consider the following conditional error correction model for $y_{1,t}$:

$$\Delta_4 y_{1,t} = \gamma_{1s}(y_{1,t-4} - \kappa_s y_{2,t-4}) + \sum_{j=1}^{p-4} \psi_{1s}\Delta_4 y_{1,t-j} + \sum_{j=0}^{p-4} \psi_{2s}\Delta_4 y_{2,t-j} + \varepsilon_{1,t},$$

$$(5.28)$$

and assume that $\Delta_4 y_{2,t}$ is generated by some AR process with no unit roots in its AR polynomial, and that $y_{2,t}$ is weakly exogenous. The latter assumption implies that the Brownian motions corresponding to $y_{2,t}$ and the cumulative sum of $\varepsilon_{1,t}$ are independent. This requires that, in the model for $y_{2,t}$, the coefficient γ_{2s} of the error correcting terms $y_{1,t-4} - \kappa_s y_{1,t-4}$ is equal to zero. If needed, for the model in (5.28) the $\Delta_4 y_{2,t}$ variables can be replaced by $\Delta_1 y_{2,t}$ variables. Notice that (5.28) together with the three assumptions puts several restrictions on multivariate PAR models like (5.1). In practice, it is therefore relevant to investigate whether at least the assumption of weak exogeneity holds, see Boswijk (1992) for a simple test procedure. Finally, it should be mentioned that all forthcoming results apply equally to models like (5.28), where the lag polynomials for $\Delta_4 y_{1,t}$ and $\Delta_4 y_{2,t}$ contain seasonally-varying parameters.

An Engle and Granger-type method

A simple empirical model specification strategy for the error correction model in (5.28) follows the well-known two-step strategy given in Engle and Granger (1987). An additional step is to test whether the various cointegration and adjustment parameters are indeed periodically varying. Periodic cointegration as in (5.28) amounts to four cointegration relationships between $y_{1,t}$ and $y_{2,t}$, that is, one cointegration relation per quarter. Denote the observation of $y_{i,t}$ in season s of year T by $Y_{s,iT}$ for $i = 1, 2$. The four cointegration relations can be written as $Y_{s,1T} - \kappa_s Y_{s,2T}$ for $s = 1, 2, 3, 4$. A first step to specify models like (5.28) may then be to regress $Y_{s,1T}$ on a constant and on $Y_{s,2T}$ for each of the seasons. In the case of cointegration between $Y_{s,1T}$ and $Y_{s,2T}$, the residuals of one or more of these four regressions should be stationary time series. Of course, it can occur that for only a few seasons does one obtain stationary residuals. In this case a partial error correction model appears. When all four residual series are stationary, one has a full error correction model (5.28).

To test for cointegration between $Y_{s,1T}$ and $Y_{s,2T}$, one may choose to check the value of the Durbin–Watson (CRDW) statistic for each season s and the Dickey–Fuller (CRDF) test. The asymptotic distributions of these test statistics can be derived from the asymptotic distributions in the case where the parameters do not vary over the seasons. This is caused by the orthogonality of the regressors $D_{s,t} y_{1,t-4}$ and $D_{s,t} y_{2,t-4}$ in (5.28). For example, the CRDF test should have the same distribution as the well-known cointegration Dickey–Fuller test in the case of two non-periodic variables, see Engle and Granger (1987). Table 9.8 of Franses (1996b) contains simulation results which support these conjectures. Critical values of the CRDW and CRDF test can be found in Engle and Granger (1987, Table II) and MacKinnon (1991).

When one obtains evidence that there is indeed cointegration in each season, a useful next step is to check whether the estimated parameters in the cointegration vectors, as well as the adjustment parameters, vary over the seasons. In other words, one may want to test the hypotheses $\kappa_s = \kappa$ and $\gamma_{1s} = \gamma_1$ in (5.28). The test for $\kappa = \kappa_s$ can be performed by comparing the residual sums of squares (RSS) of the four regressions of $Y_{s,1T}$ on a constant and $Y_{s,2T}$ with the RSS of the regression of $y_{1,t}$ on four seasonal dummies and $y_{2,t}$. Assuming cointegration, one can construct an F-test for the hypothesis $\kappa_s = \kappa$, which follows asymptotically an F distribution under the null hypothesis. This result follows from Johansen (1991, Theorem 3.1). This test will be denoted by F_κ. Furthermore, in the case of cointegration, the F statistic for the hypothesis that $\gamma_{1s} = \gamma_1$ also follows asymptotically an F distribution, as $y_{1,t-4} - \hat{\kappa}_s y_{2,t-4}$ are stationary variables, see Engle and Granger (1987). This test will be denoted by F_γ. Similar test statistics can be constructed in the case of a partial instead of a full error correction model, although one should then make sure that the F-tests for restrictions on the κ_s and γ_{1s} are only calculated for those seasons where one obtains cointegrating relationships, as otherwise these F-tests are not asymptotically F distributed.

Finally, a test for the weak exogeneity of $y_{2,t}$ for the cointegration relations can be performed via testing the significance of the periodic error correction variables in a model for $\Delta_4 y_{2,t}$. Again, as these error correction variables are stationary variables, the relevant F-test follows a standard F distribution under the null hypothesis, see Boswijk (1992).

An application of this simple empirical estimation strategy is given in Franses and Kloek (1995), where it is applied to consumption and income data for Austria. Below we will apply it to two industrial production series.

An extension of the Boswijk method

As can be observed from (5.28), periodic cointegration requires that the adjustment parameters γ_{1s} are strictly smaller than zero. Here we will discuss a class of Wald tests for the null hypothesis of no cointegration versus the alternative of periodic cointegration. Two versions of this test are considered: the Wald statistic for periodic cointegration in season s, and the joint Wald statistic. Both versions are extensions of the Boswijk (1994) cointegration test, which has been developed for non-seasonal data.

Consider again model (5.28), and define w_t as the vector containing the various differenced variables in this model, such that (5.28) can be written as

$$\Delta_4 y_{1,t} = \sum_{s=1}^{4}(\delta_{1s}D_{s,t}y_{1,t-4} + \delta_{2s}D_{s,t}y_{2,t-1}) + \psi'w_t + \varepsilon_{1,t}, \qquad (5.29)$$

where $\delta_{1s} = \gamma_{1s}$ and $\delta_{2s} = -\gamma_{1s}\kappa_s$. Notice that it follows from this definition that $\gamma_{1s} = 0$ implies $\delta_s = (\delta_{1s}, \delta_{2s}) = 0$. The null and alternative hypotheses for the season-specific Wald tests are, for some particular s,

$$H_{0s} : \delta_s = 0 \quad \text{versus} \quad H_{1s} : \delta_s \neq 0, \qquad (5.30)$$

whereas for the joint Wald test these hypotheses are

$$H_0 : \delta_s = 0 \text{ for all } s \quad \text{versus} \quad H_1 : \delta_s \neq 0 \text{ for at least one } s, \qquad (5.31)$$

where s is either 1, 2, 3, or 4. Notice that the Wald statistics are designed to test for partial periodic cointegration, whereas the joint Wald statistic concerns the full periodic cointegration hypothesis. Of course, one may expect both tests to have some power against both alternative hypotheses.

Let $\hat{\delta}_s = (\hat{\delta}_{1s}, \hat{\delta}_{2s})$ denote the OLS estimator of δ_s, and let $\hat{V}(\hat{\delta}_s)$ denote the corresponding OLS covariance matrix estimator. Similarly, define $\hat{\delta} = (\hat{\delta}_1, \hat{\delta}_2, \hat{\delta}_3, \hat{\delta}_4)$ and its estimated covariance matrix $\hat{V}(\hat{\delta})$. The Wald statistics are now given by

$$\text{Wald}_s = \hat{\delta}_s'(\hat{V}(\hat{\delta}_s))^{-1}\hat{\delta}_s = (n-l)\frac{\text{RSS}_{0s} - \text{RSS}_1}{\text{RSS}_1} \tag{5.32}$$

and

$$\text{Wald} = \hat{\delta}'(\hat{V}(\hat{\delta}))^{-1}\hat{\delta} = (n-l)\frac{\text{RSS}_0 - \text{RSS}_1}{\text{RSS}_1}, \tag{5.33}$$

where l is the number of estimated parameters in (5.29), and where RSS_{0s}, RSS_0, and RSS_1 denote the OLS residual sum of squares under H_{0s} in (5.30), H_0 in (5.31), and H_1 in both expressions, respectively.

The model in (5.29) does not contain deterministic regressors. However, if the long-run relations require an intercept, one should add seasonal dummy variables to the error correction model, that is, the Wald tests should be based on

$$\Delta_4 y_{1,t} = \sum_{s=1}^{4} \mu_{1,s} D_{s,t} + \sum_{s=1}^{4} (\delta_{1s} D_{s,t} y_{1,t-4} + \delta_{2s} D_{s,t} y_{2,t-4}) + \psi' w_t + \varepsilon_{1,t}. \tag{5.34}$$

Finally, if the variables contain a drift, the asymptotic distributions of the Wald tests change, see Park and Phillips (1988, 1989). In order to obtain distributions that are invariant to the presence of drifts, four linear trends should be added to the regressors, that is, (5.29) becomes

$$\Delta_4 y_{1,t} = \sum_{s=1}^{4} (\mu_{1,s} D_{s,t} + \tau_{1,s} D_{s,t} T_t)$$
$$+ \sum_{s=1}^{4} (\delta_{1s} D_{s,t} y_{1,t-4} + \delta_{2s} D_{s,t} y_{2,t-4}) + \psi' w_t + \varepsilon_{1,t}. \tag{5.35}$$

Notice that this also allows for a trend term to appear in the cointegration relations.

The asymptotic distributions of the Wald test statistics in (5.32) and (5.33) are nonstandard and are derived in Boswijk and Franses (1995a). To save space, we do not present these distributions in any detail, and we refer the interested reader to that paper. For practical purposes, however, we give the asymptotic critical values in the case of 2 to 4 variables, that is, 1 to 3 weakly exogenous variables, in Table C.1.

When one obtains evidence for the presence of cointegration in all or some seasons, it is of particular interest to test for the following parameter restrictions:

$$H_0 : \gamma_{1s} = \gamma \quad \text{for all } s = 1, 2, 3, 4,$$
$$H_0 : \kappa_s = \kappa \quad \text{for all } s = 1, 2, 3, 4, \tag{5.36}$$
$$H_0 : \delta_s = \delta \quad \text{for all } s = 1, 2, 3, 4.$$

Each of these hypotheses may be tested using an F-type test statistic. For the hypotheses $\gamma_{1s} = \gamma$ and $\delta_s = \delta$ these F-tests are the classical F-tests since the model is linear under the null and alternative hypotheses. These F-tests are denoted by F_γ and F_δ. For the hypothesis $\kappa_s = \kappa$ one may use the likelihood ratio-based test statistic

$$F_\kappa = \frac{n - l}{h} \frac{\text{RSS}_1 - \text{RSS}_0}{\text{RSS}_0}, \tag{5.37}$$

where RSS_0 and RSS_1 are the residual sums of squares under $\kappa_s = \kappa$ and an NLS regression under the alternative, respectively. Under weak exogeneity and given cointegration, these three F-test statistics are all asymptotically F distributed. Similar to the discussion above, a test for weak exogeneity can be performed by adding the cointegrating variables $D_{s,t}(y_{1,t-4} - \hat{\kappa}_s y_{2,t-4})$ to a model for $\Delta_4 y_{2,t}$, that is, by estimating

$$\Delta_4 y_{2,t} = \gamma_{2s}(y_{1,t-4} - \hat{\kappa}_s y_{2,t-4}) + \sum_{j=1}^{p-4} \psi_{1s} \Delta_4 y_{1,t-j} + \psi_{2s} \Delta_4 y_{2,t-j} + \varepsilon_{2,t}. \tag{5.38}$$

In Boswijk (1994) it is shown that, given cointegration, the LR-test for $\gamma_{2s} = 0$ for all s is asymptotically $\chi^2(4)$ distributed in the case of full periodic cointegration. When the null hypothesis of weak exogeneity is rejected, one may turn to alternative estimators or models. Boswijk and Franses (1995a) deal with a few such alternative approaches.

Illustration

An empirical modeling procedure for a periodic cointegration model along the lines described thus far involves four steps. The first step is an analysis of univariate time series with respect to their unit root periodicity properties. It would be useful to select those variables which play the role of $y_{2,t}$, and for which one can be reasonably confident that there are no cointegration relations amongst these variables. The second step is to specify a conditional error correction model as in (5.28), to estimate the parameters and to evaluate its empirical relevance using diagnostic measures. In the case of no misspecification, one calculates the Wald$_s$ and Wald statistics (and possibly the Engle

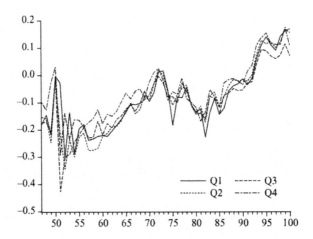

Figure 5.1: Difference between other durable goods and total industrial
production series

and Granger-type test statistics). When the null hypothesis of no cointegration
can be rejected, the third step is to test the hypotheses formulated in (5.36).
Finally, in the fourth step one tests for weak exogeneity using (5.38).

We now illustrate the above methods for other durable goods and total
industrial production series. The results in Table 4.4 suggest that both series
contain a unit root. Fig. 5.1 displays the $(1, -1)$ difference between the two
series in separate quarters, that is, $Y_{1,sT} - Y_{2,sT}$ for $s = 1, 2, 3, 4$. The difference does not seem to be a proper cointegration relation, as the series still
display a trend. To investigate whether both series are periodically cointegrated, we first consider the simple Engle and Granger (1987) approach,
that is, we regress the other durable goods series on an intercept and total
industrial production series. Table 5.1 displays the relevant results of these
regressions. The final two columns of the table show the CRDW and the
CRDF statistic. Both statistics are significant at the 1 per cent level and hence
we find evidence of cointegration. Fig. 5.2 displays the estimated cointegration
relations.

Next, we apply the Boswijk and Franses (1995a) approach to the same two
series. We first estimate (5.34), where $y_{1,t}$ corresponds to the other durable
goods series and $y_{2,t}$ to the total industrial production series. The lag order
is 8 and LM-tests for first-order and first-to-fourth-order serial correlation in
the residuals are not significant. The Wald statistic for the joint restriction
$\delta_{1s} = \delta_{2s} = 0$ for all s equals 35.722, and hence it is significant at the 5 per cent
level. To estimate the cointegration relations, we estimate the parameters of
(5.28) with seasonal dummies. The main results are given in Table 5.2. Note
that the large standard error of $\hat{\kappa}_1$ is due to the fact that the adjustment
parameter $\hat{\gamma}_{1s}$ is relatively small. The F_κ statistic for equal κ_s parameters

Table 5.1
Engle and Granger cointegration analysis for the individual quarters

Quarter	Intercept	Parameter	CRDW	CRDF
1	−0.729	1.157	0.764***	−3.435***
2	−0.867	1.190	0.709***	−3.667***
3	−0.762	1.162	1.246***	−5.070***
4	−0.623	1.138	0.821***	−3.829***

***denotes significant at the 0.01 level. Regression of other durable goods series on an intercept and total industrial production per quarter.

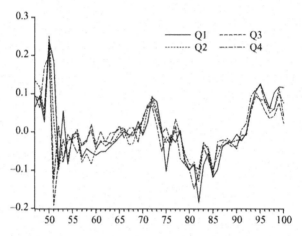

Figure 5.2: Estimated periodic cointegration relations using Engle and Granger regressions

is 0.905 with a p value of 0.44. Finally, we test whether the error correction terms in the model for $y_{2,t}$ are significant in equation (5.38), where the lag order is 11 (such that no serial correlation is present). The LR statistic for the four restrictions is 10.287 with a p value of 0.04. The results in Table 5.2 suggest that there is most evidence of periodic cointegration in the quarters two and three, as the adjustment parameters $\hat{\gamma}_{12}$ and $\hat{\gamma}_{13}$ are significant.

5.4 Cointegration testing—full-system approach

In some applications we may encounter the situation in which little is known about the properties of the variables, for example, concerning exogeneity, and

Table 5.2
Parameter estimates of the periodic error correction model
for other durable goods, with standard errors in parentheses

Quarter	Seasonal dummies	$\hat{\gamma}_{1s}$	$\hat{\kappa}_s$
1	$-0.014\,(0.054)$	$-0.004\,(0.056)$	$1.963(11.672)$
2	$-0.222\,(0.071)$	$-0.204\,(0.066)$	$1.241(0.041)$
3	$-0.287\,(0.067)$	$-0.354\,(0.070)$	$1.170(0.021)$
4	$-0.087\,(0.056)$	$-0.056\,(0.063)$	$1.350(0.264)$

The model is given in (5.28) with seasonal dummies.

it may then be wise to consider a full-system approach. Kleibergen and Franses
(1999) propose testing for cointegration in a full system like (5.24). This method
is based on testing the rank of (5.26). As parameter estimation under the
restriction of periodic cointegration is not standard, we first focus on parameter
estimation before we turn to testing.

Parameter estimation

To explain this approach we first consider, for simplicity, a PVAR(1) model
without deterministic components for the m-dimensional time series $\bar{y}_t$, that is,

$$\bar{y}_t = \bar{\phi}_{1s}\bar{y}_{t-1} + \bar{\varepsilon}_{s,t} \tag{5.39}$$

with $\bar{\varepsilon}_{s,t} \sim N(0, \Sigma_s)$, where the subscript s indicates that the variance of the
error term is assumed to be different across the seasons. This system can be
written in VQ notation as

$$\begin{pmatrix} \bar{Y}_{1,T} \\ \bar{Y}_{2,T} \\ \bar{Y}_{3,T} \\ \bar{Y}_{4,T} \end{pmatrix} = \begin{pmatrix} \bar{\phi}_{11} & 0 & 0 & 0 \\ 0 & \bar{\phi}_{12} & 0 & 0 \\ 0 & 0 & \bar{\phi}_{13} & 0 \\ 0 & 0 & 0 & \bar{\phi}_{14} \end{pmatrix} \begin{pmatrix} \bar{Y}_{4,T-1} \\ \bar{Y}_{1,T} \\ \bar{Y}_{2,T} \\ \bar{Y}_{3,T} \end{pmatrix} + \begin{pmatrix} \bar{\varepsilon}_{1,T} \\ \bar{\varepsilon}_{2,T} \\ \bar{\varepsilon}_{3,T} \\ \bar{\varepsilon}_{4,T} \end{pmatrix}. \tag{5.40}$$

If we do not impose periodic cointegration, the log likelihood function of this
system is given by

$$\mathcal{L}_m(\bar{\phi}_{11}, \bar{\phi}_{12}, \bar{\phi}_{13}, \bar{\phi}_{14}, \Sigma_1, \Sigma_2, \Sigma_3, \Sigma_4)$$

$$= c - \frac{1}{2}N\sum_{s=1}^{4}\log|\Sigma_s| - \frac{1}{2}\sum_{s=1}^{4}\sum_{T=1}^{N}\bar{\varepsilon}_{s,T}'\Sigma_s^{-1}\bar{\varepsilon}_{s,T}$$

$$= c - \frac{1}{2}N\sum_{s=1}^{4}\log|\Sigma_s| - \frac{1}{2}\sum_{s=1}^{4}\text{tr}\left(\sum_{T=1}^{N}\Sigma_s^{-1}\bar{\varepsilon}_{s,T}'\bar{\varepsilon}_{s,T}\right), \tag{5.41}$$

where $c = -2N \log(2\pi)$. It is easy to see that we can estimate the parameters of (5.39) using least squares, which results in

$$\hat{\bar{\phi}}_{1s} = \left(\sum_{T=1}^{N} \bar{Y}_{s,T} \bar{Y}'_{s-1,T} \right) \left(\sum_{T=1}^{N} \bar{Y}_{s-1,T} \bar{Y}'_{s-1,T} \right)^{-1} \tag{5.42}$$

and

$$\hat{\Sigma}_s = \frac{1}{N} \sum_{T=1}^{N} (\bar{Y}_{s,T} - \hat{\bar{\phi}}_{1s} \bar{Y}_{s-1,T})(\bar{Y}_{s,T} - \hat{\bar{\phi}}_{1s} \bar{Y}_{s-1,T})', \tag{5.43}$$

where $\bar{Y}_{0,T} = \bar{Y}_{4,T-1}$.

As we have already seen, periodic cointegration corresponds to rank reduction in the matrix $\bar{\phi}_{14} \bar{\phi}_{13} \bar{\phi}_{12} \bar{\phi}_{11} - I_m$. If the rank of this matrix is r then we can write

$$\bar{\phi}_{14} \bar{\phi}_{13} \bar{\phi}_{12} \bar{\phi}_{11} - I_m = \gamma \kappa', \tag{5.44}$$

where γ and κ are $m \times r$ matrices and $\kappa = (I_r \ -\kappa'_*)'$, with κ_* being an $(m-r) \times r$ matrix. The log likelihood of the model under the restriction of periodic cointegration is

$$\mathcal{L}_r(\gamma, \kappa, \bar{\phi}_{12}, \bar{\phi}_{13}, \bar{\phi}_{14}, \Sigma_1, \Sigma_2, \Sigma_3, \Sigma_4)$$
$$= -2N \log 2\pi - \frac{1}{2} N \sum_{s=1}^{4} \log |\Sigma_s|$$
$$- \frac{1}{2} \sum_{s=1}^{4} \sum_{T=1}^{N} (\bar{Y}_{s,T} - \bar{\phi}_{1s} \bar{Y}_{s-1,T})' \Sigma_s^{-1} (\bar{Y}_{s,T} - \bar{\phi}_{1s} \bar{Y}_{s-1,T}), \tag{5.45}$$

where $\bar{\phi}_{11} = (\bar{\phi}_{14} \bar{\phi}_{13} \bar{\phi}_{12})^{-1}(I_m + \gamma \kappa')$ and $\bar{Y}_{0,T} = \bar{Y}_{4,T-1}$. This log likelihood function is nonlinear in the parameters, and hence parameter estimation requires the use of a numerical optimization algorithm. Given the complexity of the nonlinear restriction this approach is less useful in large systems.

Therefore, Kleibergen and Franses (1999) propose estimating the parameters of the model under the restriction of periodic cointegration (5.44) using the generalized method of moments (GMM). To construct the GMM estimator it is convenient to rewrite (5.40) such that the regression parameter matrix depends on γ and κ only, that is,

$$\begin{pmatrix} \bar{\phi}_{14} \bar{\phi}_{13} \bar{\phi}_{12} \bar{Y}_{1,T} \\ \bar{\phi}_{14} \bar{\phi}_{13} \bar{Y}_{2,T} \\ \bar{\phi}_{14} \bar{Y}_{3,T} \\ \bar{Y}_{4,T} \end{pmatrix} = (I_4 \otimes (\gamma \kappa' + I_m)) \begin{pmatrix} \bar{Y}_{4,T-1} \\ \bar{\phi}_{11}^{-1} \bar{Y}_{1,T} \\ (\bar{\phi}_{12} \bar{\phi}_{11})^{-1} \bar{Y}_{2,T} \\ (\bar{\phi}_{13} \bar{\phi}_{12} \bar{\phi}_{11})^{-1} \bar{Y}_{3,T} \end{pmatrix} + \begin{pmatrix} \bar{\phi}_{14} \bar{\phi}_{13} \bar{\phi}_{12} \bar{\varepsilon}_{1,T} \\ \bar{\phi}_{14} \bar{\phi}_{13} \bar{\varepsilon}_{2,T} \\ \bar{\phi}_{14} \bar{\varepsilon}_{3,T} \\ \bar{\varepsilon}_{4,T} \end{pmatrix} \tag{5.46}$$

or

$$
\begin{pmatrix} \bar{W}_{1,T} \\ \bar{W}_{2,T} \\ \bar{W}_{3,T} \\ \bar{W}_{4,T} \end{pmatrix} = (I_4 \otimes (\gamma \kappa' + I_m)) \begin{pmatrix} \bar{V}_{1,T} \\ \bar{V}_{2,T} \\ \bar{V}_{3,T} \\ \bar{V}_{4,T} \end{pmatrix} + \begin{pmatrix} \bar{\omega}_{1,T} \\ \bar{\omega}_{2,T} \\ \bar{\omega}_{3,T} \\ \bar{\omega}_{4,T} \end{pmatrix}, \tag{5.47}
$$

where $\bar{\omega}_{s,T} \sim N(0, \Omega_s)$,

$$
\begin{aligned}
\Omega_s &= (\bar{\phi}_{14} \cdots \bar{\phi}_{1,s+1}) \Sigma_s (\bar{\phi}_{14} \cdots \bar{\phi}_{1,s+1})', \\
\bar{W}_{s,T} &= (\bar{\phi}_{14} \cdots \bar{\phi}_{1,s+1}) \bar{Y}_{s,T}, \\
\bar{V}_{s,T} &= (\bar{\phi}_{1,s-1}, \cdots, \bar{\phi}_{11})^{-1} \bar{Y}_{s-1,T},
\end{aligned} \tag{5.48}
$$

and $\bar{Y}_{0,T} = \bar{Y}_{4,T-1}$. Using (5.47), the objective function of the GMM is specified as

$$
\begin{aligned}
&G(\gamma, \kappa | \bar{\phi}_{14}, \bar{\phi}_{13}, \bar{\phi}_{12}, \bar{\phi}_{11}) \\
&= \sum_{s=1}^{4} \mathrm{tr} \left(\Omega_s^{-1} \left(\sum_{T=1}^{N} \bar{V}_{s,T} \bar{\omega}'_{s,t} \right)' \left(\sum_{T=1}^{N} \bar{V}_{s,T} \bar{V}'_{s,T} \right)^{-1} \left(\sum_{T=1}^{N} \bar{V}_{s,T} \bar{\omega}'_{s,T} \right) \right).
\end{aligned} \tag{5.49}
$$

This objective function depends on $\bar{\phi}_{1s}$ and Σ_s through Ω_s, see (5.48). To estimate the κ parameter we replace $\bar{\phi}_{1s}$ and Σ_s in the definition (5.49) of Ω_s by the estimates (5.42) and (5.43), respectively. Note that these least squares estimators are also consistent under the hypothesis of periodic cointegration. The GMM estimator of κ now follows from

$$
\frac{\partial \mathrm{vec}\, (G(\gamma, \kappa | \hat{\bar{\phi}}_{14}, \hat{\bar{\phi}}_{13}, \hat{\bar{\phi}}_{12}, \hat{\bar{\phi}}_{11}))}{\partial \mathrm{vec}\, (\kappa)'} = 0, \tag{5.50}
$$

which results in

$$
\begin{aligned}
\mathrm{vec}\, (\hat{\kappa}) &= \left(\sum_{s=1}^{4} \gamma' \hat{\Omega}_s^{-1} \gamma \otimes \sum_{T=1}^{N} \hat{V}_{s,T} \hat{V}'_{s,T} \right)^{-1} \\
&\quad \times \left(\sum_{s=1}^{4} \mathrm{vec} \left(\sum_{T=1}^{N} V_{s,T} (\hat{W}_{s,T} - \hat{V}_{s,T})' \hat{\Omega}_s^{-1} \gamma \right) \right),
\end{aligned} \tag{5.51}
$$

see Kleibergen and Franses (1999).

To estimate κ, we need a consistent estimate of γ. As we assume that $\kappa = (I_r - \kappa'_*)'$, a consistent estimator of γ is the first r columns of $\hat{\bar{\phi}}_{14} \hat{\bar{\phi}}_{13} \hat{\bar{\phi}}_{12} \hat{\bar{\phi}}_{11} - I_m$, where $\hat{\bar{\phi}}_{1s}$ is given in (5.42). Kleibergen and Franses (1999, Appendix A) show that the corresponding estimator of κ_2 is asymptotically mixed normally distributed under the hypothesis that the rank of $\bar{\psi}_4(1) \bar{\psi}_3(1) \bar{\psi}_2(1) \bar{\psi}_1(1) - I_m$ equals r.

As we have already discussed at the end of Section 5.2, the restriction for periodic cointegration becomes very complex if one just adds lagged $\bar{y}_t$. Therefore, Kleibergen and Franses (1999) consider (5.23), which can be written as

$$\bar{y}_t = \bar{\mu}_s + \bar{\tau}_s T_t + \bar{\psi}_s(1)\bar{y}_{t-1} + \sum_{i=1}^{Q-1} \bar{\psi}_{is}^* \Delta_4 \bar{y}_{t-4(i-1)-1} + \bar{\varepsilon}_{s,t}, \tag{5.52}$$

where $\bar{\psi}_{is}^* = -\sum_{j=i+1}^{Q} \bar{\psi}_{js}$, such that periodic cointegration corresponds to rank reduction in $\bar{\psi}_4(1)\bar{\psi}_3(1)\bar{\psi}_2(1)\bar{\psi}_1(1) - I_m$. Under periodic cointegration we can write

$$\bar{\psi}_4(1)\bar{\psi}_3(1)\bar{\psi}_2(1)\bar{\psi}_1(1) - I_m = \gamma\kappa'. \tag{5.53}$$

To obtain parameter estimates, we use partial regression techniques, as in Johansen (1995). We regress $\bar{y}_t$ on the deterministic components (seasonal dummy $D_{s,t}$ and seasonal trend $D_{s,t}T_t$) and lagged fourth differences, and regress $\bar{y}_{t-1}$ on the same deterministic components and lagged fourth differences. The relationship between the residuals of both regressions, denoted by $\bar{y}_t^*$ and $\bar{y}_{t-1}^*$, respectively, resembles (5.39) and is given by

$$\bar{y}_t^* = \bar{\psi}_s(1)\bar{y}_{t-1}^* + \bar{\eta}_{s,t}. \tag{5.54}$$

Parameter estimation can be done in a similar way as for the PVAR(1) model. One simply replaces $\bar{y}_t$ and $\bar{y}_{t-1}$ in the expressions by $\bar{y}_t^*$ and $\bar{y}_{t-1}^*$, respectively, see Kleibergen and Franses (1999) for a discussion.

Testing for periodic cointegration

Testing for the presence of periodic cointegration in (5.52) corresponds to testing the rank of the matrix

$$\bar{\psi}_4(1)\bar{\psi}_3(1)\bar{\psi}_2(1)\bar{\psi}_1(1) - I_m. \tag{5.55}$$

To determine the rank of this matrix, one may use sequences of likelihood ratio statistics. This, however, requires the evaluation of the log likelihood function in the parameter estimates under the hypothesis of rank reduction. As we have already discussed, ML estimation may be cumbersome due to the complex nonlinear structure imposed by periodic cointegration. Therefore Kleibergen and Franses (1999) propose the use of quasi-likelihood ratio statistics based on Kleibergen (1998), which have the same convergence properties as the likelihood ratio statistics.

These quasi-likelihood ratio statistics correspond to the objective function of GMM estimation. The statistic to test rank r versus full rank is given by

$$K(r|m) = \frac{1}{4^2} G(\hat{\gamma}, \hat{\kappa} | \hat{\bar{\phi}}_{14}, \hat{\bar{\phi}}_{13}, \hat{\bar{\phi}}_{12}, \hat{\bar{\phi}}_{11}), \qquad (5.56)$$

where $G(\gamma, \kappa | \bar{\phi}_{14} \bar{\phi}_{13} \bar{\phi}_{12} \bar{\phi}_{11})$ is defined in (5.49), $\hat{\kappa}$ is given in (5.51), $\hat{\bar{\phi}}_{1s}$ are given in (5.42), and $\hat{\gamma}$ are the first r columns of $\hat{\bar{\phi}}_{14} \hat{\bar{\phi}}_{13} \hat{\bar{\phi}}_{12} \hat{\bar{\phi}}_{11} - I_m$. The test statistic for rank 0 is equal to (5.56) evaluated for $\gamma = 0$ and $\kappa = 0$.

The quasi-likelihood ratio statistics have the same asymptotic distribution as the Johansen (1991) trace statistics. Critical values are tabulated in Table B.1 with $q = m - r$, at least for the case with no deterministics. The asymptotic distribution depends on the deterministic elements included in the PVAR model in the usual way. If one includes seasonal dummies and seasonal trends, one has to consider Tables B.3 and B.5, respectively.

Illustration

We apply this procedure to the same series as before. If we only include seasonal dummies and 1 lag, that is $Q = 1$, the test statistic for rank 0 versus rank 2 is 237.18, while the test for rank 1 versus rank 2 is 1.87. If we compare these values with the critical values in the first two rows of Table B.3 we conclude that there is a single cointegration relation across the two periodic series. The GMM estimate of κ_* is 1.150 and this corresponds very well to the estimated parameters in Table 5.1.

The multivariate PAR model under the restriction of periodic cointegration can be rewritten as (5.21) with seasonal dummies, where the covariance matrix of the error terms varies across the quarters. Table 5.3 shows the ML estimates of the model parameters. Note the restriction of periodic cointegration, that is, the rank of $\hat{\bar{\phi}}_{14} \hat{\bar{\phi}}_{13} \hat{\bar{\phi}}_{12} \hat{\bar{\phi}}_{11} - I_2$ is 1, implies that there are only $3 \times 4 + 3 = 15$ parameters identified. This means that we can estimate the three α_{is} parameters of the periodic differencing filters of the two series, two times four adjustment parameters γ_{is} and only one cointegration relation parameter κ_s. The values of the cointegrating vector in the other seasons follow from the relation $\kappa_{s-1} = \alpha_{1s}\kappa_{s-2}/\alpha_{2s}$, as discussed before. The cointegration relation parameters κ_s correspond reasonably well with the corresponding parameters in Table 5.1. Fig. 5.3 displays the four cointegration relations, and indeed they look stable.

5.5 Discussion

In this chapter we reviewed various representation, estimation, and inference issues concerning multivariate models for periodic data. These appeared to

Table 5.3

Parameter estimates of the periodic error correction model for other durable goods and total industrial production series, with standard errors in parentheses

Quarter	Seasonal dummies	$\hat{\alpha}_{is}$	$\hat{\gamma}_{is}$	$\hat{\kappa}_s$	
		Other durable goods			
1	$-0.046\,(0.064)$	$1.027\,(0.008)$	$0.123\,(0.079)$	1.180	–
2	$-0.219\,(0.067)$	$1.028\,(0.009)$	$-0.143\,(0.072)$	1.207	–
3	$-0.040\,(0.085)$	$0.989\,(0.008)$	$-0.084\,(0.085)$	1.175	–
4	$0.316\,(0.082)$	0.957 –	$0.111\,(0.093)$	$1.152\,(0.024)$	
		Total			
1	$0.043\,(0.039)$	$1.003\,(0.006)$	$0.075\,(0.047)$	1.180	–
2	$0.059\,(0.035)$	$1.004\,(0.005)$	$0.078\,(0.037)$	1.207	–
3	$0.059\,(0.037)$	$1.016\,(0.005)$	$0.128\,(0.036)$	1.175	–
4	$0.165\,(0.041)$	0.977 –	$0.069\,(0.045)$	$1.152\,(0.024)$	

The model is given in (5.21) with seasonal dummies and normally distributed error terms with a different covariance matrix across the quarters. Note that only one of the κ_s parameters is estimated, as discussed after (5.21).

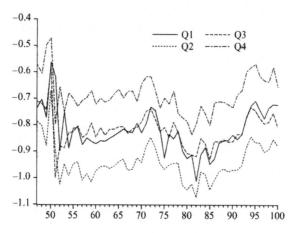

Figure 5.3: Estimated periodic cointegration relations using model (5.21)

be quite complicated, and most inference issues depend heavily on the chosen representation. The analysis of time series with a stochastic trend is even more cumbersome, although we showed that simple extensions of available methods could be usefully applied for empirical data. Admittedly, the illustrations concerned bivariate series, and we expect that applications to larger systems might give empirical results that are less easy to interpret. In summary, we expect that more research is needed for the analysis of systems of seasonal time series. Indeed, the literature on seasonal cointegration, where one examines if two or more seasons have the same seasonal stochastic trends, also indicates that there are reasons for modifying the methods and models. Hence, we think that future research should reveal how one can handle systems of seasonal time series in a useful and relevant way.

There is some evidence in the literature on the forecasting capacities of cointegration models for seasonal time series. Herwartz (1997) evaluates periodic error correction models and finds that these do not forecast very well, relative to more simple models. One reason for this finding might be that the periodic models require quite a number of parameters to be estimated, and this increases the uncertainty. Löf and Franses (2001) compare various multivariate models for seasonal time series for seven bivariate systems concerning consumption and income. Their finding is that seasonal cointegration models give better forecasts than periodic cointegration models. Further empirical and simulation results are needed to better understand the results so far documented in the literature.

Finally, the analysis of common properties in this chapter was confined to stochastic trends. It is also possible that periodic stationary time series share common features. One example can be that two or more series have similar periodicity in their autocorrelation functions. It seems possible to build on the work of Engle and Kozicki (1993) and Vahid and Engle (1993) to examine such similarities. This is also of practical relevance as it perhaps facilitates the analysis of, say, monthly data with periodic properties.

This chapter also concludes our book on periodic models. We have tried to summarize everything we know about these models, and, in particular, their application to economic data with stochastic trends. Looking back, we see that univariate models are fairly easy to construct, but that multivariate models are more difficult to analyze. We also see that the models are a good competitor in terms of forecasting. Combining this with the observation that periodic models may match with theoretical insights into economic behavior, we believe that periodic time series models are a useful addition to the tool kit of applied economists.

Appendix A

Critical values of the Dickey and Fuller statistics

Table A.1
Quantiles of the Dickey and Fuller distribution

	1%	5%	10%	20%
No deterministics	−2.58	−1.95	−1.62	−1.20
Intercept	−3.43	−2.86	−2.57	−2.21
Intercept + trend	−3.96	−3.41	−3.12	−2.78

Source: Fuller (1976, Table 8.5.2).

Appendix B

Critical values of the Johansen trace statistics

Table B.1
Quantiles of the Johansen trace statistics in
the case of no deterministic elements

q	80%	90%	95%	99%
1	1.89	2.98	4.14	7.02
2	8.41	10.35	12.21	16.16
3	18.83	21.58	24.08	29.19
4	33.10	36.58	39.71	46.00
5	51.25	55.54	59.24	66.17
6	73.27	78.30	82.61	91.12
7	99.12	104.93	109.93	119.58
8	128.61	135.16	140.74	151.70

Source: Johansen (1995, Table 15.1).

Table B.2
Quantiles of the Johansen trace statistics for
restricted intercept parameters under H_0

q	80%	90%	95%	99%
1	5.85	7.50	9.13	12.73
2	15.31	17.79	19.99	24.74
3	28.65	31.88	34.80	40.84
4	45.86	49.92	53.42	60.42
5	66.92	71.66	75.74	83.93
6	91.75	97.17	101.84	111.38
7	120.52	126.71	132.00	142.34
8	152.75	159.74	165.73	177.42

Source: Johansen (1995, Table 15.2).

Table B.3
Quantiles of the Johansen trace statistics for
unrestricted intercept parameters under H_0

q	80%	90%	95%	99%
1	1.64	2.71	3.84	6.64
2	11.06	13.31	15.34	19.69
3	23.72	26.70	29.38	34.87
4	40.08	43.83	47.21	53.91
5	60.23	64.74	68.68	76.37
6	84.10	89.37	93.92	102.95
7	111.79	117.73	123.04	133.04
8	143.19	149.99	155.75	166.95

Source: Johansen (1995, Table 15.3).

Table B.4

Quantiles of the Johansen trace statistics for
restricted trend parameters under H_0

q	80%	90%	95%	99%
1	8.59	10.56	12.39	16.39
2	20.22	22.95	25.47	30.65
3	35.58	39.08	42.20	48.59
4	54.73	58.96	62.61	70.22
5	77.65	82.68	86.96	95.38
6	104.29	110.00	114.96	124.61
7	134.77	141.31	146.75	157.53
8	168.85	176.13	182.45	194.12

Source: Johansen (1995, Table 15.4).

Table B.5

Quantiles of the Johansen trace statistics
for unrestricted trend parameters under H_0

q	80%	90%	95%	99%
1	1.64	2.71	3.84	6.64
2	13.53	15.94	18.15	22.78
3	28.28	31.57	34.56	40.61
4	46.41	50.67	54.11	61.28
5	68.76	73.62	77.79	86.11
6	94.43	99.97	104.76	114.23
7	123.95	130.39	135.66	146.05
8	157.25	164.24	170.15	181.62

Source: Johansen (1995, Table 15.5).

Appendix C

Critical values of the Boswijk and Franses statistic

Table C.1

Asymptotic critical values of the Wald$_s$ and Wald test statistics for periodic cointegration

No.	Significance level					
	Wald$_s$			Wald		
	0.20	0.10	0.05	0.20	0.10	0.05
Regression contains no constants and trends						
2	4.80	6.48	8.10	16.17	19.09	21.65
3	7.40	9.38	11.18	25.26	28.73	31.75
4	9.87	12.10	14.20	34.02	38.03	41.50
Regression contains constants and no trends						
2	7.49	9.50	11.36	25.34	28.75	31.82
3	9.92	12.18	14.24	34.13	38.07	41.51
4	12.29	14.79	16.99	42.85	47.22	51.06
Regression contains constants and trends						
2	10.13	12.38	14.39	35.00	38.97	42.49
3	12.45	14.89	17.11	43.50	47.92	51.73
4	14.78	17.39	19.78	51.93	56.72	60.78

Based on the regression models (5.29), (5.34), and (5.35), where the number of lags is zero. The quantiles are obtained through Monte Carlo simulations using 50,000 replications, where Brownian motions are approximated by Gaussian random walks of 500 observations.

References

Abraham, A. and Ikenberry, D. L. (1994). The individual investor and the weekend effect. *Journal of Financial and Quantitative Analysis*, **29**, 263–78.

Adams, G. J. and Goodwin, G. C. (1995). Parameter estimation for periodic ARMA models. *Journal of Time Series Analysis*, **16**, 127–45.

Akaike, H. (1969). Fitting autoregressive models for prediction. *Annals of the Institute of Statistical Mathematics*, **21**, 243–7.

Andel, J. (1983). Statistical analysis of periodic autoregression. *Aplikace Matematiky*, **28**, 364–85.

Anderson, P. L. and Vecchia, A. V. (1993). Asymptotic results for periodic autoregressive moving-average models. *Journal of Time Series Analysis*, **14**, 1–18.

Bac, C., Chevet, J. M., and Ghysels, E. (2001). Time-series model with periodic stochastic regime switching—Part II: Applications to 16th and 17th century grain prices. *Macroeconomic Dynamics*, **5**, 32–55.

Balcombe, K. (1999). Seasonal unit root tests with structural breaks in deterministic seasonality. *Oxford Bulletin of Economics and Statistics*, **61**, 569–82.

Bentarzi, M. and Hallin, M. (1994). On the invertibility of periodic moving-average models. *Journal of Time Series Analysis*, **15**, 263–8.

———— (1996). Locally optimal tests against periodical autoregression: Parametric and nonparametric approaches. *Econometric Theory*, **12**, 88–112.

Bessembinder, H. and Hertzel, M. G. (1993). Return autocorrelations around nontrading days. *Review of Financial Studies*, **6**, 155–89.

Birchenhall, C. R., Bladen-Hovell, R. C., Chui, A. P. L., Osborn, D. R., and Smith, J. P. (1989). A seasonal model of consumption. *Economic Journal*, **99**, 837–43.

131

Bloomfield, P., Hurd, H. L., and Lund, R. B. (1994). Periodic correlation in stratospheric ozone data. *Journal of Time Series Analysis*, **15**, 127–50.

Bollerslev, T. and Ghysels, E. (1996). Periodic autoregressive conditional heteroskedasticity. *Journal of Business and Economic Statistics*, **14**, 139–51.

—— Chou, R., and Kroner, K. (1992). ARCH modeling in finance: A review of the theory and empirical evidence. *Journal of Econometrics*, **52**, 5–59.

Boswijk, H. P. (1992). Cointegration, identification and exogeneity. Ph.D. thesis. Tinbergen Institute, Amsterdam.

—— (1994). Testing for an unstable root in conditional and structural error correction models. *Journal of Econometrics*, **63**, 37–60.

—— and Franses, P. H. (1992). Dynamic specification and cointegration. *Oxford Bulletin of Economics and Statistics*, **54**, 369–81.

—— —— (1995a). Periodic cointegration—representation and inference. *Review of Economics and Statistics*, **77**, 436–54.

—— —— (1995b). Testing for periodic integration. *Economics Letters*, **48**, 241–8.

—— —— (1996). Unit roots in periodic autoregressions. *Journal of Time Series Analysis*, **17**, 221–45.

—— —— and Haldrup, N. (1997). Multiple unit roots in periodic autoregression. *Journal of Econometrics*, **80**, 167–93.

Box, G. E. P. and Jenkins, G. M. (1970). *Time series analysis; forecasting and control*. Holden-Day, San Francisco.

Breitung, J. and Franses, P. H. (1997). Impulse response functions for periodic integration. *Economics Letters*, **55**, 35–40.

—— —— (1998). On Phillips–Perron type tests for seasonal unit roots. *Econometric Theory*, **14**, 200–21.

Burridge, P. and Taylor, A. M. R. (2001). On regression-based tests for seasonal unit roots in the presence of periodic heteroskedasticity. *Journal of Econometrics*, **104**, 91–117.

—— and Wallis, K. F. (1990). Seasonal adjustment and Kalman filtering: Extension to periodic variances. *Journal of Forecasting*, **9**, 109–18.

Canova, F. and Hansen, B. E. (1995). Are seasonal patterns constant over time? A test for seasonal stability. *Journal of Business and Economic Statistics*, **13**, 237–52.

Cipra, T. (1985). Periodic moving average processes. *Aplikace Matematiky*, **30**, 218–29.

Cleveland, W. P. and Tiao, G. C. (1979). Modelling seasonal time series. *Revue Economique Appliquee*, **32**, 107–29.

Dezhbakhsh, H. and Levy, D. (1994). Periodic properties of interpolated time series. *Economics Letters*, **44**, 221–8.

Dickey, D. A. and Fuller, W. A. (1979). Distribution of the estimators for autoregressive time series with a unit root. *Journal of the American Statistical Association*, **74**, 427–31.

——— ——— (1981). Likelihood ratio statistics for autoregressive time series with a unit root. *Econometrica*, **49**, 1057–72.

Diebold, F. X. and Inoue, A. (2001). Long memory and regime switching. *Journal of Econometrics*, **105**, 131–59.

Engle, R. F. and Granger, C. W. J. (1987). Co-integration and error correction: Representation, estimation, and testing. *Econometrica*, **55**, 251–76.

—— and Kozicki, S. (1993). Testing for common features (with discussion). *Journal of Business and Economic Statistics*, **11**, 369–95.

—— Granger, C. W. J., Hylleberg, S., and Lee, H. S. (1993). Seasonal cointegration: The Japanese consumption function. *Journal of Econometrics*, **55**, 275–98.

Foster, D. F. and Viswanathan, S. (1990). A theory of the interday variations in volume, variance, and trading costs in security markets. *Review of Financial Studies*, **3**, 593–624.

Franses, P. H. (1991). A multivariate approach to modeling univariate seasonal time series. Econometric Institute report 9101. Erasmus University, Rotterdam.

—— (1993). Periodically integrated subset autoregressions for Dutch industrial production and money stock. *Journal of Forecasting*, **12**, 601–13.

—— (1994). A multivariate approach to modeling univariate seasonal time series. *Journal of Econometrics*, **63**, 133–51.

—— (1995*a*). A vector of quarters representation for bivariate time series. *Econometric Reviews*, **14**, 55–63.

—— (1995*b*). The effects of seasonally adjusting a periodic autoregressive process. *Computational Statistics and Data Analysis*, **19**, 683–704.

—— (1995*c*). On periodic autoregressions and structural breaks in seasonal time series. *Environmetrics*, **6**, 451–6.

Franses, P. H. (1996a). Multi-step forecast error variances for periodically integrated time series. *Journal of Forecasting*, **15**, 83–95.

—— (1996b). *Periodicity and Stochastic Trends in Economic Time Series*. Oxford University Press.

—— (1998). *Time Series Models for Business and Economic Forecasting*. Cambridge University Press.

—— and Kloek, T. (1995). A periodic cointegration model of quarterly consumption. *Applied Stochastic Models and Data Analysis*, **11**, 159–66.

—— and Koehler, A. B. (1998). A model selection strategy for time series with increasing seasonal variation. *International Journal of Forecasting*, **14**, 405–14.

—— and Koop, G. (1997). A Bayesian analysis of periodic integration. *Journal of Forecasting*, **16**, 509–32.

—— and Kunst, R. M. (1999). On the role of seasonal intercepts in seasonal cointegration. *Oxford Bulletin of Economics and Statistics*, **61**, 409–33.

—— and McAleer, M. (1997). Testing nested and non-nested periodically integrated autoregressive models. *Communications in Statistics—Theory and Methods*, **26**, 1461–75.

—— and Ooms, M. (1997). A periodic long-memory model for quarterly UK inflation. *International Journal of Forecasting*, **13**, 117–26.

—— and Paap, R. (1994). Model selection in periodic autoregressions. *Oxford Bulletin of Economics and Statistics*, **56**, 421–40.

—— —— (1996). Periodic integration: Further results on model selection and forecasting. *Statistical Papers*, **37**, 33–52.

—— —— (2000). Modelling day-of-the-week seasonality in the S&P 500 index. *Applied Financial Economics*, **10**, 483–8.

—— —— (2002). Forecasting with periodic autoregressive time series models. In *A Companion to Economic Forecasting* (ed. M. P. Clements and D. F. Hendry), Chapter 19, pp. 432–52, Basil Blackwell, Oxford.

—— and Romijn, G. (1993). Periodic integration in quarterly UK macroeconomic variables. *International Journal of Forecasting*, **9**, 467–76.

—— and Taylor, A. M. R. (2000). Determining the order of differencing in seasonal time series processes. *Econometrics Journal*, **3**, 250–64.

—— and van Dijk, D. J. C. (2000). *Non-linear Time Series Models in Empirical Finance*. Cambridge University Press.

Franses, P. H. and Vogelsang, T. J. (1998). On seasonal cycles, unit roots and mean shifts. *Review of Economics and Statistics*, **80**, 231–40.

—— Hylleberg, S., and Lee, H. S. (1995). Spurious deterministic seasonality. *Economics Letters*, **48**, 249–56.

—— Hoek, H., and Paap, R. (1997). Bayesian analysis of seasonal unit roots and seasonal mean shifts. *Journal of Econometrics*, **78**, 359–80.

—— van der Leij, M., and Paap, R. (2002). Modeling and forecasting level shifts in absolute returns. *Journal of Applied Econometrics*, **17**, 601–16.

French, K. R. (1980). Stock returns and the weekend effect. *Journal of Financial Economics*, **8**, 55–69.

—— and Roll, R. (1986). Stock return variances: The arrival of information and the reaction of traders. *Journal of Financial Economics*, **17**, 5–26.

Fuller, W. A. (1976). *Introduction to Statistical Time Series*. Wiley, New York.

Gersovitz, M. and MacKinnon, J. G. (1978). Seasonality in regression: An application of smoothness priors. *Journal of the American Statistical Association*, **73**, 264–73.

Ghysels, E. (1994). On the periodic structure of the business cycle. *Journal of Business and Economic Statistics*, **12**, 289–98.

—— (2000). Time-series model with periodic stochastic regime switching—Part I: Theory. *Macroeconomic Dynamics*, **4**, 467–86.

—— and Osborn, D. R. (2001). *The Econometric Analysis of Seasonal Time Series*. Cambridge University Press.

—— Hall, A., and Lee, H. S. (1996). On periodic structures and testing for seasonal unit roots. *Journal of the American Statistical Association*, **91**, 1551–9.

—— McCulloch, R. E., and Tsay, R. S. (1998). Bayesian inference for periodic regime-switching models. *Journal of Applied Econometrics*, **13**, 129–44.

Gladyshev, E. G. (1961). Periodically correlated random sequences. *Soviet Mathematics*, **2**, 385–8.

Granger, C. W. J. (1986). Developments in the study of cointegrated variables. *Oxford Bulletin of Economics and Statistics*, **48**, 213–28.

—— and Hyung, N. J. Y. (1999). Occasional structural breaks and long memory. Technical report 99-14. University of California, San Diego.

—— and Joyeux, R. (1980). An introduction to long-memory time series models and fractional differencing. *Journal of Time Series Analysis*, **1**, 15–39.

Granger, C. W. J. and Teräsvirta, T. (1993). *Modelling Nonlinear Economic Relationships*. Oxford University Press.

Hamilton, J. D. (1989). A new approach to the economic analysis of non-stationary time series and the business cycle. *Econometrica*, **57**, 357–84.

——— (1994). *Time Series Analysis*. Princeton University Press, NJ.

Hansen, L. P. and Sargent, T. J. (1993). Seasonality and approximation errors in rational expectations models. *Journal of Econometrics*, **55**, 21–56.

Harvey, A. C. (1993). *Time Series Models*. MIT Press, Cambridge, MA.

Herwartz, H. (1997). Performance of periodic error correction models in forecasting consumption data. *International Journal of Forecasting*, **13**, 421–31.

Hosking, J. R. M. (1981). Fractional differencing. *Biometrika*, **68**, 165–76.

Hurd, H. L. and Gerr, N. L. (1991). Graphical methods for determining the presence of periodic correlation. *Journal of Time Series Analysis*, **12**, 337–50.

Hylleberg, S. (1995). Tests for seasonal unit roots: General to specific or specific to general. *Journal of Econometrics*, **69**, 5–25.

——— Engle, R. F., Granger, C. W. J., and Yoo, B. S. (1990). Seasonal integration and cointegration. *Journal of Econometrics*, **44**, 215–38.

Jaditz, T. (2000). Seasonality in variance is common in macro time series. *Journal of Business*, **73**, 245–54.

Johansen, S. (1988). Statistical analysis of cointegration vectors. *Journal of Economic Dynamics and Control*, **12**, 231–54.

——— (1991). Estimation and hypothesis testing of cointegration vectors in Gaussian vector autoregressive models. *Econometrica*, **59**, 1551–80.

——— (1992a). A representation of vector autoregressive processes integrated of order 2. *Econometric Theory*, **8**, 188–202.

——— (1992b). Determination of cointegration rank in the presence of a linear trend. *Oxford Bulletin of Economics and Statistics*, **54**, 383–97.

——— (1994). The role of constant and linear terms in cointegration analysis of nonstationary variables. *Econometric Reviews*, **13**, 205–29.

——— (1995). *Likelihood-Based Inference in Cointegrated Vector Autoregressive Models*. Oxford University Press.

——— and Shaumburg, E. (1999). Likelihood analysis of seasonal cointegration. *Journal of Econometrics*, **88**, 301–39.

Jones, R. H. and Brelsford, W. M. (1967). Time series with periodic structure. *Biometrika*, **54**, 403–7.

Keim, D. B. and Stambaugh, R. (1984). A further investigation of the weekend effect in stock returns. *Journal of Finance*, **39**, 819–35.

Kleibergen, F. (1998). Reduced rank regression using GMM. In *Generalized Method of Moments Estimation* (ed. L. Matyas), Chapter 7, pp. 171–210, Cambridge University Press.

—— and Franses, P. H. (1999). Cointegration in a periodic vector autoregression. Econometric Institute report 9906/A. Erasmus University Rotterdam.

Koopman, S. J. and Franses, P. H. (2002). Constructing seasonally adjusted data with time-varying confidence intervals. *Oxford Bulletin of Economics and Statistics*, **64**, 509–26.

Kunst, R. M. (1993). Seasonal cointegration in macroeconomic systems: Case studies for small and large European countries. *Review of Economics and Statistics*, **75**, 325–30.

—— (1997). Testing for cyclical non-stationarity in autoregressive processes. *Journal of Time Series Analysis*, **18**, 123–35.

Kurozumi, E. (2002). Testing for periodic stationarity. *Econometric Reviews*, **21**, 243–70.

Kwiatkowski, D., Phillips, P. C. B., Schmidt, P., and Shin, Y. (1992). Testing for the null hypothesis of stationarity against the alternative of a unit root. *Journal of Econometrics*, **54**, 159–78.

Laroque, G. (1977). Analyse d'une méthode de désaissonnalisation: Le programme X-11 du Bureau de Census, version trimestrielle. *Annales de l'INSEE*, **28**, 105–27.

Lee, H. S. (1992). Maximum likelihood inference on cointegration and seasonal cointegration. *Journal of Econometrics*, **54**, 351–65.

Lewis, P. A. W. and Ray, B. K. (2002). Nonlinear modelling of periodic threshold autoregressions using TSMARS. *Journal of Time Series Analysis*, **23**, 459–71.

Löf, M. and Franses, P. H. (2001). On forecasting cointegrated seasonal time series. *International Journal of Forecasting*, **17**, 607–21.

Lütkepohl, H. (1991). *Introduction to Multiple Time Series Analysis*. Springer-Verlag, Berlin.

MacKinnon, J. G. (1991). Critical values for co-integration tests. In *Long-Run Economic Relationships* (R. F. Engle and C. W. J. Granger, eds.), Oxford University Press, Oxford, pp. 267–276.

McLeod, A. I. (1993). Parsimony, model adequacy and periodic correlation in time series forecasting. *International Statistical Review*, **61**, 387–93.

—— (1994). Diagnostic checking of periodic autoregression models with application. *Journal of Time Series Analysis*, **15**, 221–33.

Mills, T. C. (1991). *Time Series Techniques for Economists*. Cambridge University Press.

Nelson, D. B. and Cao, C. Q. (1992). Inequality constraints in the univariate GARCH model. *Journal of Business and Economic Statistics*, **10**, 229–35.

Noakes, D. J., McLeod, A. I., and Hipel, K. W. (1985). Forecasting monthly riverflow time series. *International Journal of Forecasting*, **1**, 179–90.

Ooms, M. and Franses, P. H. (1997). On periodic correlations between estimated seasonal and nonseasonal components in German and US unemployment. *Journal of Business and Economic Statistics*, **15**, 470–81.

—— —— (2001). A seasonal periodic long memory model for monthly river flows. *Environmental Modelling and Sofware*, **16**, 559–69.

Osborn, D. R. (1988). Seasonality and habit persistence in a life-cycle model of consumption. *Journal of Applied Econometrics*, **3**, 255–66.

—— (1991). The implications of periodically varying coefficients for seasonal time-series processes. *Journal of Econometrics*, **48**, 373–84.

—— (1993). Comment on Engle *et al.* (1993). *Journal of Econometrics*, **55**, 299–303.

—— (2000). Cointegration for seasonal time series processes, unpublised working paper, University of Manchester.

—— and Rodrigues, P. M. M. (2002). Asymptotic distributions of seasonal unit root tests: A unifying approach. *Econometric Reviews*, **21**, 221–41.

—— and Smith, J. P. (1989). The performance of periodic autoregressive models in forecasting seasonal U.K. consumption. *Journal of Business and Economic Statistics*, **7**, 117–27.

—— Chui, A. P. L., Smith, J. P., and Birchenhall, C. R. (1988). Seasonality and the order of integration for consumption. *Oxford Bulletin of Economics and Statistics*, **50**, 361–77.

Paap, R. and Franses, P. H. (1999). On trends and constants in periodic autoregressions. *Econometric Reviews*, **18**, 271–86.

Pagano, M. (1978). On periodic and multiple autoregressions. *Annals of Statistics*, **6**, 1310–17.

Pantula, S. G. (1989). Testing for unit roots in time series data. *Econometric Theory*, **5**, 256–71.

Park, J. Y. and Phillips, P. C. B. (1988). Statistical inference in regressions with integrated processes: Part I. *Econometric Theory*, **4**, 468–97.

———————— (1989). Statistical inference in regressions with integrated processes: Part II. *Econometric Theory*, **5**, 95–131.

Parzen, E. and Pagano, M. (1979). An approach to modeling seasonally stationary time series. *Journal of Econometrics*, **9**, 137–53.

Proietti, T. (1998). Spurious periodic autoregressions. *Econometrics Journal*, **1**, 1–22.

Sakai, H. (1982). Circular lattice filtering using Pagano's method. *IEEE Transactions on Acoustics, Speech and Signal Processing*, **30**, 279–87.

Salas, J. D., Boes, D. C., and Smith, R. A. (1982). Estimation of ARMA models with seasonal parameters. *Water Resources Research*, **18**, 1006–10.

Schwarz, G. (1978). Estimating the dimension of a model. *Annals of Statistics*, **6**, 461–4.

Smirlock, M. and Starks, L. (1986). Day-of-the-week effect and intraday effects in stock returns. *Journal of Financial Economics*, **17**, 197–210.

Smith, R. J. and Taylor, A. M. R. (1998*a*). Additional critical values and asymptotic representations for seasonal unit root tests. *Journal of Econometrics*, **85**, 269–88.

——— ——— (1998*b*). Likelihood ratio tests for seasonal unit roots. Discussion paper 98/444, University of Bristol.

——— ——— (1999). Likelihood ratio tests for seasonal unit roots. *Journal of Time Series Analysis*, **20**, 453–76.

——— ——— (2001). Recursive and rolling regression-based tests of the seasonal unit root hypothesis. *Journal of Econometrics*, **105**, 309–36.

Taylor, A. M. R. and Smith, R. J. (2001). Tests of the seasonal unit-root hypothesis against heteroskedastic seasonal integration. *Journal of Business and Economic Statistics*, **19**, 192–207.

Tiao, G. C. and Grupe, M. R. (1980). Hidden periodic autoregressive-moving average models in time series data. *Biometrika*, **67**, 365–73.

Todd, R. (1990). Periodic linear–quadratic methods for modeling seasonality. *Journal of Economic Dynamics and Control*, **14**, 763–95.

Tong, H. (1990). *Nonlinear Time Series: A Dynamic System Approach*. Oxford University Press.

Troutman, B. M. (1979). Some results in periodic autoregression. *Biometrika*, **66**, 219–28.

Vahid, F. and Engle, R. F. (1993). Common trends and common cycles. *Journal of Applied Econometrics*, **8**, 341–60.

Vecchia, A. V. (1985). Maximum likelihood estimation for periodic autoregressive moving average models. *Technometrics*, **27**, 375–84.

—— and Ballerini, R. (1991). Testing for periodic autocorrelations in seasonal time series data. *Biometrika*, **78**, 53–63.

—— Obeysekera, J. T., Salas, J. D., and Boes, D. C. (1983). Aggregation and estimation for low-order periodic ARMA models. *Water Resources Research*, **9**, 1297–306.

Author Index

Abraham, A. 55, 57
Adams, G. J. 42
Akaike, H. 43
Andel, J. 29, 42
Anderson, P. L. 42

Bac, C. 59
Balcombe, K. 20
Ballerini, R. 35, 39
Bentarzi, M. 39
Bessembinder, H. 55, 57, 58
Birchenhall, C. R. 6, 37, 66
Bladen-Hovell, R. C. 6
Bloomfield, P. 39,
Boes, D. C. 6, 54, 55
Bollerslev, T. 54, 55
Boswijk, H. P. 7, 43, 46, 67–69 79,
    80, 82–85, 88, 104, 110–116,
    129
Box, G. E. P. 39
Breitung, J. 20, 74
Brelsford, W. M. 6, 29
Burridge, P. 40

Canova, F. 20
Cao, C. Q. 55
Chevet, J. M. 59
Chou, R. 54
Chui, A. P. L. 6, 37, 66

Cipra, T. 29, 35, 42
Cleveland, W. P. 29

Dezhbakhsh, H. 59
Dickey, D. A. 21, 63, 79, 81, 125
Diebold, F. X. 70

Engle, R. F. 14, 18, 20–22,
    25, 64, 65, 86, 110, 112,
    113, 115–117, 124

Foster, D. F. 54
Franses, P. H. 1, 3, 4, 7, 9, 14,
    19, 20, 25, 29, 32, 40,
    42–44, 46, 47, 49, 50, 59, 67–
    70, 74, 79, 80, 82–85, 88, 98,
    99 104, 105, 107,
    110–116, 129
French, K. R. 54
Fuller, W. A. 3, 21, 63, 79–81, 125

Gerr, N. L. 39
Gersovitz, M. 8, 30
Ghysels, E. 3, 4, 11, 18, 20, 54, 55,
    59, 84
Gladyshev, E. G. 29, 31
Goodwin, G. C. 42
Granger, C. W. J. 14, 18, 20–22, 25,
    59, 64–66, 69, 70, 74, 86,
    110, 112, 113, 115–117
Grupe, M. R. 6, 31

Subject Index